HISTORIC RESTAURANTS *of*

Washington D.C.

CAPITAL EATS

John DeFerrari

AMERICAN PALATE

Published by American Palate
A Division of The History Press
Charleston, SC 29403
www.historypress.net

Copyright © 2013 by John DeFerrari
All rights reserved

First published 2013

Manufactured in the United States

ISBN 978.1.62619.126.6

Library of Congress CIP data applied for.

This book, once again, is for Sue

CONTENTS

PREFACE

I f the way to a man's heart is through his stomach, as the old proverb goes, then the way to a city's heart must be through its restaurants. Good restaurants offer both sensory and spiritual delights: good food and good company. The ones you remember are the ones that make you feel at home, the places where you celebrate special occasions and cement relationships, where you propose to someone or are proposed to, where you go when you are down and want to forget your troubles. Beyond what's on your plate, the important thing is the overall experience. The décor, the ambience, the manners of the wait staff, the owner's eccentricities and even the other customers' behavior—it all adds up. Looking back over the past two hundred years, it is these qualities that stand out in the city's most notable historic restaurants and make them a unique window into how our local culture has developed and changed.

Conventional wisdom has it that Washington's meager restaurants, until very recently, were an embarrassment to the city and a sign of its profound cultural shortcomings. But this narrow view considers only the food itself and judges it from the perspective of today's eclectic and demanding customers. In fact, the historical record shows an astonishing diversity of eateries, restaurateurs, chefs and cuisines, and the best places were as loved back then as the finest spots are today—or maybe more so.

In many ways, the development of restaurants in Washington has closely followed developments in New York City, to which our town has so often been compared unfavorably. The first true restaurants—places where you could choose when to eat, select items from a menu and be served at a private table—appeared here by the 1830s, not long after they got started in New York. The Swiss-born Delmonico brothers opened one of the first and most famous French restaurants in New York City in about 1830, but only eight years later, John Privaux, a former White House chef, opened a French-style eatery on Pennsylvania Avenue. The banquet at the celebrated Napier Ball, held at the Willard Hotel in 1859, was as grandly excessive as any served at the time in the Big Apple. And while New York in the nineteenth century was famous for its abundant oysters, Washington's proximity to the Chesapeake Bay gave it an equally endless supply, with oyster houses at one time seemingly on every corner. Even the eccentricities of popular New York eateries found echoes in the nation's capital. New York's notorious Cobweb Hall, a dark Dickensian haunt hung with thick cobwebs, found an imitator in Andrew Hancock's Old Curiosity Shop on Pennsylvania Avenue, where the famous African American bartender Dick Francis held forth amid a cobwebbed museum of moldering historic artifacts.

Washington restaurants in the mid-nineteenth century offered a bountiful assortment of local delicacies, including terrapin and canvasback duck from the Chesapeake Bay, two emblems of haute cuisine. However, the dawn of the twentieth century brought dramatic changes. Terrapin and canvasbacks became scarce, and extravagant formal dinners fell out of fashion. Lunchrooms and diners began filling the need for cheap food quickly served. The tearoom craze of the 1910s and 1920s brought a whole new genre of charming and informal restaurants that catered primarily to women, while men retreated to clubby steakhouses and traded insults with their hosts. The arrival of Prohibition wiped out a generation of venerable old watering holes and eateries, but new places in tune with the economics of the Depression years took their places. The prolonged food rationing of World War II and subsequent years dampened the restaurant business straight through the 1950s, but in 1960, the election of a new, young president with a taste for fine dining brought resurgence.

The president of the United States, the city's foremost resident, probably has had a more profound influence on the city's eateries than any other single person. Thomas Jefferson, an epicure of the highest order, followed prevailing European fashion by hiring French chef Honoré Julien to serve at the White House in 1801. Several later White House chefs, including John Privaux, would follow their Executive Mansion service by opening D.C. restaurants. Any visit by a sitting president to a local restaurant became a notable event; Abraham Lincoln's first meal of steamed oysters at Harvey's was an occasion the restaurant's owners would celebrate for years to come. Almost one hundred years later, John F. Kennedy's visits to the Rive Gauche and the fledgling Jockey Club helped ensure their lasting success. George H.W. Bush, Bill Clinton and

Barack Obama have likewise boosted the fortunes of a privileged few D.C. restaurants in more recent years.

This book covers two centuries of D.C. history, from 1800 to 2000; my goal was to illustrate the vast changes that have occurred in the restaurant business over two hundred years' time, and in doing so I've had to pick and choose among hundreds of restaurants. This book does not include any recently established places, though there are arguably more good restaurants in Washington now than ever in the past. With a few notable exceptions, it also does not include places that were primarily oriented toward drinking or entertainment. Some people surely will flip through this book looking for a particular haunt and not find it. With apologies to them, I hope the assortment I've included will offer a wide array of entertaining glimpses into the city's culinary past. Vintage recipes are included primarily for their historical interest and appear as they did in original sources; they have not been professionally tested for this book. I've also included several intriguing recipes graciously provided by restaurants that are still in business today.

Speaking of graciousness, this book benefited from the help of many people in ways both large and small, including Mohammed Abu-El-Hawa (Mama Ayesha's), Katy Adams and Maureen Hirsch (Clyde's Restaurant Group), Nizam Ali (Ben's Chili Bowl), Marcellus Arnold, Lawrence Berry, Sallie Buben (Bistro Bis), Reverend Sandra Butler-Truesdale, Evelyn Cuttino, Mel Davis (Michel Richard Citronelle), Patricia DeFerrari, Will Fleishell, Pat Fowler, Martin Garbisu, James Goode, Donét Graves, Bill Holmes, Michael Horsley, Todd Kliman and Denise Wills (*Washingtonian* magazine), Jeff Krulik, Richard Longstreth, Michele Mount (General Federation of Women's Clubs), Savino Recine (PrimiPiatti), Ruth Simpson Redmond, Bill Rice, Beth Schuster (Marriott International, Inc.), Lindsay Smith (the Palm Restaurant Group), John Valanos (the Monocle) and Felicia Wivchar (U.S. House of Representatives Clerk's Office).

In addition, the staff of the Washingtoniana Division of the D.C. Public Library, including Michele Casto, Derek Gray, Mark Greek, Faye Haskins, Jerry McCoy and Jason Moore, provided extensive assistance. Likewise, the staff of the Historical Society of Washington, D.C., including Jennifer Krafchik, Anne McDonough and Anne Rollins, was also indispensible, as were Patsy Fletcher, Kim Williams and Bruce Yarnell of the D.C. Historic Preservation Office.

I am especially indebted to Frances White for patiently and insightfully reviewing chapter drafts and providing invaluable comments. My thanks also to Austin Cuttino, who took a number of exquisite photographs for the color section, and to Hannah Cassilly, my editor at The History Press, who provided very gracious and helpful advice, particularly in the early stages of the book's development. Lastly, Susan

Decker's abiding support and encouragement were as crucial to this book's successful completion as they were to *Lost Washington, D.C.*, and once again I dedicate this volume to her with all my love.

A Note on Notes

Regrettably, space limitations have prevented me from including the endnotes I originally prepared for this book. However, I have deposited a manuscript version of this book, complete with footnotes, at the Washingtoniana Division of the D.C. Public Library and at the Kiplinger Research Library of the Historical Society of Washington, D.C.

JOHN DeFERRARI
June 2013

Chapter 1

FROM TAVERNS TO RESTAURANTS

A traditional part of British and Dutch culture, taverns sprang up in the American colonies from their earliest days. The story of restaurants in Washington, D.C., begins with these taverns, which were around before there even was a Washington, and progresses through the early decades of the nineteenth century to the public eating houses that first focused on providing good food and service to their customers. From these, the modern restaurants would emerge in D.C. by the time of the Civil War.

EARLY TAVERNS

Early Washington's taverns were not true restaurants as we conceive of them today—far from it. They didn't have menus or waiters and were not primarily oriented toward meals. Instead, they were first and foremost drinking houses that also offered room and board. Drinking was the most popular form of public entertainment in the late eighteenth and early nineteenth centuries, when the average person drank three times as much alcohol as we do today. The food available at a tavern, usually only at set meal times, seems to have been of little interest to either tavern keepers or their patrons, even though important public dinners might take place there. Press accounts might describe a notable formal banquet at a tavern as "elegant" but generally did not bother to mention what kind of food was served. In contrast, a complete list of all the numerous toasts that had been offered—as many as fifteen or twenty at a fancy dinner—would frequently be included. In newspaper advertisements, tavern keepers vying for patronage were much more likely to describe their fine stocks of Madeira than the type of food they served, which did not vary from place to place.

Because of the emphasis on drinking, it is difficult to find precise information about the dishes that were served in Washington's early taverns. Generally, the food was potluck and would be served buffet style, laid out on a long table in a big dining room. Guests—both boarders and local customers—would all be seated around the same table together. New Englander Samuel Vaughan listed in his diary in 1787 the kinds of food and drink that one would be likely to find at a country tavern, and the items might well have been found in Washington's early taverns as well:

> *Ham, bacon & fowl pigeon of one sort or another always to be had upon the road & often fresh meat or fish, dried Venison Indian or Wheaten bread, butter eggs milk, often cheese, drinks Rum, Brandy or Whisky, resembling Gin.*

Game was much more frequently encountered then than it is today, including venison, wild turkey, duck, pigeon and even bear. Pork was the primary type of meat served, often in the form of heavily salted ham. Potatoes, cabbage, beans, squashes and cucumbers were also common. But one didn't usually go to a tavern anticipating a delectable meal. One went to learn the news, to socialize and to drink. Eating seems to have played little more than a supporting role.

It seems only fitting to start a book about the history of Washington restaurants with the tavern that served as the city's birthplace—the site where an agreement was signed in 1791 to purchase the land for the new capital city. Suter's Tavern, also known as the Fountain Inn, was operated by John Suter (1744–1794) and hosted a number of key events connected with the founding of Washington. George Washington, John Adams, Thomas Jefferson and James Madison all dined there and often transacted important business within its walls. Georgetown had more than a dozen taverns in those days, but Suter's was the best known and remains the most celebrated to this day.

Scottish-born John Suter opened the Fountain Inn in 1783, taking over an older tavern known as the King's Arms, which had gone out of business. Suter seems to have quickly garnered a very good reputation for his exceptional liquor cabinet. He was said to have imported whiskey from his native Scotland, rum from Jamaica and brandy from the London docks. Thomas Jefferson once stated, "No man on the Atlantic coast can bring out a better bottle of Madeira or Sherry than old Suter."

A fanciful drawing of Suter's Tavern, as it appeared in *Perley's Reminiscences of Sixty Years in the National Metropolis*, published in 1886.

George Washington's diaries indicate that he first dined at Suter's in August 1785, on a day when he came up to Georgetown for a meeting of the Potowmack Company, of which he was president. The company was building a canal to improve transportation along the Potomac River. Washington followed a similar pattern in October 1787, coming up from Mount Vernon for a Potowmack Company meeting, dining afterward at Suter's (dinner in those days was served between noon and 3:00 p.m.) and then heading back into Virginia in the evening. Washington visited again for three days in March 1791 to finalize arrangements with key landholders to acquire the territory that would be designated the District of Columbia. Later, the sale of house lots in the new city would also take place at Suter's, no suitable accommodations yet being available within Washington City itself. The tavern, like many of its kind, was an important community focal point, hosting meetings of Georgetown's commissioners, operating a lending library and even staging productions of several dramatic plays.

John Suter died in 1794 at age fifty, perhaps after contracting cancer. His wife took over the tavern for a year or so before it passed into the hands of a succession of later owners. The wooden frame building eventually fell into disrepair and may have been torn down around 1835. At some point toward the end of the nineteenth century, people seem to have lost track of exactly where Suter's Tavern had been located, and strenuous arguments were subsequently made advancing several different sites. The most likely location based on current scholarship is on the east side of Wisconsin Avenue (formerly Water Street), immediately north of the Chesapeake & Ohio Canal. Christian Hines (1781–1874), a prominent early Georgetown resident, located Suter's at this spot in his *Early Recollections of Washington City,* and historian Oliver Wendell Holmes offered compelling evidence that this was the tavern's most likely site in an article he wrote in 1974. However, we will probably never have conclusive evidence proving the famous tavern's precise location.

Perhaps the most famous early tavern within the city limits of Washington was RHODES TAVERN, on the northeast corner of Fifteenth and F Streets, Northwest. F Street was one of the few streets in L'Enfant's plan that was actually laid out in the early days of the city, and it became the city's first residential core in the 1800s and 1810s. Rhodes Tavern, opposite the Treasury Department, was a natural public gathering point. Constructed in 1801, its first tenant was William Rhodes, who ran it as a tavern and boardinghouse. Like the Georgetown taverns, it became a de facto town hall for the new city, with city commissioners meeting there in 1801. The tavern served as the first polling place for a municipal election in 1802.

The building's tavern days were few, however. In March 1814, the newly established Bank of the Metropolis purchased it, and it served as a bank for many years. Two-thirds of the building was torn down in 1957, but the corner section survived until 1984. A herculean effort to save the remnant was undertaken by a committed group of preservationists in the late 1970s. Appeals were made to influential officials, demonstrations were held and court suits were filed, all delaying the demolition for several years. In a citywide referendum held in November 1983, voters overwhelmingly endorsed saving the historic tavern, but it was not enough. The Supreme Court ruled in September 1984 that there was no legal basis for continuing to block the demolition, and the ancient building quickly came down. An office building now fills the site.

Opposite, top: Rhodes Tavern, 1979. *Library of Congress.*

Opposite, bottom: Tunnicliff's Tavern in its 1880s beer hall days. *Library of Congress.*

Pennsylvania Avenue, the "Nation's Main Street," hosted several important early taverns, including TUNNICLIFF'S TAVERN, at what is now the southwest corner of Pennsylvania Avenue and Ninth Street Southeast. Constructed in 1796 in anticipation of the arrival of the federal government four years later, Tunnicliff's was one of the first taverns in Washington City. It was built by Lewis Deblois, a Boston merchant who came to Washington to open both a store and tavern on land owned by Philadelphia speculator John Nicholson. In those early days, many people thought the eastern side would become the city's central business district. Instead, the western part of Pennsylvania Avenue, on the other side of Capitol Hill, took on that role.

Deblois and Nicholson both encountered much frustration and bad luck in their real estate development efforts, but the tavern survived. When Deblois's first tavern keeper quit on him, he hired William Tunnicliff, an Englishman. Tunnicliff ran the tavern from 1796 to 1799. Like Rhodes Tavern, Tunnicliff's was more than just a place to room and board; it was also a multipurpose community center. An early social group, the Washington Dancing Assembly, met there. Most of the inn's guests came from Maryland, traveling across the Anacostia River (then known as the Eastern Branch) via ferry, and the tavern became known as the Eastern Branch Hotel. It survived for more than one hundred years, being turned into a private residence in the 1820s and staying that way until after the Civil War. It served as a beer hall in the 1880s and later as a storage building. When it was torn down in 1931, it was being used as a gas station, and there is a gas station on the site to this day.

Taverns might be located at any key spot along a stagecoach route into or out of the city. An example was the GOOD HOPE TAVERN, built around 1820 on a hill just across the Eastern Branch River from the bustling Navy Yard on the southeast waterfront. The tavern's location was near the current intersection of Naylor Road and Alabama Avenue Southeast. Not much is known about the tavern, including how it got its cheerful name, but perhaps it was meant to hearten weary travelers who had almost made it to the capital city. The tavern gave its name to the local community and a major Anacostia road. As a well-known landmark just outside the city proper, it became one of several popular dueling grounds, and in 1835, Francis Scott Key's son Daniel was killed in a duel there with a fellow navy midshipman. The tavern survived at least until the 1920s, when the *Sunday Star*'s "Rambler," J. Harry Shannon, sarcastically noted that the Good Hope Tavern had the distinction of not being one where George Washington had slept. It's unclear when this modest establishment was finally torn down.

The tavern tradition, particularly in Georgetown and on Capitol Hill, has continued into modern times, though contemporary taverns bear little resemblance to their

Martin's Tavern on Wisconsin Avenue in Georgetown. *Photo by the author.*

eighteenth-century forbears. Probably best known of today's neighborhood taverns is MARTIN'S, located at 1264 Wisconsin Avenue Northwest in Georgetown. William G. "Billy" Martin (1894–1949), a Georgetown native and star athlete, opened Martin's Tavern in April 1933, just as Prohibition was finally coming to an end. Georgetown was quite different in the 1930s, with few other restaurants competing for customers. As the first tavern keeper to open after Prohibition, Martin made a point of establishing a "respectable" joint. His dour, no-nonsense waiters enforced a conservative dress code and refused to let women sit at the bar (for their own good, of course). Men were prohibited from table-hopping, lest Martin's gain a reputation as a pickup joint. It never did.

Martin's featured hearty, inexpensive fare and was popular from the start. As early as the World War II years, people would wait in long lines on weekend evenings. Every president from Harry S Truman through George W. Bush has dined at Martin's, and John F. Kennedy is said to have proposed to Jackie Bouvier in booth three. In 1961, *Evening Star* writer Richard Slusser recommended the veal cutlet, calf's liver sautéed with

17

bacon and the "Old Virginia" crab cakes. Like many others, Slusser also liked Martin's coleslaw, which he found "not at all vinegary and made of shredded cabbage instead of the blender-inspired mush swimming in liquid that is served in too many places."

When the original Billy Martin, known as "Old Billy," passed away in 1949, his son, William A. Martin, took over, and grandson Billy Martin runs the tavern to this day, making Martin's one of the oldest continually operating restaurants in the city. Martin's recently held a gala celebration of its eightieth anniversary, attended by the mayor.

THE FIRST RESTAURANTS

Returning to the first few decades of the 1800s, we find early restaurants emerging as a distinctly different kind of eatery from the city's long-established tavern culture. Several factors played a role in the rise of this new style of public dining. The first modern restaurants, as we now know them, developed in France in the late 1700s. The French word *restaurant* originally referred to a type of meat bouillon that supposedly had restorative powers, the idea being that bouillon consisted of only the purest and most healthful "essence" of meat, which could be easily absorbed by the body and would not require digestive effort on the part of someone who was ailing. Sipping these "restaurants" became very fashionable among sophisticated elites in late eighteenth-century France. Further, in contrast to the rough-and-tumble taverns and cafés with their questionable clientele sanitation, the restaurateurs offered a more refined product and setting, individualized service and an appealing focus on customers' health and well-being. These pioneers offered an entirely new and modern kind of dining experience, and soon businesses modeled on them were springing up everywhere in large cities.

In contrast to earlier taverns, restaurants were uniquely customer-oriented. They were open for extended periods of time, allowing customers to arrive and be served according to their own schedules, not just at fixed times. Parties of customers were seated at separate tables where they could receive individual attention from wait staff rather than being grouped at a communal table. And finally, restaurants allowed patrons to order dishes à la carte—from a menu—rather than offering only fixed meals (known as table d'hôte service). Empowered to tailor their dining experiences to their own tastes and whims, the new restaurant-goers must have been quite taken by the experience.

Delmonico's, perhaps New York's most famous restaurant, was one of the first to allow patrons to order dishes à la carte when it opened as a restaurant around 1830. Washington's first restaurants opened soon thereafter. GEORGE KENSETT, an early restaurateur, ran an eating-house at Tenth Street Northwest and Pennsylvania Avenue. In 1833, he advertised in the *National Intelligencer*:

> ON THE FOURTH OF JULY, *and at all hours of every other day during the summer, will be served up, a la mode, at the corner of Tenth street and Pennsylvania Avenue, Beef Soups, Turtle Soup, Tripe, Fresh Oysters, Fresh Crabs, and all kinds of Eatables in season, and seasoned to be in season—so that any person wishing to enjoy the luxury of "something comfortable," will be good enough to call and try for himself, at the said Restorateur.*
>
> GEORGE KENSETT.
>
> N.B.—Bull Frogs for the Epicures this day.

In 1838, JOHN PRIVAUX, a former White House cook under Andrew Jackson, offered his services to the citizens of Washington "as a skillful and professed cook, either at their dwellings or at his own restaurant," located on Pennsylvania Avenue several blocks west of the White House. Another former White House cook was JOSEPH BOULANGER (1791–1862), a Belgian native from the city of Liège. Boulanger had learned the art of cooking at the famous Maison Chevet restaurant in Paris and came to Washington to be head chef at the White House during the Jackson administration. He was a talented confectioner, known for his cakes, ice cream and candy. After leaving the Executive Mansion during the Martin Van Buren administration, Boulanger set up his first restaurant on the south side of Pennsylvania Avenue at Sixth Street Northwest. Later he moved to G Street Northwest, just west of the White House and War Department building.

Newspaperman Benjamin Perley Poore (1820–1887) claimed in his 1886 *Reminiscences*, with some exaggeration, that Boulanger's was the first restaurant in Washington. Poore noted that Boulanger's "soups were gastronomic triumphs, and he was adept in serving oysters, terrapin, reed-birds, quails, ortolan [tiny birds that the French liked to roast—and eat—whole], and other delicacies in the first style of culinary perfection." Henry Clay (1777–1852) was one of the luminaries who frequented Boulanger's, and he was said to have enjoyed introducing guests there to Old Crow bourbon, which came from his home state of Kentucky.

Boulanger and most of the other early D.C. restaurateurs were also cooks/caterers. Catering services were a big business in Washington in the early to mid-nineteenth century, offering much more than just food service for large social events. Many government officials—senators, representatives, Supreme Court justices and their myriad clerks—came to Washington for just part of the year, when Congress or the court was in session, and they would leave their families back home. They lived in boardinghouses and small hotels, mostly along Pennsylvania Avenue or on Capitol Hill, and were not in a position to cook for themselves. For a fixed monthly fee, caterers would deliver two boxed meals a day—breakfast and dinner—to these grateful customers. While Washington was unusual in hosting its annual crop of transient officials, the profession of cook/caterer was not unique to the city. Other large metropolitan areas had similar professionals.

The cooking/catering profession—and by extension the operation of a café or restaurant—was one of the few lines of business open to African Americans in these years. Historian Barbara G. Carson notes that in 1822, the first year a city directory was published for Washington, at least one African American was listed as a "cook," and by 1830, two black-owned oyster houses were listed in the city directory. Whites probably saw the dinner services offered by caterers and their early restaurants as an extension of the kind of domestic service that they were used to having performed in their own homes by African American servants or slaves, and many of the early caterers would prepare meals at private residences if so desired.

Former slaves who had gained skills in both cooking fine meals and waiting on their masters would be well prepared to enter the hospitality business once they gained their freedom. Such was the case with Beverly Snow (1799–1856), who opened Snow's Epicurean Eating House and National Restaurateur at Sixth Street and Pennsylvania Avenue Northwest in 1832. Strategically located between two major hotels (the Indian Queen and the National), the restaurant was very popular. In announcing the opening of his "eating house," Snow offered his customers "an opportunity of regaling themselves on the choicest of fresh Venison, Canvass Backs [ducks], Pheasants, Partridges, Woodcocks, Snipes, and every other Luxury that the season can afford." Appealing to sophisticated diners and their French-influenced tastes, Snow went on to promise a complete culinary experience: "His Tables will be found well furnished with all the necessary articles to give the Epicurean finish to the luxuries of his Larder, such as Chafing Dishes, Plate Heaters, &c."

On July 4 of the following year—directly opposite George Kensett's ad in the *National Intelligencer*—Snow proudly announced, "Just received at the Epicurean Eating House, a fat lot of green Turtle, which will be served up in the best style this day at 11 o'clock." Later that year, under the heading "Health Bought Cheap," Snow advertised that the fine green turtle he was offering had "been recommended by some of our

A drawing of Snow's Epicurean Eating House. *Historical Society of Washington, D.C.*

most eminent physicians as a restorative." To give a "finishing touch" to delicacies such as this, "Currant and other Jellies, French and domestic Sauces…will be served at the request of the guest."

While Snow prospered and built up a supportive and appreciative clientele, his days as one of Washington's earliest restaurateurs would be unfairly cut short. In August 1835, an incident occurred on F Street in downtown Washington in which a slave, Arthur Bowen, became inebriated late one night and entered the bedchamber of his owner, Mrs. Anna Thornton, carrying an axe. News of the incident sparked hysteria among fearful whites, who had grown insecure after the Nat Turner rebellion in nearby Virginia, which had occurred only four years earlier. A throng of angry young whites known as "Mechanics" (skilled laborers) gathered and vandalized several black-owned houses and other buildings, including, most notably, Beverly Snow's restaurant. Snow had no direct connection with the Bowen affair, but the Mechanics were looking for an easy target. Word circulated that Snow had insulted the wives of the Mechanics, and they converged at his restaurant at the corner of Sixth and Pennsylvania Avenue. Snow himself was not to be found; he apparently had been taken to safety by sympathetic patrons of his restaurant. The Mechanics then vandalized the place, tearing down its sign, breaking up furniture and kitchen equipment, helping themselves to Snow's stocks of liquor and dumping what they couldn't drink out in the street. The building itself was spared only because it was understood that Snow didn't own it. All in all, several days of disorder, violence and confrontation between the Mechanics and authorities took place that would forever after be known as the Snow Riot of 1835.

Though Snow wrote a letter to the newspapers protesting his innocence regarding the alleged slur against the wives of the Mechanics, his reputation nevertheless had been ruined. The newspapers reported that when he showed up one day on Pennsylvania Avenue a year after the riots, he was recognized, and an angry crowd began to form. He had to seek police assistance to avoid harm. He could not have reopened his restaurant anyway; the city's common council, reacting to the civil unrest of the Snow Riot, had enacted a new ordinance restricting free blacks to driving carts and hackneys and prohibiting them from running taverns or eating-houses. Undaunted, Snow moved to Canada and opened another successful restaurant in Toronto.

The ordinance against blacks running restaurants did not last long, and the Epicurean Eating House itself survived and was eventually reopened under the supervision of another African American, Absalom Shadd. Rechristened the NATIONAL EATING HOUSE, it stayed in business under a succession of owners well into the 1850s. An 1856 ad by owner William Coke for "this old, well-known and popular establishment" made it sound very much like Beverly Snow's old place: "The Lovers of Good Things will find at the National Eating House, corner Sixth Street and Pennsylvania avenue, just received fresh and on hand HARD and DEVILED CRABS, OYSTERS, CLAM SOUP, SPRING CHICKENS, GREEN PEAS, and all other delicacies of the season, served up at the shortest notice, in the most approved style, and suited to the nicest taste."

By mid-century, restaurants were no longer a newfangled invention. Washington sported a variety of eateries, ranging from humble oyster houses to elegant dining rooms with haughty waiters and menus written entirely in French. Many were along Pennsylvania Avenue, while others clustered near the Capitol or the White House. The best restaurants featured popular delicacies such as canvasback duck and diamondback terrapin. A new era of haute cuisine was coming.

Chapter 2

CULINARY TRIUMVIRATE

Oysters, Diamondback Terrapin
and Canvasback Duck

Washington's proximity to the Chesapeake Bay, one of nature's most bountiful food sources, strongly influenced local cuisine in the nineteenth century, and three dishes above all others became the benchmarks of culinary excellence among the city's epicureans: Chesapeake Bay oysters, diamondback terrapin and canvasback duck—all of which thrived in parts of the bay and its tributaries. A meal composed of all three—oysters as an appetizer, terrapin soup to start and roast duck as the entrée— was the ultimate feast. And while all three began as inexpensive dishes that everyone could enjoy, they were far less so by the end of the century. Terrapin and duck became luxury items affordable only to the city's top tier of diners, and oysters grew far scarcer and more expensive.

CHESAPEAKE BAY OYSTERS

To prevent squalls and bring peace and happiness to your family, carry home with you a box of those superior fried oysters from John's restaurant.

The tiny ad for JOHN'S RESTAURANT, located at Seventh and D Streets Northwest, appeared in January 1878 in the *Critic-Record*, one of Washington's smaller newspapers. John's had a great location, right in the heart of Washington's Seventh Street business district, across the street from the Hub Furniture Store. "Prime Norfolk oysters are daily received at John's, and families are supplied with shucked oysters at liberal prices," an 1877 ad boasted. Afflicted with strabismus, the proprietor was affectionately known as "Dirty John" and had been a D.C. bartender since pre–Civil War days.

John's oyster house had no pretensions to elegance, and it epitomizes the central role that oysters once had in Washingtonians' eating habits. Oysters were for everybody in those days; they were plentiful, and they were dirt-cheap. You could enjoy steamed oysters at an elegant restaurant on Pennsylvania Avenue, or you could take home a bag of fried oysters from John's to keep the kids and the wife happy. Another John's ad from 1877 crowed, "Vhen dot phryed oysters from John's restaurant come aroundt mine house, der frau holds her tongue and der children whoops mit joy"—perhaps aiming in its primitive way at the growing community of German immigrants who lived in that neighborhood.

Historically, the greatest concentrations of eastern American oysters were in New York Harbor and the Chesapeake Bay. Many, many thousands of undersea acres along the coasts of these estuaries were covered with billions of oysters, making them an exceptionally abundant food source. In fact, Native Americans had been harvesting and consuming oysters in large quantities long before the arrival of Europeans, leaving massive piles of shells behind that laced the coastal landscape. Despite this substantial consumption, the oyster beds were so extensive and resilient that they remained undiminished. Europeans had also consumed oysters since ancient times, but the bivalves on the other side of the Atlantic had never been so large and plentiful. Colonists quickly learned how easy it was to harvest eastern American oysters and how tasty they could be.

As populations grew in the nineteenth century, the oyster industry also grew. New York consumed so many oysters—and shipped so many around the country and to Europe—that its beds became overharvested, increasing demand for Chesapeake Bay product. The Chesapeake oyster industry mushroomed shortly after the Civil War, when a particularly farsighted entrepreneur by the name of John W. Crisfield (1808–1897), a native Marylander, invested in a railroad to the shores of Tangier Sound, one of the richest oyster grounds in the world. The town of Crisfield sprang up on the edge of the bay, a tawdry assortment of hellish workhouses devoted to processing millions of oysters for shipment by rail all over the country. Crisfield grew rich, and Chesapeake Bay oysters were soon ubiquitous. In the 1870s and 1880s, the bay produced 40 percent of the world's oysters, and by the 1890s, over seven thousand oyster boats were on the tax rolls of the Maryland Oyster Commission.

Oyster shuckers at Crisfield, Maryland. *From* Harper's Weekly, *March 16, 1872.*

Oysters were the signature dish of HARVEY'S OYSTER HOUSE, one of the most famous of all Washington restaurants. Harvey's was the creation of George Washington Harvey (1840–1909) and his brother, Thomas (1830–1872), native Washingtonians who opened their restaurant in 1858 at Eleventh and C Streets Northwest. The restaurant quickly became a big hit, particularly after the onset of the Civil War. Large numbers of soldiers passed through the city, either to guard the nation's capital or on their way to Southern battlefields. Poorly provisioned, many of these troops sought out cheap, satisfying meals. Harvey's offered them delicious oysters in every style, but its signature dish was steamed oysters, for which it became famous far and wide.

Harvey's gained prestige in 1863, when Secretary of State William Seward and his wife invited President and Mrs. Lincoln to dine there. In a special room made up for them in the back of the restaurant, Mr. Lincoln enjoyed his first meal of Harvey's steamed oysters, instantly becoming a Harvey's enthusiast—or so the story is told. By then, the restaurant was steaming five hundred wagonloads of oysters a week and producing huge fifty-foot-high piles of shells that had to be trucked away by a dedicated fleet of wagons. Throughout the war years, the restaurant advertised that its plucky little pung boats ran the Confederate blockade of the Potomac River on a daily basis, bringing a constant supply of fresh oysters to the restaurant's insatiable customers.

In 1866, Harvey's moved to a newly remodeled building with a stylish cast-iron front on the southeast corner of Eleventh Street and Pennsylvania Avenue Northwest, where it would stay for sixty-five years. At this point, Harvey's had fully transitioned from a simple oyster house like John's to one of Washington's most elegant restaurants. After a remodeling in 1884, a newspaper article called the restaurant "the finest south of New York." "Pushing aside new and handsome ground glass entrance doors," a visitor would discover an elegant dining room with artistically frescoed walls and chandeliers of "hand-hammered brass with colored globes." Upstairs, the ladies' dining room included a "magnificent stuffed peacock in full and brilliant plumage" and specially designed tableware.

In May 1906, Harvey estimated that Washingtonians had consumed a billion oysters over the season (September to April) that had just finished. That would be enough oysters to make a pile as tall as the Capitol building. Harvey retired from the business that same year and died from a heart ailment three years later, leaving his heirs a $200,000 fortune.

Even after Harvey's passing, his restaurant continued to dominate the Washington dining scene for decades to come. Every president from Ulysses S. Grant to Franklin D. Roosevelt dined at Harvey's. In 1931, pushed out of its longtime home on Pennsylvania Avenue by construction of the Federal Triangle, the restaurant moved to larger and more modern quarters at 1107 Connecticut Avenue Northwest, next to the Mayflower Hotel. There, under the watchful eye of owner Julius Lulley (1893–1951), a native Washingtonian who had started out as a wine steward at Harvey's in 1908, Harvey's continued to be the haunt of presidents, dignitaries and anyone looking for the finest in seafood—or other—dinners. J. Edgar Hoover, for example, used to frequent Harvey's with his assistant, Clyde Tolson, and he would usually order steak or roast beef and a Caesar salad.

The restaurant moved again in 1970, this time pressured by Metro construction, and settled at Eighteenth and K, where it remained for another twenty-one years. Always an expensive restaurant, it went bankrupt during the recession of the early 1990s. A branch restaurant opened in Rockville, Maryland, in the early 1980s but has also since closed.

A typical downtown place known for its oysters was the OLMSTED GRILL, at 1336 G Street Northwest, founded by Bert L. Olmsted (1878–1940) in 1926. Behind its

Harvey's Restaurant, circa 1915. *Author's collection.*

Chef Rene Roux dishing out the 300,000th Order of OLMSTED'S OYSTERS CASINO

1336 G St., N. W.   DI. 8235   WASHINGTON, D. C.

Your Order is

Number 356579

SINCE

OLMSTED'S

INTRODUCED ITS

FAMOUS

OYSTERS CASINO

Prepared from a
Sacred Family Recipe

OLMSTED RESTAURANT

A NATIONAL INSTITUTION

A postcard advertising Olmsted's Oysters Casino. *Author's collection.*

distinctive Gothic windows, Olmsted's featured a dining room said to be one of the largest in Washington. Its kitchen was equipped with all the latest fixtures, including "automatic refrigeration." Olmsted quickly earned a reputation for offering excellent seafood obtained daily from the Chesapeake Bay and nearby Atlantic coastal waters.

Oysters remained a particular specialty throughout the Olmsted's history. Olmsted himself had claimed to own oyster beds off Chincoteague Island in the Chesapeake that were washed over by ocean waters and thus acquired a pleasant salty taste. Using these select oysters, Chef René Roux prepared Baked Oysters Casino according to a "300-year-old family recipe." The dish remained a major draw for the restaurant for many years until the Olmsted Grill finally closed in 1962.

Oysters, of course, are far less plentiful these days than when the great oyster restaurants of the past were in their heyday. In 1885, near the peak, some fifteen million bushels of oysters were harvested from the Chesapeake Bay. As early as 1892, adverse weather conditions resulted in a much smaller oyster harvest, and industry insiders began worrying that overharvesting would seriously damage the bay's numerous beds. Throughout the twentieth century and into the twenty-first, oysters continued a slow, steady decline, besieged by overharvesting, disease and pollution.

While the Chesapeake Bay still produces oysters, at the rate they are being harvested and with the threats they face, that may not continue long into the future.

DIAMONDBACK TERRAPIN

Oysters were often eaten as appetizers, followed by terrapin stew, a favorite dish of many prominent Washingtonians. Margaret Leech opens her classic book on the Civil War, *Reveille in Washington*, with a vivid 1860 vignette of proud General Winfield Scott, nicknamed "Old Fuss 'n' Feathers." At seventy-five years old, Scott loved sophisticated cuisine. "Yet nothing, to his taste, equaled the delicacy he called 'tarrapin,'" she notes.

> *He would hold forth on the correct method of preparing it: "No flour sir—not a grain." His military secretary could saturninely foresee that moment, when, leaning his left elbow on the table and holding six inches above his plate a fork laden with the succulent tortoise, he would announce, "The best food vouchsafed by Providence to man," before hurrying the fork to his lips.*

The colorful General Scott was not alone in his fondness for terrapin, specifically diamondback terrapin (*Malaclemys terrapin*), which was acclaimed as one of the finest delicacies of the East Coast and said to have a subtle and complex taste like no other. The animal thrives in brackish waters from New England to the Gulf states; it is the only species of turtle that is comfortable living in the waters of an estuary, where salt water from the sea mixes with fresh water from rivers. George Harvey asserted that the very finest of these "birds" were to be caught at the mouth of the Potomac River, just before it empties into the Chesapeake Bay. Such is the historical importance of the diamondback to the state of Maryland that it was declared the official state reptile, and these days it is probably best known to locals, not as a menu item, but as the mascot of the University of Maryland.

All the elegant Washington restaurants of the late nineteenth century offered terrapin, priding themselves on their skill in preparing it. "'Stewed terrapin, Maryland style,' forms an important part of any Washington dinner laying claim to being a pretentious affair," intoned the *Post* in 1880. Soup or stew made from terrapin was especially sought after in the winter months. A New Year's Day 1901 menu from the WILLARD HOTEL features "Stewed Terrapin, Maryland Style in Cases," while a 1906 dinner menu from the elegant RALEIGH HOTEL, just down the avenue, headlines

John F. Chamberlin. *From* Washington: A Not Too Serious History *(1930).*

"Chesapeake Diamond Back Terrapin à la Maryland" on its list of entrées. The delicacy cost $2.50, one of the most expensive dishes.

Terrapin was featured at CHAMBERLIN'S, a Gilded Age landmark on the southeast corner of Fifteenth and I Streets Northwest, owned by John F. Chamberlin (1837–1896), one of the best-known and most-beloved restaurateurs of his age. It seems that all of Washington's VIPs frequented Chamberlin's to both gamble at high-stakes card games and enjoy gourmet dinners. Chamberlin's practice was to bring out live terrapins for special guests to inspect before they were cooked for them, and one story printed in the *Post* in 1898 told of a terrapin at Chamberlin's that recognized a certain retired army major from so many visits to the restaurant that he rose up on his hind legs and bowed to him three times. The article noted that Chamberlin didn't much care for this fanciful story, as it seemed to reflect poorly on the freshness of his terrapins.

John Chamberlin was a consummate high roller even in an age of excess. "He made money easily and spent it with a lavish hand," the *Post* observed. According to the *New York Times*, "He was a bon vivant, a raconteur, a most loyal friend, debonnaire, [*sic*] facile, straightforward, and as silent on other people's affairs as the Egyptian sphinx." Born in Lansingburgh, New York, he grew up in New York City and was involved in a number of successful businesses before moving to Washington in the 1870s and opening Chamberlin's in 1880. The small hotel with a grand dining room was located in a former Victorian mansion exquisitely designed for entertaining. The first floor held an English bar and tables for regular restaurant patrons. Upstairs were private dining rooms and a spacious banquet hall, lined with paintings, which became the scene of numerous fine banquets for distinguished guests. One, from 1895, was written up in detail in the *Post*, which marveled at the huge circular table adorned with "a magnificent floral mass" and noted that "the 'old mutton' and the terrapin in particular came in for unlimited praise." Chamberlin died from Bright's disease in 1896; his exclusive inn lasted another decade, until 1906.

By the time of the diamondback terrapin's greatest popularity in the Victorian age, many were already concerned that the docile and reclusive animal might be harvested to extinction. The *Post* worried in 1902 that the diamondback was "rapidly disappearing, so that the danger of complete extinction within the next ten years is not only within the bounds of possibility, but highly probable." By that time, Maryland had enacted strict laws limiting the harvesting of the reptiles to the winter months, protecting diamondback eggs and banning non-Marylanders from catching the state reptile. Most terrapins were grown in enclosed "farms" near the town of Crisfield, with few remaining fully in the wild anywhere in the Chesapeake Bay.

The *Post*'s grim forecast of extinction might well have come true if a variety of factors hadn't conspired to dramatically decrease consumption. By the early 1900s, terrapin was seen as an expensive and even extravagant delicacy, something that was very difficult to prepare and that would be found only at the most exclusive restaurants. Popular interest in the dish declined considerably.

Still, to this day, a few aficionados remain committed to this rare reptilian delicacy. As recently as 1979, *Post* writer Hank Burchard observed that "terrapin is a tough act to follow. The pungent aroma and deep, rich flavor are like nothing else on earth." But in a side piece to the same article, food critic Phyllis Richman commented on a recent meal of diamondback stew, observing that

> *terrapin consists of a very small amount of stringy, tough meat, and larger quantities of black, gelatinous, fatty skin that tastes like lard stored in a cat-food can. Well-made as the stew was, it did not successfully overcome the problems of tiny little terrapin toes that stick in the teeth, muscle that turns into terrapin chewing gum, and floating bits of disturbing curled black fat. I would have enjoyed that terrapin stew if it hadn't bothered with the terrapin.*

Perhaps we should thank reviewers like Richman for keeping diners away from the diamondback. It still survives in the Chesapeake in numbers large enough to not be considered endangered.

CANVASBACK DUCK

The canvasback completes the culinary trio of Chesapeake Bay treats that were once the pride of Washington and other Atlantic Coast cities. With oysters as an appetizer and terrapin soup as a first course, canvasback duck (*Aythya valisineria*) would reign as the pièce de résistance of Washington's finest dinners, an intensely gamey dish that appealed to discriminating epicureans. "The canvas-back duck is the gastronome's favorite fowl," the *New York Times* declared in 1896.

> *Nothing so crowns a feast. Senator Cameron once paid $16 a pair for all that a Havre de Grace* [Maryland] *dealer had, in a time of scarcity, to grace a dinner he was giving in Washington. Prince Bismarck, until his recent failing health, had a consignment of canvas-backs sent to him from Havre de Grace every year…Queen Victoria has served them at State dinners, and the Prince of Wales is always pleased to receive a gift of them. To the epicure's imagination they convey the most confortable and exhilarating ideas…*

Indeed, Alessandro Filippini, the world-renowned chef of Delmonico's in New York City, was said to have dubbed canvasback the "king of birds."

What made the canvasback such a delicacy were its fastidious eating habits. "The favorite food of the canvas back, which imparts to it the peculiar flavor so highly esteemed by epicures, is, on the Atlantic Coast, the valesneria [*sic*], an aquatic plant popularly called the wild celery," the *Washington Post* explained in 1905. Canvasbacks would dive into the marshy Chesapeake Bay waters where vallisneria thrived below the surface and grab the plants' tuberous roots, which are the tasty parts. They would eat other foods if necessary but preferred vallisneria.

In the nineteenth century, canvasbacks were especially abundant around Havre de Grace and the upper reaches of the Chesapeake, known as the Susquehanna Flats, which had large beds of submerged vallisneria. The birds would summer in central Canada and the Midwest, where they nested and raised their young, and then migrate south to the Chesapeake and a few other southern spots for the winter. Duck hunters from all over the country would descend on the Chesapeake during the season to take on the challenge of hunting for canvasbacks, although only the wealthiest could afford to join the exclusive clubs that held dominion over the best hunting grounds. President Benjamin Harrison was one canvasback aficionado who loved nothing better than to get up very early on a brisk November morning in the 1890s and sit in the marshes of the Chesapeake to wait for canvasbacks to appear.

Like oysters and terrapins, canvasback ducks were served in the best Washington restaurants. In the eighteenth and early nineteenth centuries, they were abundant and very cheap. A tasty canvasback dinner was easily obtained at Washington taverns and eating-houses. George Washington was among many who enjoyed duck hunting and had a keen appreciation for canvasback. Once, when dining at Gadsby's Tavern in Alexandria, Washington was told by the proprietor that "there was good store of canvass-back ducks in the larder."

"Very good, sir," Washington replied, "give us some of them, with a chafing-dish, some hominy, and a bottle of good Madeira, and we shall not complain."

"TERRAPIN TOM" MURREY'S FRIED OYSTERS (C. 1900)

Beat up three eggs thoroughly; add half a pint of oyster juice, a pepper-spoonful of cayenne, a salt-spoonful of black pepper, a tablespoonful of salt and a teaspoonful of English mustard. Work the mixture to a batter and gradually add a gill of oil. Now comes the most particular part of the formula. Cover a board or part of a table with a layer of cracker crumbs half an inch deep. Drain fifty oysters free from liquid, place them on the cracker crumbs and dredge over them more cracker crumbs. See to it that one oyster is not on top of another. Pick up each oyster by its beard and dip it in the batter. Have ready a quantity of breadcrumbs grated from the white part of stale bread; spread this out on the table, and after the oysters have been dipped in batter, lay them carefully on the breadcrumbs two inches apart. After they are all spread out, turn them over neatly, which will breadcrumb the other side. Dip them in the batter again by taking hold of the beard, and again spread them out on the breadcrumbs. Under no circumstances place one oyster on top of another, nor in any way press them together; this would make them heavy. When the fat is so hot that the smoke from it would light a match, then fry them by again taking hold of the beard, one at a time, and dropping them into the fat. When they are dark brown, take them up and strew over them a quantity of salt.

By the later part of the nineteenth century, the king of ducks had grown quite scarce and very expensive. Accordingly, it was found at only the most exclusive restaurants, such as the Willard Hotel, Chamberlin's and Harvey's. One famous group of VIPs—the Canvasback Club—met regularly to enjoy dinners punctuated with canvasback duck as the main course. It was organized "immediately after the Civil War" and lasted until the twentieth century, gaining fame for all the celebrities who were invited to join in the feasts. The group originally met at Chamberlin's but later moved to Harvey's. Speakers among its distinguished guests included Ralph Waldo Emerson, Thomas Nast and Stephen A. Douglas. It was said to be similar to and a precursor of today's Gridiron Club.

Overhunting irrevocably decimated canvasback duck populations. "Formerly ducks were very abundant on the [Susquehanna] flats, but the immense multitudes, which covered acres and acres of the flats and produced a noise resembling thunder as they rose in a body, are no longer seen," the *Washington Post* lamented in 1911. The scarcity of canvasbacks was exacerbated during World War I, when the army started testing ordnance in and around the flats, scaring most of them off. By that time, the Migratory Bird Treaty Act had banned all commercial harvesting of the canvasback and other species and had given the federal government the power to regulate canvasback hunting. By 1936, the wild populations had become so low that all hunting of canvasbacks was banned. In subsequent years, the ban would be partially lifted, only to be reinstated later.

The greatest threat to canvasbacks these days is not the few remaining hunters but the loss of their prized habitat. Erosion and silting of the Chesapeake has severely curtailed the former underwater fields of vallisneria, dramatically reducing canvasback numbers. Some 250,000 of the majestic birds visited the Chesapeake in the 1950s; now, about 50,000 remain. Much of their nesting habitats in the Midwest and Canada have also been destroyed. It's been many years since canvasback duck has appeared on a Washington restaurant menu, and it is unlikely ever to return.

Chapter 3
On Pennsylvania Avenue and Elsewhere in the Nineteenth Century

In the mid-nineteenth century, Washington, like other cities, had few fine restaurants. French cuisine was synonymous with fine dining in those days, and the best restaurants catered exclusively to the upper classes that had the sophistication, resources and leisure time to enjoy them. At such places, simply ordering a meal took formidable skills that were well beyond most people's abilities. The menus were entirely in French, using numerous specialized culinary conventions, and all items had to be ordered separately and assembled into a meal. Attentive, well-trained waiters would discreetly assist patrons whom they perceived to be worthy and reserve the best food for them while treating others with chilly contempt. Multicourse dinners lasted for hours, involved elaborate manners and could be enormously expensive. Such was the setting at Delmonico's in New York City, which set the standard for fine dining in the United States and was known internationally as one of the best French restaurants. Located in the country's richest city, it became a showplace for conspicuous upper-class consumption, staffed by the best French chefs, offering the rarest and most exquisite dishes and hosting extraordinarily lavish banquets.

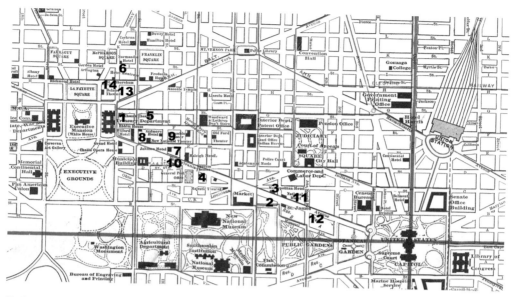

Early Washington restaurants: 1. Rhodes Tavern; 2. Boulanger's; 3. Snow's Epicurean Eating House; 4. Harvey's; 5. Olmsted Grill; 6. Chamberlin's; 7. Gautier's; 8. Gerstenberg's; 9. Perreard's; 10. Hancock's; 11. Fritz Reuter's; 12. Mades; 13. Welcker's; and 14. Wormley's.

DENIZENS OF THE AVENUE

Washington, of course, was not New York City, and very few Washington restaurants aspired to the airs (or prices) of Delmonico's. But contrary to popular opinion, Washington did have its own fine restaurants. In addition to the dining rooms at Willard's and several other hotels, Washington's two best restaurants at mid-century were Hammack's and Gautier's, both near the White House on Pennsylvania Avenue.

JOHN D. HAMMACK, a successful and well-known D.C. restaurateur, opened one of the city's finest Civil War–era restaurants in 1861 at Fifteenth Street and Pennsylvania Avenue Northwest. An *Evening Star* review of the new eatery admired the "handsome vestibule, rich with stained glass" at the entrance, the "really handsome still-life and other paintings in oil" decorating the main dining saloon and the big marble tables "set out with beautiful Bohemian wares, cut glass, &c." The spacious quarters included separate upstairs supper rooms and bars, a billiards room and a modern kitchen in the rear fitted up with the latest ranges "by Dove," where "Hammack's famous good things are dished up for epicures." As is typical of nineteenth-century commentary, nothing in the *Star*'s article discussed the food specifically, other than a few general references that it was very good. After the First Battle of Manassas, one of the Confederate Quaker guns seized by Union troops at Manassas was put on display at Hammack's. John Hammack died in 1867.

CHARLES GAUTIER (1811–1884) was a fashionable Washington caterer and perhaps its most prominent restaurateur from the 1840s until after the Civil War. Gautier arrived in the United States in 1838 and first settled in Georgetown before moving into Washington City in the early 1840s. Like Joseph Boulanger, he was particularly noted as a confectioner, and he also offered catering services. In 1846, he advertised a "Great Christmas Display" at his VILLE DE PARIS on the northeast corner of Eleventh Street and Pennsylvania Avenue Northwest, promising he could "supply parties and balls with every thing that is rich and good and needed on such occasions, at reasonable rates," and invited visitors to see his display of "a large number of superb Cakes, most tastefully and richly ornamented, ranging in weight from five pounds up to near twelve hundred pounds!"

In 1853, Gautier built a new place at Twelfth Street and Pennsylvania Avenue, and it was fitted up as all the best restaurants of the time were, with separate large dining rooms for men and women, as well as a number of smaller rooms for private parties. Gautier's new establishment was capable of the highest levels of French-style finery. In 1855, he advertised that his "Ladies' and Gentlemen's Elegant Saloon and Restaurant" was "conducted on the plan of Taylor & Delmonico's New York" and offered breakfast, lunch, dinner and supper—all "served in the best style at a few minutes' notice." Also offered were "elegant dining rooms and parlors for the accommodation of messes or parties of gentlemen desirous of taking their meals together." Beyond his day-to-day offerings, Gautier catered inaugural parties for James Buchanan in 1857 and Abraham Lincoln in 1861. For Buchanan's fête, he reportedly served up four hundred gallons of oysters, 500 quarts of chicken salad, 500 quarts of jellies, 1,200 quarts of ice cream, eight rounds of beef, seventy-five hams, sixty saddles of mutton and four saddles of venison.

A March 1865 advertisement proclaimed Gautier's to be "the restaurant of this city, where a gentleman can take a lady to enjoy the luxuries of the season, as no improper characters are admitted here." Ironically, that very month, one of the most improper characters in U.S. history, John Wilkes Booth, had met with his co-conspirators at Gautier's to plan the kidnapping of President Lincoln. Gautier was later questioned about the plotters, but he had no involvement in the conspiracy. After the war, Gautier got out of the confectionery and catering business and concentrated on wholesale liquor sales, including his trademarked Native Wine Bitters. He died at his home in Washington in 1884.

Many of the city's restaurants, both fine and casual, were clustered along Pennsylvania Avenue, where the bulk of the city's commercial life took place in the nineteenth century. Toward the end of the century, a string of quirky but much-loved eateries took hold along the avenue. While Gautier's and Hammack's offered their sophisticated fare in the block nearest the Treasury Department, the next block east, from Fourteenth to Thirteenth Streets Northwest, was in sharp contrast.

Known as "Rum Row," the stretch of the avenue between Thirteenth and Fourteenth Streets was home to a variety of "bohemian" restaurants and saloons. As the name suggests, Rum Row was a place for drinking—and naturally an assortment of other vices, particularly gambling. Originally a line of federal town houses housing early residents and professionals, Rum Row changed character dramatically during the Civil War, when soldiers swarmed the streets looking for cheap entertainment. Previously respectable homes and commercial establishments were replaced with saloons and gambling joints. After the war, the row became less notorious but was still a focal point for eating and drinking. Its central location made it the rendezvous for all elements of society. "On the row a man met and mingled with the elite, the bon-ton, the busy man-about-town, the Bohemian, the poet laureate, the soldier of fortune, and everything but the bootlegger, a type that at that date had not come into existence," wrote the *Washington Post* in 1921.

One of Rum Row's quirkiest fixtures was also one of the city's best-known German restaurants, GERSTENBERG'S, which opened in 1887 in the former barroom of Rum Row denizen George W. Driver at 1343 E Street Northwest. The proprietor of this resort, Ernst Gerstenberg, emigrated from Germany in 1883 when he was twenty-eight years old, around the same time he married his wife, Augusta. It was Frau Gerstenberg's culinary skills that made the food at his restaurant so tasty. One of her most celebrated dishes was a *hasenpfeffer* (rabbit stew), and she was also noted for her wiener schnitzel, veal chops, sour beef and German pancakes, all distributed to waiters from a little window in the back of the dining room.

While Mrs. Gerstenberg was ensuring that the guests were all served with hearty German fare, Mr. Gerstenberg, a large and formidable-looking man, would tend to other matters, such as the beer. He was famous for his homemade pilsner, and in time his establishment became known among locals as the "University of Gerstenberg," perhaps because it seemed like a student beer hall in old Heidelberg.

Gerstenberg's Restaurant, circa 1910. *Library of Congress.*

Aside from good food and drink, Gerstenberg had a fondness for dogs—big dogs. Lena, Daisy and Laura were three of his Great Danes, and many Washingtonians knew them well. When Daisy died in 1905, the *Post* reported that Gerstenberg received many letters of condolence, including a poem celebrating her loyalty to her master. But the most famous of Gerstenberg's dogs was a bulldog named Bismarck.

"There is probably not a canine in the city that possesses such a wide acquaintance among men about town as does the massive bulldog owned by Ernst Gerstenberg, the restaurant-keeper," the *Post* remarked one day in August 1895. The article was entitled "Dog Bismarck Must Die" and told the sad story of how the vigilant dog had mistaken

Caricature of Ernst Gerstenberg. *After a drawing published in the* Washington Herald.

a young newsboy for a burglar and bit him on the leg. The boy was taken to Emergency Hospital, but doctors said he had only a slight scratch and was not hurt. Things went less well for poor Bismarck. Gerstenberg was served a warrant charging him with "keeping a biting dog." A trial was held, and Gerstenberg appeared, explaining that Bismarck "was a gentle creature and never attacked people without provocation." Nevertheless, the judge was unsympathetic, decreeing that Bismarck was to be put down. Gerstenberg was enraged and vowed never to let anyone onto his premises to carry out the court's order.

The newspapers followed the story breathlessly for days. It seemed almost everyone, except the authorities, was on Bismarck's side in the dispute. When the police duly arrived at the restaurant one day with the intention of shooting the dog, Gerstenberg refused to let them in. He was hauled back into court on contempt charges (which were dropped), and the judge reaffirmed the canine death sentence. But by this time, Gerstenberg had spirited Bismarck away to refuge in Cabin John, Maryland, while his lawyer worked the legal system. Finally, in early November, more than two months after the original incident, the D.C. Court of Appeals overturned the ignominious death sentence, and Bismarck was joyfully returned to E Street, much to the delight of numerous supporters throughout the city. The dog finally died of natural causes about a year later, an event duly noted by the *Washington Post*, which claimed that he had devoured fourteen thousand pounds of tenderloin in his nine years of life.

Gerstenberg's continued to thrive through the early years of the twentieth century but received its own death sentence with the dawning of Prohibition in the District in

November 1917. The beloved eatery closed in December 1918 and was converted to a Chinese restaurant, the Canton Pagoda. The Gerstenbergs' plans for retiring to a life of ease at their summer home in Suitland, Maryland, were cut short when Mrs. Gerstenberg died suddenly in January 1919. Ernst Gerstenberg survived for at least another decade.

Perhaps even more eccentric than old Gerstenberg was "Count" Jean Marie Perreard (1844–1918), a proud Frenchman whose restaurant and hotel at 1206 E Street Northwest (just off the avenue) celebrated all things French. A native of Savoy, Perreard came to Washington as a chef for the French legation and decided to stay on and open his own hotel, officially dubbed the "French Bastille" but known to everyone as PERREARD'S.

Every year on July 14, the affable Count would throw a lavish celebration at his "castle" to commemorate the storming of the Bastille. He insisted he was "one damn good republican," despite the implications of his assumed title and his other contradictory statements, such as "I do not cater to the rabble." His famous Bastille Day banquets were indeed highly exclusive affairs, "events of rare enjoyment, where assemble only the most prominent and aristocratic people of Washington." His 1905 event included an elaborate banquet, speeches by dignitaries including Samuel Gompers of the American Federation of Labor, vocal and instrumental music and, finally, a "clever, realistic representation of the crash of the falling of the historic Paris prison."

Perreard's was known for its fine French food, especially the delicious soups prepared by Perreard's wife, Alice, known as the "Countess." Despite its French elegance, Perreard's was also known as a beer hall, perhaps more so than a traditional French restaurant. Perreard—short, flamboyant and energetic—liked to mix with his customers. He was credited with inventing the "Bismarc" cocktail, which is simply a small glass of beer. "He will give you desserts—ah, *sacre dieu*—desserts that are beyond the dream of any one but a Perreard," James Frank Lyman rhapsodized in the *Washington Herald* in 1911. "And if you desire the count will sit down and drink at your expense and tell you stories of his native country and the glorious America." Special guests might be invited to sit at the *en famille* table with the Count and Countess, where Perreard would prepare exquisite salads.

With the rise of the Anti-Saloon League in the 1910s, places like Perreard's were increasingly under pressure. Under influence from the league, Congress passed the Jones-Works Excise Law in 1913 that put severe restrictions on saloons in the District. The law went into effect on July 1, 1913, just days before Bastille Day. The Count was devastated and decided not to hold his famous celebration that year. As Mme. Perreard explained to the *Washington Herald*:

Ze excise law will not permit ze ladies to join in ze celebration, and what ees ze celebration sans ladies? Rien de tout. We weel celebrate notre tres cher quatorze Juillet en famille, entre nous. No songs, no musique, no speeches, no enthusiasm, no nothing. My husban' weel go to Baltimore, 'e ees so disgust' avec toutes les choses. Mais oui, oui, we weel fly ze flag de la belle France, oh, oui, but c'est tout.

Then, in November 1917, the Sheppard Act went into effect, bringing Prohibition to the District. Perreard took the dry law as a blow to his personal liberty, and according to the newspapers, passage of the law marked the beginning of a severe decline in Perreard's health. When he died two months later, in January 1918, his wife was heartbroken and "between sobs said, 'I may go back home now—to France.'"

On the south side of Pennsylvania Avenue, about a block to the east, stood another notable culinary rendezvous known as HANCOCK'S, at 1234 Pennsylvania Avenue Northwest. Andrew Hancock (1804–1881), a native of Occoquan, Virginia, came to Washington as a child and founded his namesake restaurant in 1840. Daniel Webster, Henry Clay and John C. Calhoun were among the famous men who were habitués of Hancock's, along with countless other statesmen, military officers and other important people (but never women). Centrally located on Pennsylvania Avenue, Hancock's was famed for its excellent food and drinks.

Hancock was an eccentric individual, known in later years for his long, snow-white beard. His cramped, low-ceilinged eatery was jam-packed with knickknacks and historic souvenirs. "In early life Mr. Hancock developed a fondness for what was queer and curious in art, and hence his collection of all kinds of curiosities, with which the place is lined, gave it the name of the 'Old Curiosity Shop,'" the *Post* explained in 1881. Some items visitors found grim and macabre, such as the wanted poster for John Wilkes

Jean Marie Perreard. *From the* Washington Times, *July 14, 1905.*

Booth and the photos of the hanging of the Lincoln conspirators. There were many old weapons—guns, sabers, pistols—hung on the walls or even dangling from the heavy oak ceiling beams. A tall white hat that Zachary Taylor wore at the Battle of Okeechobee, Florida, in 1837 sat in a glass case, and hanging nearby was Andrew Jackson's umbrella. There was even a pair of bedroom slippers supposedly belonging to George Washington.

As to its cuisine, Hancock's was known primarily for one dish: sizzling hot "Chicken à la Maryland" (fried chicken served with a cream-based gravy) with hoecakes (cornmeal pancakes traditionally fried on a hoe). To wash it down, a large cut-glass pitcher of beer would be set in the middle of the table. As simple as the dish sounds, commentators of all stripes routinely raved about it. As one newspaper put it, if you didn't know any better, you probably wouldn't go into Hancock's and expect to get a fine meal, but once you tried the chicken, you would be a believer. All the cooking and serving was done by African Americans, which doubtless allowed many white Washingtonians to imagine that they were still living in the Old South.

Hancock's would likely never have been so famous if it weren't for the exceptional talents of Dick Francis (1827–1888), an African American who took over as bartender in 1848 and stayed for nearly forty years. Hancock's was known for its mixed drinks served in sugar-frosted glasses, the most famous of which was the Hancock Punch (ingredients are a secret). Francis knew how to give the drinks just the right kick, whether they be mint juleps (a favorite in this southern town), gin rickeys, milk punches, whiskey smashes or, in the wintertime, hot toddies and buttered rum. Francis's winning personality and mixological skills made him widely beloved, and his bar had the kind of edgy charm that makes saloons endearing. On the wall behind Francis hung a portrait of Jack Sheppard (1702–1724), the ruthless English criminal who was notorious for his multiple escapes from prison. Here was a place to revel in the exploits of the world's most infamous rapscallions.

Hancock retired and turned the restaurant over to his son, John, in 1863. John's son, Andrew W. Hancock, ran it after John passed away in 1885. Descending through the Hancock generations, the restaurant was likely the oldest continuously in existence in Washington when it finally closed in 1914. After seventy-four years in business, it was yet another victim of the anti-saloon crackdown (its liquor license had been terminated). The old building, however, remained standing until 1931, when all the structures on the south side of Pennsylvania Avenue were torn down for the Federal Triangle project. What became of the many priceless documents and relics that cluttered the Old Curiosity Shop is anybody's guess.

Farther east, on the northwest corner of Fourth Street and Pennsylvania Avenue Northwest, stood the hotel and restaurant of FRITZ REUTER (1862–1906). Reuter was

Hancock's Restaurant, circa 1914. *Library of Congress.*

born in Hanover and came to the United States when he was twenty-one years old. After spending a year in Baltimore, he came to Washington to work in a saloon. When he opened up his own *gasthaus* (inn and restaurant) in 1889, it was in an area that was developing as Washington's first Chinatown. The building he took over had been a boardinghouse for many years in the early part of the century, hosting luminaries such as John Marshall and other Supreme Court justices, as well as Henry Clay and John C. Calhoun.

The Fritz Reuter restaurant was very flashy for its day, featuring an unusual serpentine-edged bar and a large, refrigerated showcase behind the plate-glass window on Pennsylvania Avenue. According to George Rothwell Brown, Reuter's was "a memorial to the small hot bird and the large cold bottle, to terrapin, and to the broiled, live lobster." In 1902, Reuter offered table d'hôte meals for just fifty cents, advertising them as "the best dinner in the city for the money" and claiming "a large number of people enjoy it rather than go to the trouble of home cooking." That same year, Prince Henry of Prussia dined at Reuter's during his much-ballyhooed state visit to Washington.

Sadly, Reuter was plagued with depression, and after being treated for it for over a year, he committed suicide in 1906 by shooting himself in the second-floor parlor of his hotel. The hotel and restaurant were subsequently taken over by Henry Achterkirchen (1875–1914), another native of Hanover. Achterkirchen promoted the restaurant extensively, including its famous planked steak à la Fritz Reuter, "a dish fit for a king." Achterkirchen died in 1914, and later that same year, the District excise board, in a foretelling of the coming Prohibition era, closed Reuter's down.

In 1858, Prussian-born CHARLES MADES (1831–1915) opened his small hotel and restaurant on the southwest corner of Third Street and Pennsylvania Avenue Northwest, a block to the east of where Reuter's would stand. A "stout and powerful" man, Mades got his start in Washington as a sculptor, carving decorations for the U.S. Capitol and other public buildings. His restaurant, located just northwest of the Botanic Garden (which was in the middle of the Mall in those days), was frequented by soldiers during the Civil War and grew in popularity in the postwar years.

One of the unique curiosities of Mades's was its frog pond in the backyard; customers were invited to select their dinners from it. Of course, you could get more than just frog legs. "Chicken dinners were the attraction at Mades," the *Washington Post* declared in a 1921 reminiscence.

> *It was the rival of Hancock's at the other end of the Avenue. The two places stood in classes by themselves. They were, in fact, the class of Washington; quaint little out-*

of-the-way places where a tired soul might go and partake of choice viands, foodstuffs cooked and served in the manner and method that a gentleman of the old school demanded—and secured.

As Charles Mades grew older, he delegated much of the day-to-day operations of the restaurant and hotel to his sons. Journalist Buck Bryant wrote in the *Post* in 1929 that Mades would sit for hours every day by a window looking out on Third Street and feed the birds that came over from the Botanic Garden. "While distinguished members of Congress and well-known newspaper men made merry at the tables or the counter, he would whistle for the blue jays, the mockers, the catbirds and other feathered friends who appreciated his generosity."

Mades's closed in 1925, long past its heyday, and all its furnishings were auctioned off to pay debts. The building burned down in 1931, just as the entire south side of Pennsylvania Avenue was being cleared for construction of the Federal Triangle office buildings.

OFF THE AVENUE

Of course, not all of Washington's notable restaurants were on Pennsylvania Avenue, although most were there or somewhere nearby. A few blocks north on Fifteenth Street, between New York Avenue and H Streets Northwest, stood two of the most prestigious restaurants of the late nineteenth century, both connected with boutique hotels. One was WELCKER'S HOTEL AND RESTAURANT, at 727 Fifteenth Street Northwest. John Welcker (1836–1875), a native of Prussia, immigrated to the United States at a young age and first learned the hospitality trade as a waiter at Delmonico's in New York City. He came to Washington in 1861, when he was involved in supplying provisions to the Union army, and got into the restaurant business by taking over Buhler's Restaurant on Pennsylvania Avenue before opening his namesake establishment on Fifteenth Street. Welcker's featured a large banquet hall that could seat over six hundred dinner guests, as it did on the day of Ulysses S. Grant's inauguration in 1869. The hall attracted large groups, especially alumni associations, including the Harvard Club and the Princeton Club. Frederick Douglass spoke at the first annual dinner of the Howard University Alumni Association at Welcker's in 1886. Finally, the Gridiron Club, the exclusive dinner club of Washington news correspondents famous for its satires of the rich and famous, had its first meeting at Welcker's in 1885.

According to journalist George Alfred Townsend (1841–1914), John Welcker was "a youthful, florid, stoutish man with a hearty address, a ready blush, and a love for the open air and children." The fare at his restaurant was widely praised as among the very best in Washington. Charles Dickens stopped at Welcker's during his second trip to Washington in 1868, and Townsend says that Welcker had a letter signed by Dickens proclaiming that Welcker "kept the best restaurant in the world."

Townsend quizzed Welcker about the best local foods and recorded the following observations: the best local fish, in Welcker's opinion, was Spanish mackerel, then fairly abundant in the Potomac. D.C. markets carried superior celery, asparagus and lettuce, but local potatoes and carrots were subpar. Virginia mutton was "the best in the world," better even than English Southdown mutton, widely considered the *ne plus ultra*. Virginia also produced excellent partridge and pheasant. Welcker was very enthusiastic about the snipe and canvasback duck found along the Potomac, while the best local oysters, in his opinion, were from Tangier Island in the Chesapeake and the York and Elizabeth Rivers in Virginia. The most expensive dish Welcker offered was "Philadelphia capon au sauce Goddard, stuffed with truffles," the capon coming from New Jersey and the truffles from France or northern Italy.

Welcker died suddenly from pneumonia at age thirty-nine. However, his hotel and restaurant continued to operate for many years afterward under the control of Welcker's widow, who had always manned the cash register in the restaurant. A six-story addition, designed by noted architect Adolf Cluss (1825–1905), was completed in 1884. Finally, in 1900, J. Barton Key, a descendant of Francis Scott Key, leased the hotel and reopened it as Barton's, although he ran into financial difficulties within months and was forced to close. The Barton Hotel was torn down to make way for the headquarters of the W.B. Hibbs Banking Company in 1906.

The other exclusive Fifteenth Street eatery was even more celebrated than Welcker's. It was run by JAMES WORMLEY (1819–1884), an African American who became a prominent Washington businessman. Wormley was truly an exceptional individual in the history of the city. As a young man in the 1840s, Wormley learned the hospitality trade as a steward on ships and riverboats and opened his first boardinghouse and restaurant on I Street Northwest when he returned to Washington in the 1850s. At the same time, he served as head steward of the exclusive Washington Club on Lafayette Square, where he built friendships with many of the city's most influential citizens. When wealthy statesman Reverdy Johnson (1796–1876) was named minister to England in 1868, Wormley accompanied him briefly to help set up his London household. Wormley brought live terrapins with him on the transatlantic voyage and greatly impressed the British with his delicious terrapin

Wormley's Hotel, circa 1898. *D.C. Public Library, Washingtoniana Division.*

stew. It was on the heels of this triumph that Wormley returned to Washington to open his famous five-story hotel and restaurant on the southwest corner of Fifteenth and H Streets Northwest in 1869.

Wormley was widely celebrated as a sophisticated caterer and restaurateur, and his hostelry was frequented by the rich and powerful. In later years, the *Evening Star* called him "one of the most widely known stewards and hotel proprietors in the country." The *Boston Herald* observed that his hotel, "while not the largest, was the most strictly aristocratic of any in the city, its quiet elegance and high prices attracting a very select circle of patronage."

A fervent supporter of the cause of African American equality, Wormley was a close friend of Massachusetts senator Charles Sumner (1811–1874), who had steadfastly championed the rights of African Americans both before and after emancipation. One of Wormley's prize possessions was a portrait of Charles Sumner painted by

Henry Ulke and originally intended for the Charles Sumner School on M Street Northwest. Wormley acquired it after Sumner's death. The State of Massachusetts reportedly offered to purchase the Sumner portrait from Wormley, but he refused. "Never shall any one say that I parted with the picture of the man who befriended me and my race, for any money consideration," he was quoted as saying. He later decided to donate the portrait to Massachusetts rather than sell it.

When President James Garfield was fatally shot in 1881, Wormley was the natural choice to minister to his needs, including preparing special meals for him. According to an article in the *New York Herald-Tribune*, Wormley had a "patented" method of making beef tea (beef broth), which was thought to have restorative powers. Wormley prepared the special tea for Garfield as he had previously done for the stricken Charles Sumner. The special tea "was made by broiling the tenderloin of a porterhouse steak, and while the meat was yet smoking putting it into an iron receiver heated for the purpose. A crank was then turned which brought hundreds of pounds of pressure on the steaming steak, causing every particle of its juice to stream forth. A little seasoning and the tea was ready." Wormley also prepared chicken broth for Garfield, using the chickens grown on his farm out in the suburbs near Tenleytown. Garfield, of course, did not recover from his wounds, but not for any shortcomings in the food prepared by Wormley.

Probably the most famous historical event to occur at Wormley's hotel was the so-called Wormley Conference, which was held in secret in February 1877. The "conference" was in reality an informal meeting among representatives of the Democratic and Republican Parties to agree on the outcome of the close 1876 presidential election. A deal had emerged whereby Democratic congressmen agreed not to fight an electoral vote count that would put the Republican candidate, Rutherford B. Hayes, in office in exchange for the Republicans agreeing that the Reconstruction constraints they had previously imposed on the South (which had protected the rights of African Americans) would be abandoned. While this infamous deal was supposedly struck at the meeting at Wormley's hotel, where Democratic congressmen were staying, it had in fact already been made by the time the Wormley Conference occurred. Wormley himself certainly did nothing to abet such deal making and surely would have done what he could to thwart it if it had been in his power.

Wormley renovated and expanded his posh hotel in the early 1880s. However, he was afflicted with kidney stones and died after an operation for them in 1884. His passing was mourned across the country. Wormley's heirs debated what to do with the hotel and finally decided to sell it in 1893. Competition from larger and grander hotels, such as the Shoreham, built directly across H Street in 1887, had eclipsed its prestige. A sheriff's auction was held in 1895, and all of the rare furnishings that Wormley had accumulated were sold at bargain-basement prices to customers who seemed indifferent to their historical value. Two divans that had been owned by Charles Sumner sold for three dollars apiece. The two-hundred-room building later reopened for a few years as the Colonial Hotel but was finally razed in 1906, when it was replaced by the massive neoclassical Union Trust Company building that stands on the site today.

Chapter 4

THE EXCLUSIVE DINING ROOMS
OF THE GREAT HOTELS

Just as most people dined almost exclusively at home—or as guests in other people's homes—in the nineteenth century, so when they traveled they almost always expected to eat in the dining rooms of their hotels. Accordingly, most hotels included the cost of meals in their room prices. While many of the early taverns seemed to care as little about the food they served as they did about the quality of their sleeping accommodations, later hotels adopted a much more customer-oriented approach, vying with one another to provide the most luxurious away-from-home experience possible, both in living quarters and in dining. The shift was a gradual one. By the 1830s and 1840s, Washington's first large hotels started to build their reputations with dining rooms that offered tasty and even (at times, at least) elegant fare but were not quite full-fledged restaurants. Patrons still dined together at set times in table d'hôte style rather than being served individually à la carte. Later in the century, hotel restaurants would largely surpass all of the city's other eateries in the quality of their cuisine, the refinement of their service and the elegance of their furnishings, deliberately setting their standards well above the reach of the common man.

One of the first great hotels in Washington was directly connected to the earlier tavern era through its owner, John Gadsby (1766–1844), who had operated Gadsby's Tavern in Alexandria from 1796 to 1808. Gadsby came to Washington in the early 1820s, taking over a tavern and rooming house at Nineteenth and I Streets Northwest. That place was too small and out of the way, however, so in 1827, he purchased a row of Federal town houses on the northeast corner of Pennsylvania Avenue at Sixth Street Northwest and combined them to create what was the city's largest hostelry at the time, which he called the NATIONAL HOTEL. To mark its opening, Gadsby organized a grand ball in celebration of George Washington's birthday. "The extensive rooms of the National Hotel were crowded with a company of ladies and gentlemen never surpassed on any occasion here in numbers or brilliance," the *National Intelligencer* reported. President John Quincy Adams opened the ball and stayed to its close, dancing with all the pretty ladies.

Gadsby, by all accounts, was a gracious host. The dining room was renowned for its terrapin dinners and rare old wines. Although guests continued to eat at set hours at a large communal table at the National, Gadsby made sure both the food and the service were impeccable. Nathan Sargent, a visitor to Washington City in the 1820s, recalled the "military style" displayed at John Gadsby's dinners:

> *The guests being all seated, and an army of colored servants standing behind the chairs, Mr. Gadsby, a short, stout gentleman, standing at the head of the table, the guests silent with expectation, the word was given, "Remove covers!" when all the servants moved like automata, each at the same moment placing his hand upon the handle of a cover, each at the same instant lifting it, stepping back in line and facing to the head of the table, and, at a sign from Mr. Gadsby, all marching and keeping regular step to the place of depositing the covers, and then back, to commence waiting on the guests.*

The National stood as a major landmark for much of Washington's early history, one of several important hostelries along Pennsylvania Avenue, the city's main street. Henry Clay lived there for many years and died in his room in 1852. Presidents Andrew Jackson, James K. Polk and Abraham Lincoln all frequented the place. A lavish post-inaugural banquet was held for Lincoln at the National, as were many of the finest Washington dinners before the Civil War. In later years, as postwar prosperity took hold and Washington grew, the National was increasingly unable to compete with newer, grander establishments, and the hotel finally closed in 1931. The Newseum now occupies the hotel's old site.

One block west of the National, also on the north side of Pennsylvania Avenue, stood another of Washington's famous early hotels, the INDIAN QUEEN. The first inn on this site, the Pennsylvania House and Myer's City Tavern, opened as early as 1806. James Madison's second inaugural ball was held here in 1813, as were both of James Monroe's inaugural balls (1817 and 1821).

Jesse B. Brown (1767–1847), a native of Havre de Grace, Maryland, and a protégé of John Gadsby, bought the hotel in 1820. He remodeled and enlarged it and then rechristened it the Indian Queen, a name in common use among early American

NATIONAL HOTEL WINTER GARDEN, WASHINGTON, D.C.

A circa 1912 view of the National Hotel's main dining room. *Author's collection.*

hotels. "No pains shall be spared to accommodate customers, travellers, and others, nor any care or expense omitted in procuring the best of viands, liquors, and forage, with good beds and stabling," Brown promised. He hung a large sign out front with a "lurid" picture of Pocahontas brightly painted on it.

Brown was a classic entrepreneur, styling himself "the prince of landlords." He was known for his officious and personal attention to every guest and for the large decanters of brandy and whiskey that he would ensure were placed at every table setting. Like the National, Brown's Indian Queen kept many of the customs of traditional taverns and inns. Meals were served at a large communal dining table, with everyone sharing and passing plates. A great bell was rung whenever meals were ready, and it was said that the bell could be heard all across Washington City. As Ben Perley Poore recalled years later:

> When the next meal was ready the newly arrived guest was met at the door of the dining-room by Mr. Brown, wearing a large white apron, who escorted him to a seat and then went to the head of the table, where he carved and helped the principal dish.

The excellences of this—fish or flesh or fowl—he would announce as he would invite those seated at the table to send up their plates for what he knew to be their favorite portions; and he would also invite attention to the dishes on other parts of the table, which were carved and helped by the guests who sat nearest them. "I have a delicious quarter of mutton from the Valley of Virginia," Mr. Brown would announce in a stentorian tone, which could be heard above the clatter of crockery and the din of steel knives and forks. "Let me send you a rare slice, Mr. A." "Colonel B., will you not have a bone?" "Mrs. C., send up your plate for a piece of the kidney." "Mrs. D., there is a fat and tender mongrel goose at the other end of the table." "Joe, pass around the sweet potatoes." "Colonel E., will you help to that chicken-pie before you?"

After Brown died in 1847, his two sons took over the hotel, and in 1850 they hired celebrated Philadelphia architect John Haviland (1792–1852), a major proponent of the Greek Revival style, to enlarge the structure to a full five stories and to add a grand, neoclassical façade made of white marble reportedly from the same quarry as had supplied the Capitol Building. The beautiful, renovated building reopened as Brown's Marble Hotel in 1851. In 1865, the Brown family sold the hotel, and the new owners renamed it the Metropolitan, a moniker it would keep until it closed in 1932. The *Washington Post* remarked the following year that it "had been in continuous operation longer than any other hotel in America."

THE WILLARD AND THE EBBITT

The WILLARD HOTEL began very much like the National and the Indian Queen, but by the time of the Civil War, it outclassed them both, and in the latter part of the nineteenth century, it rose to become the ultimate public dining spot in Washington City.

There had been a hotel on the northwest corner of Fourteenth Street and Pennsylvania Avenue Northwest since 1818, almost three decades before the Willard brothers showed up to take over its operations. The prominent early Washington landowner John Tayloe (1770–1828), whose elegant Octagon House is one of Washington's great mansions, acquired this property and built a row of six town houses here as an investment in 1816, renting out the corner building to be used as a hotel two years later.

By 1847, Benjamin Ogle Tayloe (1796–1868), John Tayloe's son and heir, had grown dissatisfied with the condition of the hotel and was looking for a new manager.

He chose Henry A. Willard (1822–1909), a shrewd and energetic young entrepreneur whom his fiancée, Phoebe Warren, had recommended. A native of Vermont, Willard had learned the hospitality trade as a steward on a Hudson River steamboat, where he had impressed Miss Warren. He was eager for a new and challenging venture.

As part of the arrangement to bring Willard on, extensive improvements were made to the hotel. It was expanded to 150 rooms from 40 and had elegant gentlemen's and ladies' dining rooms and parlors and three large halls in front, connected to the rooms above by two broad oak staircases. Willard soon brought on his brother Joseph (1820–1897) to help run the hotel, and as it prospered, they acquired additional property along F Street until the Willard Hotel complex eventually spanned the entire block from Pennsylvania Avenue to F Street along Fourteenth.

Henry Willard made a point of ensuring that he had the freshest available meat and produce for his dining room. According to Garnett Laidlaw Eskew, who chronicled the Willard Hotel's early years, Willard "rose every day before dawn and went down to Center Market…to order the day's supply of fresh meat. That duty he would entrust to no one else, nor would he let another supervise the slicing of roasts in the kitchen." Willard also made use of nearby vacant lots as garden space to grow his own produce. "Lettuce, spring onions, snap beans, radishes, asparagus—they all seemed to jump from the ground straight to Willard's tables, said a wag in the dining room."

As the hotel matured, it became known as one of the best sites in the city for elegant, catered events. One of the most famous was the farewell ball for Lord Francis Napier (1819–1898), British minister to the United States, and his wife, Lady Anne Napier, held in February 1859. The ball was a sensational event, one of the largest ever given in Washington City, with some 1,800 guests paying a steep ten dollars each to get in. The Willard's 150-foot ballroom, draped in British and American flags and adorned with portraits of George Washington and Queen Victoria, was barely big enough to contain all the revelers.

At midnight, a curtain was raised on the dining room, which adjoined the ballroom and seated three to four hundred. "The supper and wines were upon a scale of magnificence such as is rarely seen at such an entertainment on this side of the Atlantic," marveled the *Star*. "Immediately in front of Lady Napier stood a pyramid of confectionery six feet high…and ornamented at the top with the figure of Brittania; and another similar ornament, at a different part of the table, emblematical of the United States." Dining went on until 3:00 a.m., and dancing continued virtually unabated until 4:00 a.m. For weeks afterward, the magnificent ball was the talk of the town.

The Napier Ball, as drawn for *Harper's Weekly* magazine. *Library of Congress.*

To handle the immense undertaking of the Napier Ball, Henry Willard enlisted the help of Charles Gautier. In those days, all refined, restaurant-style cooking had to be French, of course, and Gautier's participation gave the event added cachet. In fact, the French influence dominated all fine public dining in America in the mid- to late 1800s, as upper-class Americans increasingly strove to cement their social ranks. "By consuming the cuisine of Old World elites, society leaders of the late nineteenth century believed they were asserting a claim to membership in a European-style aristocracy. If you are what you eat, then eating like the French nobility made you an aristocrat," restaurant historian Andrew P. Haley has observed.

Restaurants—and the best hotel dining rooms were often the finest examples—developed an elaborate code of conduct designed to reinforce the feeling of exclusivity and privilege that upper-class patrons would feel when they dined there. Menus were written entirely in French, under the assumption that anyone attending would be able to read them. Diners were also expected to adhere to an elaborate code of manners, both for ordering food and eating it. Waiters were attuned to the sophistication of their patrons and would vary their service based on it. Above all else, the elaborate, multi-course dinners served in these restaurants were simply far too costly for most Americans to afford. While these restaurants officially remained open to everyone, the system made sure that only a select few could actually patronize them.

The Willard's dining rooms remained Washington's most exclusive into the early years of the twentieth century. The hotel reached its peak of ostentation upon completion of its new building in 1900–04. Architect Henry Janeway Hardenbergh (1847–1918), who designed New York City's Waldorf-Astoria and Plaza Hotels, created the Willard's iconic Beaux-Arts structure with its stately mansard roof that has been a landmark on Pennsylvania Avenue since its completion.

The new Willard's lavish main restaurant was "one of the largest and most elegant dining halls to be found anywhere," according to the *Washington Times*. Decorated in green and brown with mottled green marble columns and heavy oak furniture, it was an emblem of Edwardian opulence and self-satisfaction. The first time Mark Twain stayed at the new Willard, he supposedly took the elevator downstairs for dinner and was surprised to discover that it slipped him quietly into the rear of the restaurant. Vexed by this, he promptly climbed back upstairs one flight and crossed over to the grand staircase, where he made a much more ostentatious descent and was besieged by numerous female admirers, much to his satisfaction.

The Willard's preeminence faded in the twentieth century as more stylish and modern hotels farther uptown eclipsed it. By the 1960s, dining at the Willard had become a rather pedestrian affair. A dinner menu from 1963 offered mostly steaks and sandwiches and a "Chef's Special" that consisted of baked elbow macaroni, Canadian cheddar cheese, mixed green salad and coffee or tea for $1.05—a far cry from the days of the dining room's culinary excesses. The Willard closed abruptly in 1968 and spent almost two decades as an abandoned shell, its interior spaces left in shambles. Preservationists mounted a tremendous effort to save the historic landmark from the wrecking ball, and finally in the 1980s, it was renovated, enlarged and restored to its former glory.

With its reopening in 1986, the hostelry's restored Willard Room restaurant revived its old tradition of rarified, upper-class restaurants. Phyllis Richman, reviewing the Willard Room for the *Washington Post* in 1996, remarked, "This is simply the most magnificent dining room in Washington, outside of the White House and the State Department." But fine hotel dining was already in sharp decline by the 1990s, and the Willard Room would not last long. Recently, it was converted exclusively for use as special event space.

A "sister" hotel to the Willard was the EBBITT HOUSE across the street. William E. Ebbitt established his boardinghouse in 1856 on the southeast corner of Fourteenth

The Willard dining room, circa 1910, photographed by Frances Benjamin Johnston. *Library of Congress.*

and F Streets Northwest, in a neighborhood of old residences that had become boardinghouses. Like the National, Indian Queen and Willard's, the Ebbitt House was created by linking together several existing Federal-style town houses. Ebbitt ran it for only eight years, selling it to Caleb C. Willard (1834–1905) in 1864. Caleb was the younger brother of Henry and Joseph and had worked with his brothers at the Willard Hotel before striking out on his own. His hotel continued to grow after he took over. In 1872, he incorporated the old structure's several parts into a much larger "New" Ebbitt, a stylish Second Empire building six stories tall. Then, in about 1895, the building was enlarged again with a dramatic new mansard roof that hid servants' quarters in the attic. The lobby of the elegant hotel featured massive chandeliers, a marble floor, a marble-topped walnut reception desk and a twenty-five-foot-high coved ceiling, supported by four Corinthian columns.

Dinner.

SATURDAY, MARCH 3, 1866.

SOUP.

Puree of Fowl a la Rhine.

FISH.

Baked Cod, Port Wine sauce.

BOILED.

Leg of Mutton, Caper sauce.   Corned Beef and Cabbage.
Boiled Capons, Pork sauce.   Chicken, Parsley sauce.
Cincinnati Ham.   Beef Tongue.

COLD DISHES.

Ham.   Pressed Corned Beef, with Slaugh   Spiced Beef.

ENTREES.

Wild Red Head Duck broiled, with Currant Jelly sauce.
Croquettes of Rice, flavored with Lemon, French style.
Fricassee of Chicken in Croustade, a la St Martial.
Beef Steak Pot Pie, saute in Fine Herbs, a la Mex'can.
Turkey Hash, in Borders of Potatoes, a la Financiere.
Stewed Veal, with Small Onions, Country stlye.

ROAST.

South Down Mutton.   Ham, Champagne sauce.   Ribs of Beef.
Pork, Apple sauce.   Turkey.

VEGETABLES.

Mashed Potatoes.   Turnips.   Boiled Rice.   Potatoes.
Baked Mashed Potatoes.   Cabbage.   Hominy
Squash.   Oyster Plants.   Beets.   Onions.   Parsnips.

RELISHES.

Pickles.   Parker & Bro.'s London Club sauce.;   Olives.
Cont'nental Sauce.   Tomato Catsup
Shaker Apple sauce.   Horse Radish.

PASTRY.

Lemon Pie.   Fruit Pudding, Wine sauce.   Peach Pie.

DESSERT.

Almonds.   Apples.   Raisins.
Walnuts   Filberts.
Ice Cream.
COFFEE   CHEESE AND CRACKERS

Menu from the Ebbitt House, dated March 3, 1866.
Library of Congress.

A menu from the Ebbitt House, dated March 3, 1866, in the Library of Congress shows that it offered typical fare for a hotel dining room in post–Civil War days. Pretentiousness is muted here; for one thing, the menu is in English. The "Wild Red Head Duck Broiled, with Currant Jelly Sauce" might be quite nice, but it isn't canvasback. The chicken fricassee, beef pot pie, turkey hash and "country style" stewed veal were all dishes that a wide range of travelers would recognize and find appealing.

By the end of the nineteenth century, economic pressures were working to break down the exclusivity of the elite hotel restaurants. It was expensive to maintain these lavish establishments, and there weren't enough rich people to keep them going. Middle-class hotel guests resisted the traditional practice of including meal costs with room charges (called the "American plan"), which had helped subsidize the dining rooms. Having lost this support, hotel restaurants were forced to broaden their appeal to remain economically viable.

In 1910, the hotel opened its New Ebbitt Café in a bid to offer its dining services to a broader clientele, including the many newspapermen who worked in the neighborhood. The café was decidedly less formal than the hotel's main dining room, known as the Crystal Room; there were no high-backed leather chairs or chandeliers. Instead of plush red carpeting, the floors had mosaic tiles. Nevertheless, "the new café is fitted with elegant furnishings and profusely decorated with palms and ferns," the *Post* observed.

Despite such efforts, the Ebbitt struggled. The hospitality business, then as now, was highly competitive, with new hotels continually leapfrogging older ones by offering more fashionable, more up-to-date and/or more prominent quarters. In 1925, the year the new Mayflower Hotel opened on Connecticut Avenue, the venerable Ebbitt House finally closed, and its many opulent but old-fashioned furnishings were sold at auction for fire-sale prices. The hotel was torn down and replaced by the National Press Building.

Swedish-born Anders R. Lofstrand (1886–1966) acquired the elaborately paneled bar from the Ebbitt along with other assorted fixtures, such as a collection of antique beer steins, a wooden bear said to have been owned by Alexander Hamilton, several stuffed animal heads and a two-hundred-year-old clock with wooden works. Adopting the slogan "Allegiance to Reputation," Lofstrand set about using all the old artifacts to re-create the Ebbitt House's old bar and café in a small Victorian building at 1427 F Street Northwest, less than a block from the site of the hotel. He even hired bartenders who had worked at the Ebbitt House. The new eatery, opened in 1926, included an "Old Ebbitt Buffet" downstairs and a separate "Old Ebbitt Cafeteria" upstairs, but they were soon combined and renamed the OLD EBBITT GRILL. From a culinary viewpoint, Lofstrand aimed to provide good, simple food at low prices, pledging not to charge more than ten cents for any one order.

The Old Ebbitt Grill gradually gained a following, as much for its motley collection of historic artifacts as for the quality of its food. A late-night fire in 1941 could have destroyed much of the collection, but passersby were alerted to it by the barking of Prince, the eatery's Great Dane watchdog, and firefighters soon had the blaze under control with little permanent damage.

Lofstrand retired and sold the Old Ebbitt in 1961 to Peter Bechas (1932–1988), who ran it until 1970, when it was seized by the Internal Revenue Service for failure to pay back taxes. By that point, the interior, with all its historic trappings, had been designated a historic landmark, and there was much handwringing as the date approached in June 1970 for the IRS to auction everything off. After almost all of the items had been sold, one by one, to different buyers, a "white knight" appeared with a bid of $11,250 for the entire lot, enough to supersede all the previous individual bids, pay off the back taxes that were owed and keep the restaurant together. The Old Ebbitt's savior was Stuart Davidson (1922–2001), the owner of CLYDE'S RESTAURANT in Georgetown.

Davidson and partner John Laytham kept the Old Ebbitt much the way it had been physically but improved the food, drawing praise from restaurant critics and earning a new following for the venerable eatery. Then, in 1983, the Old Ebbitt's historic storefront home, along with nearby Rhodes Tavern, was demolished to make way for the massive Metropolitan Square office complex. A new Old Ebbitt was constructed within Metropolitan Square, and selected relics from the old restaurant were incorporated. The historic sixty-five-foot mahogany bar, over one hundred years old, was deemed too rotted to be saved, although a replica was built in the new eatery.

The new Old Ebbitt opened in October 1983 at 675 Fifteenth Street Northwest, where the Keith's Theater used to stand. The Clyde's Restaurant Group continues to operate the spacious eatery, which seats 390 and does a booming business. It serves a mix of "classic" American fare and is known for its hamburgers and crab cakes, as well as its oyster bar.

OLD EBBITT GRILL CRAB CAKES

1 pound jumbo lump crabmeat
1/3 cup mayonnaise
2 teaspoons Old Bay seasoning
1 tablespoon chopped parsley
1 tablespoon Dijon mustard
4 saltine crackers

Pick over the crabmeat gently to remove excess shells and cartilage. Combine the mayonnaise, Old Bay, parsley, mustard and water (as needed) until smooth. Add the mayonnaise mixture to the crabmeat and mix, being careful not to break up the lumps of crabmeat. With your hands, break up the saltines into crumbs and mix into the crab mixture. Form into four patties and pan-fry or broil the cakes until golden brown. Serves 2.

"UPTOWN" HOTELS

One of the most elegant hostelries of the Victorian era was the ARLINGTON HOTEL, located on Vermont Avenue just a block north of Lafayette Square. At its height, it was the most prestigious (and possibly most expensive) hotel in the city. "The fame of the Arlington is only bounded by the circumference of the globe," proclaimed the *Evening Star* in December 1902. William W. Corcoran (1798–1888), whose grand Italianate mansion was right around the corner on Lafayette Square, built the hotel in 1869. It was designed by E.G. Lind, architect of the Peabody Institute in Baltimore, in a restrained but very fashionable Second Empire style using pressed red brick with brownstone trim.

From the start, the hotel was exclusive and luxurious. Vermont Avenue outside the hotel became the first street in Washington to receive asphalt paving, in hopes of deadening noise and making guests more relaxed. There were no fewer than five dining rooms on the first floor, to accommodate multiple private parties. Notable guests included many senators and representatives, as well as the great capitalists of the day, including Andrew Carnegie and J.P. Morgan, the latter maintaining a permanent suite of rooms specially decorated to his tastes. State visitors included Dom Pedro, the "emperor" of Brazil; President Porfirio Diaz of Mexico; and Queen Kapiolani of Hawaii, who visited President Cleveland in 1887 and received Mrs. Cleveland at her quarters in the Arlington.

Of course, the dinners at the Arlington were universally acclaimed as "splendid," remarkable as much for their extravagant floral display as their fine cuisine. An 1890 dinner for the Business Men's Club featured "huge mounds of flowers" on each of the tables and a twenty-one-course meal of salmon, terrapin, quail, venison, turkey, pheasant and "many other delicacies." Given the large number of foreign dignitaries who stayed at the Arlington, the hotel's famous manager, Theophilus E. Roessle (1834–1904), adapted his kitchen to accommodate their cooks; it was said that the Arlington hosted more international chefs than any other hotel. Among his various innovations, the *Post* credited Roessle with introducing the five o'clock dinner to Washington, a welcome change for businesspeople that meant the large, formal meal of the day no longer inconveniently took up time in the middle of working hours.

In 1911, the decision was made to replace the old building with a new one. By that time, the Arlington's pressed red brick, Second Empire building was woefully out of date. However, the project ran into financing problems, and although the old hotel was torn down in 1912, the new one was never built. The site remained a huge open pit covered with weeds until the federal government stepped in to build a headquarters for its War Risk Bureau (predecessor of the Department of Veterans Affairs) in 1918. The VA has remained there ever since.

In its day, the posh Arlington marked fashionable Washington's shift away from Pennsylvania Avenue and the streets of old downtown. That shift continued in the early twentieth century as Connecticut Avenue between Farragut Square and Dupont Circle transitioned from imposing Victorian-era mansions and embassies to posh stores, restaurants and elite apartment houses, what some considered Washington's Fifth Avenue. In the center of this elegant stretch, the MAYFLOWER HOTEL was completed in 1925.

The hotel was the dream project of Allan E. Walker (1880–1925), one of Washington's most prominent real estate developers in the years after World War I. In

Dining room of the Arlington Hotel, circa 1890s. *Author's collection.*

1920, Walker purchased much of the former site of the Academy of the Visitation, a large Gothic Revival school building designed by Adolf Cluss that had filled the east side of the 1100 block of Connecticut Avenue Northwest. On this site, Walker planned to build the largest, most lavish and most up-to-date hotel the city had ever seen. Envisioning it as the Hotel Walker, he put $1 million of his own money into the $11 million project, but it encountered construction delays and cost overruns that forced Walker to give up his interest and lose his entire investment. When the hotel was finally completed and opened in February 1925, it was renamed the Mayflower, and Walker was no longer involved. He died of an apparent heart attack just a few months later.

The new 1,059-room hotel, designed by the prestigious New York firm of Warren and Wetmore, managed to lure highly regarded chef Nicholas Sabatini (1881–1936) from the recently closed Delmonico's in New York City to be its first chef de cuisine. Sabatini had cooked in prestigious hotels throughout Europe before heading up New York City's finest restaurant, and by some accounts it was he who invented chicken tetrazzini to honor opera singer Luisa Tetrazzini (1871–1940). As his assistant, Sabatini brought along Nicholas Marchitelli (1900–1969), a fellow Italian who had learned his craft from his father while only a boy. In the early 1930s, Marchitelli took over as chef de cuisine at the Mayflower, a position he would hold for several decades, serving presidents, diplomats and countless other important people at banquets of sometimes two thousand or more. Franklin D. Roosevelt was particularly fond of Marchitelli's terrapin, which the Mayflower would deliver to the White House for him to snack on.

Through the years, many changes were made to the layout and décor of the hotel's restaurants and cafés. The hotel's original tearoom, known as the Palm Court, became the Mayflower Lounge in 1934. Though not limited to just women, the lounge was an informal eatery and meeting place where female guests could feel comfortable meeting. In contrast, the hotel's original coffee shop along Connecticut Avenue was converted at around the same time into the Men's Lounge, which was strictly for men and designed with lots of clubby dark wood and leather. Partly a throwback to earlier times—when many restaurants and cafés were designed primarily for men—and partly a reaction to the popular women-oriented tearooms, men's lounges were common in hotels in this era.

In 1948, the Men's Lounge was converted into the Town and Country Lounge, a celebrated watering hole and "power" meeting spot for over six decades that offered 101 different kinds of martinis. The Town and Country Lounge closed in 2011.

In 1963, after a change in hotel management, the hotel's old coffee shop was transformed into the Rib Room, a conservative eatery in the Washington steakhouse tradition that proudly offered "roast rib of prime prize beef." The Rib Room was most famous as the spot frequented on a regular basis by J. Edgar Hoover whenever he was not having lunch at Harvey's next door. Beginning around 1952, Hoover famously sat at the same table and ordered the same thing each time: chicken soup, buttered toast and cottage cheese on a lettuce salad with grapefruit. No prime ribs. In 1971, after another management change, the Rib Room became the Carvery,

A matchbook cover from the Mayflower Men's Lounge. *Author's collection.*

named for John Carver, a passenger on the original *Mayflower*, and in 1984 it was renovated and reopened again as Nicholas Restaurant, named after Nicholas Sabatini. Though it was much smaller than the hotel's original formal dining room, with space for just ninety-two guests, Nicholas served as the hotel's flagship formal dining room for the next decade, offering sophisticated cuisine prepared by top chefs. Nevertheless, by the early 1990s, competition from nearby fine restaurants was steadily increasing, and fewer and fewer guests were eating in the hotel. Nicholas closed in the mid-1990s, ending the era of haute cuisine at the Mayflower. Its space is now used for a retail shop.

Washington's other notable hotel dining rooms ranged from the distinguished restaurants of the HAY-ADAMS HOTEL on Lafayette Square, opened in 1927, which continues to offer elegant but expensive dining in a variety of settings, to the Art Deco–themed Pall Mall Room of the Raleigh Hotel on Pennsylvania Avenue at Twelfth Street Northwest, a popular night spot in the 1940s and 1950s (discussed in *Lost Washington, D.C.*), and the Polynesian-themed Trader Vic's, with its giant tiki heads, located in the basement of the Statler Hotel (now the Capital Hilton) at 1001 Sixteenth Street Northwest from 1961 to 1995.

One standout was the sophisticated Montpelier Room at Fifteenth and M Streets Northwest, which made a splash when it opened in the new Madison Hotel in 1963. Finished in red leather and rosewood with crystal chandeliers, the restaurant was one of the best formal French restaurants of its day, holding its own against the likes of the Rive Gauche, Sans Souci and Jockey Club (see later chapters). The Montpelier Room featured excellent cuisine but was very expensive, and critics sometimes wondered whether it was worth the cost. Like many of Washington's other formal hotel restaurants, it closed in the mid-1990s, replaced by more casual dining options.

Chapter 5

THE LASTING LEGACY OF WASHINGTON'S TEAROOMS AND INNS

In the nineteenth century, restaurants were understood to be male bastions, places established by and for men where they could eat, drink and smoke without having to worry about behaving properly in mixed company. Such places were seen as dangerous for women, geared as they were toward sensory pleasures that threatened the morals of the fairer sex. As a result, respectable women ate out infrequently and, except for lunches with other female companions, generally only in the company of their husbands. Larger restaurants often had separate dining rooms set aside for the ladies who lunched, while the most exclusive eateries, including most hotel dining rooms, generally refused to seat women at all unless accompanied by a man.

By the turn of the century, many women began to feel hemmed in by their limited options for dining out. Drawn on the one hand to the social opportunities and the excitement of being out and about in the big city, they were on the other hand self-conscious about public exposure and fearful of the potential damage to their reputations. In a letter printed in the *Washington Post* in 1902, a young New York City society woman who had moved to D.C. notes that her uncle "shares mamma's old-fashioned views about girls and even married women being seen too often at a restaurant" and concedes that "personally, I am seldom allowed to lunch at a restaurant, even when closely chaperoned." But in another breath she declares enthusiastically: "We New York girls and women…go down-town to lunch precisely as the men of the family do. We have our lunching money in our purse and sally forth toward noon, or at an earlier hour, for shopping, with the firm intention of not returning home until at least the afternoon tea hour."

A Charles Gibson drawing of women lunching in New York, from *Scribner's Magazine*, September 1898. *Library of Congress*.

Dissatisfaction with the constraints on public dining for women was a key factor in the rise in the 1910s and 1920s of women-operated tearooms that repudiated the male-dominated conventions of the nineteenth century. There were many reasons why restaurants changed dramatically—the ascendancy of the middle class, changes in daily work and home life patterns, the impact of the automobile culture—but much can be attributed directly to the aesthetic and social choices of the pioneering women who opened these first popular tearooms, broadly influencing the cuisine and décor of restaurants ever since.

While hotels opened the first tearooms—the Willard had one in the late 1890s—they were operated by men and designed largely as exclusive, formal settings for elite patrons. By the 1910s, tearooms had broken out of that mold to become informal eateries designed and operated independently by women and often exuding a lively, bohemian atmosphere. The tearoom concept became the perfect model for light, alcohol-free, casual eating and socializing in a cozy, home-like setting. Once the new breed of tearooms became firmly established, women began eating out much more often. In fact, while women made up just 20 percent of all restaurant patrons in 1917, that share rose to an estimated 60 percent by the mid-1920s. By that time, tearooms were widespread and became a fixture of department stores catering to their predominantly female shoppers.

One of the first Washington tearooms was the LOTOS LANTERN TEA HOUSE, which opened in 1914 at 731 Seventeenth Street Northwest, little more than a block from the White House. The Lotos Lantern was the creation of Ida E. Steger (1880–1950), a native of Richmond, Virginia. Steger had come to Washington as a teenager to attend the exclusive Gunston Hall School for girls, graduating in 1895. She worked for several years as a nurse at Garfield Memorial Hospital in the 1900s before deciding to open her teahouse with the assistance of her younger sister, Mary. Steger's first location, at 1622 H Street Northwest, a tiny, cramped basement space, was a big hit, and within a few years, Steger moved around the corner to a much larger commercial storefront at 731 Seventeenth Street. A photo of the eatery from the mid-1920s, when it had been expanded to include a cafeteria as well as the teahouse, shows plate-glass storefront windows filled with "antique" vases, candlesticks, furniture and even a shiny copper kettle. It was typical of teahouses to feature quaint household objects, most of which were usually for sale. Tearoom operators often made as much money from selling antiques and souvenirs as they did from serving food.

Steger prospered as the owner of the Lotos Lantern, which was featured in motorists' guidebooks and undoubtedly drew much of the tourist trade. (By 1930, there was another tearoom just around the corner in the basement of the Blair Mansion, called the LA FAYETTE ARMS TEA ROOM, also run by two sisters.) "The Public wants just what we have to give. Good wholesome food properly cooked," a Lotos Lantern advertisement from 1928 proclaimed. Steger became a prominent businesswoman and a founding member of the local Zonta Club, a group of female professionals and business owners formed in 1922. She continued to run the Lotos Lantern Tea House and adjoining cafeteria until the federal government seized the property (along with other lots in this block) in December 1941, shortly after the attack on Pearl Harbor.

Divinations of various types were a popular diversion at early tearooms. In 1928, two young women from Wilmington, North Carolina—Ashley Curtis and Annie Murchison—came to Washington to open a southern-style tearoom. They initially leased an old mansion at 1643 Connecticut Avenue Northwest just north of Dupont

Circle for their PARROT TEA ROOM, which they advertised as "a delightful place to entertain your friends at Tea," with the added incentive of "the city's foremost palmist available to our guests during Tea hours on Mondays, Wednesdays, and Fridays." The divinations must have proven popular; by 1931, free tealeaf readings were being offered every day from noon to 8:00 p.m. The following year, Curtis and Murchison moved their successful venture just a few doors to the north, to the former Fraser House, a grand and distinguished 1890 mansion at 1701 Twentieth Street Northwest. The Parrot was noted for its delicious fresh hot breads, including "tender pocketbook rolls, rolled cinnamon rolls filled with raisins and currants, and golden corn sticks," all baked in the former pantry adjoining the mansion's elegant dining rooms. "Will you have some hot breads right out of the oven?" the waitresses in their sharp, ruby-red uniforms would ask.

The Parrot Tea Room continued in business until 1950, when it was taken over by Johnnie and Hilda Goldstein, who transformed it into the GOLDEN PARROT RESTAURANT, called "a pretty plush establishment that has many features of a swank town house or private club with all the facilities of a modern dining room," according to the *Washington Post*'s nightlife reporter, Paul Herron. President Eisenhower ate there in 1953 with boxer Rocky Marciano. The Golden Parrot continued into the mid-1970s and was replaced in turn, after an extensive renovation, by the sophisticated FOURWAYS RESTAURANT in 1981. The Church of Scientology purchased the landmark building in 1994, ending its career as a restaurant.

Another prominent early tearoom proprietor was Olive Blanche Kreuzburg (1877–1960), known to generations of Washingtonians as "Mrs. K." Kreuzburg, who was born in Cincinnati, Ohio, and came to Washington in 1926 with her husband, Harvey. The couple opened their first tearoom, known simply as MRS. K's, at 1721 K Street Northwest. In 1927, they added the BRICK WALL INN, located in a picturesque old town house two blocks to the west at 1905 K Street Northwest. The two quaint inns featured candlelit dinners beside open fireplaces and were known as Mrs. K's K Street teahouses. Like other tearooms, Kreuzburg stressed fresh, home-style cooking. "Mrs. K not only gives you FRESH VEGETABLES in and out of season, but knows no can opener nor soup stock pots," she advertised. "Everything is actually cooked as

Opposite, top: The Lotos Lantern Tea House, circa 1925. *Library of Congress.*

Opposite, bottom: Postcard from the Parrot Tea Room, circa 1931. *Author's collection.*

within the home." Furthermore, she didn't scrimp on serving sizes, a common male complaint about tearooms. "That we are Tea Houses of plenty as well as daintiness is attested by our great number of men patrons," she wrote. In 1930, the Kreuzburgs expanded to Silver Spring, Maryland, purchasing a former tollhouse at 9201 Colesville Road that became MRS. K's TOLL HOUSE and which remains in business to this day. Kreuzburg was an avid gardener and collector of antiques, and many patrons enjoyed strolling her gardens and perusing her collections after downing a satisfying, home-cooked meal.

One of the prime attractions of early tearooms was that they offered a refuge from city life, which by the end of the nineteenth century was seen to be hectic, alienating, overly industrialized and unsanitary. Many tearooms sprang up on country roads outside major cities throughout the Northeast. Smart tearoom proprietors would choose locations that were just far enough out to make for a delightful automobile drive, allowing pleasure seekers to flee tiresome city life and enjoy some fresh home cooking in a quaint, rustic setting, such as an old farmhouse, stable or mill.

In 1906, at the very dawn of the tearoom era, a teahouse opened in one of the city's most charmingly rustic spots, the old Peirce Mill on Tilden Street Northwest. The mill was in Rock Creek Park, a national park created in 1890 from a large swath of woodland in the northwest section of the city. In the late eighteenth century, many gristmills had operated along the creek, but by 1906 the only one not in ruins was Peirce Mill. The new PEIRCE MILL TEAHOUSE occupied an enclosed porch that was built on the side of the mill where the water wheel had once turned. Upon its opening, the *Washington Post* announced that "the public in general will be served with ices and soft drinks, tea and sandwiches and cake from 2 o'clock onward each day" under the management of the "Misses Todd, who are well known to prominent residents of the city." The teahouse was a great success, in no small measure because the old mill was a popular destination for afternoon outings, both on horseback and by motorcar. In 1912, the *Aberdeen American* noted that "President Taft and members of Washington's smart set often stop and sip tea" at the mill and that "many elaborate social functions" were held there.

Over its thirty-year existence, the Peirce Mill Teahouse had a number of proprietors, including Hattie L. Sewell, an African American who took over in 1920 and reportedly offered good service and was able to increase business over what her predecessors had achieved. She unfortunately ran afoul of an influential neighbor, E.S. Newman, who complained that with Sewell there the mill would become "a rendezvous for colored people, soon developing into a nuisance." Newman's

The tearoom at Peirce Mill, circa 1934. *Library of Congress.*

influence forced Sewell out after only one year in business. The local Girl Scouts, who also ran a teahouse at Hains Point, then took over. Among the items on their menu were "Harding waffles," named after the president. The Hardings, as well as the Coolidges, enjoyed stopping at the Girl Scout teahouse on Hains Point and likely visited Peirce Mill as well. Popular as it was, the teahouse was finally forced to close in 1934, when the Works Progress Administration began a project to restore the mill to working order.

The popularity of tearooms led to the broader development of quaint, country-style inns, often run by women, which offered a relaxing dining experience in a romantic environment that conjured nostalgic images of the past. The TABARD INN at 1739 N Street Northwest, near Dupont Circle, is a good example. Marie Willoughby Rogers (1885–1970) opened the Tabard Inn in 1922, naming it after the famous country inn featured in Chaucer's *Canterbury Tales*. Rogers, a native of South Carolina, had opened her first restaurant, the Dixie Cupboard, in

New York City after the death of her husband, geologist Dr. Gaillard Rogers. She brought experience from that brief undertaking to Washington, where she acquired a distinguished circa-1900 Classical Revival town house for her new inn, which served as a small hotel as well as a public tearoom. Rogers told the *Washington Post* in 1963 that she had originally wanted the place "just to give parties" and that in its early days it "was full of debutantes running back and forth all the time." The Tabard Inn soon became a popular meeting place for women's groups, and Rogers gradually expanded it, adding an adjacent town house in 1928 and another in 1936.

The inn was temporarily taken over by the navy during World War II as quarters for female volunteers, but Rogers resumed control after the war and continued there until her death in 1970. After being closed for a while and threatened with demolition, the inn was restored and reopened in the late 1970s to once again become an elegant hostelry and notable restaurant. "What's so refreshing about the inn," the *Christian Science Monitor* commented in 1986, "is that the place is so homelike, cozy, and genuinely welcoming."

Directly across N Street from the Tabard Inn is the stately former mansion of General Nelson A. Miles (1839–1925), who had been commander-in-chief of the army during the Spanish-American War. General Miles loved horses—he had presented "Buffalo Bill" Cody with the prize horse, Duke, that Cody subsequently rode in his famous *Wild West Show*—and to house his beloved equines, Miles built elegant stables behind his N Street mansion. After the mansion became the headquarters of the General Federation of Women's Clubs in 1922, the clubwomen decided to convert the stables into a "demonstration" teahouse where young women could refine their social and culinary skills. With a few alterations, such as the installation of a fireplace to add to the homey atmosphere, the teahouse was soon ready, complete with original iron hay racks, feed boxes, harness hooks and saddle trees. "The stalls where 'Golden Pebbles,' 'Denver,' and 'General Wool,' the three thoroughbreds of Gen Miles, once whinnied in coaxing tones for their oats and hay, now frequently entertain groups of young debutantes who make waffles, 'perk' coffee and fix toast just as though they were at home," the *Washington Post* reported in 1924.

By 1928, the teahouse had acquired the name IRON GATE INN. Its first proprietor, Marie Mount (1888–1957), was dean of the University of Maryland's School of Home Economics, and the Iron Gate Inn was just one of several rustic inns she ran. The inn became a well-known fixture in Washington and was sought by visitors, particularly after legendary restaurant critic Duncan Hines (1880–1959) featured

The Iron Gate Inn, circa 1925. *Library of Congress.*

it in his widely read dining guide for travelers, *Adventures in Good Eating* (1935). Like many teahouses and inns of its day, the early Iron Gate Inn did not offer fancy cooking. A typical menu might include baked tenderloin steaks smothered in mushrooms, fried chicken or broiled Maine lobster. For lunch, one might order tuna salad sandwiches or maybe a pineapple and cottage cheese salad. A few of the inn's more intriguing delicacies included butterscotch rolls, Kentucky beaten biscuits and pecan mint mousse. Hines liked the butterscotch rolls, and they became one of the inn's signature dishes.

IRON GATE INN BUTTERSCOTCH ROLLS

2½ cups milk
½ cup butter or shortening
¼ cup sugar, heavy (heaping)
2 yeast cakes (yeast packets)
2 eggs
7 cups flour
2½ teaspoons salt
1 cup light brown sugar per dozen rolls
¼ cup butter per dozen rolls
Melted butter
Cinnamon

Scald milk and melt the shortening in it as it cools. Separately mix sugar and yeast until it liquefies. When milk is lukewarm, add to yeast mixture. Beat the eggs and add them to the mixture, and then beat in flour and salt until you have a soft dough. Sprinkle with flour and pat into a ball in the mixing bowl. Cover and set bowl in an icebox until 3 hours before using.

Generously grease muffin tins, making sure they are heavily greased. For every dozen rolls, mix 1 cup light brown sugar with ¼ cup butter and drop a spoonful in the bottom of each section of a muffin tin.

Roll the dough into an oblong shape about ¼ inch thick, spread with melted butter and sprinkle with cinnamon. Roll into a long roll and cut into pieces about 1 inch thick. Place in muffin tin and let rise in a warm room for 2 to 3 hours or until double in bulk. Bake in a 375-degree Fahrenheit oven for about 25 minutes, being careful not to burn the sugar. Before removing from the oven, have a large, flat pan ready and turn the tin over immediately onto this. Lift and let sugar run onto the rolls. Makes 3 to 4 dozen.

Many patrons especially enjoyed the restaurant's outdoor garden seating beneath a sprawling wisteria vine. After Mount's death, the Iron Gate Inn was acquired by Palestinian-born Charles M. Saah (1906–1980). Saah was an authority on Arab cuisine and had served as the personal chef and food consultant for King Saud of Saudi Arabia. Working with his two sons, Saah soon replaced the Iron Gate Inn's traditional tearoom fare with Middle Eastern favorites like hummus, baba ghanoush, stuffed grape leaves and shish kebab. Though *Washington Post* critic Donald Dresden wasn't impressed with the cooking when he tried the place in 1973, it improved over the years. Its mainstay was the Arabian Nights Platter, consisting of a sampling of various classic Middle Eastern dishes.

The Saah family continued to run the Iron Gate Inn until 1991, when it was acquired by Nabeel David, son of Ameen David, the Lebanese-American who had operated the Blue Mirror Club and Blue Mirror Grill (see next chapter). David enhanced the cuisine at the Iron Gate, adding more Mediterranean dishes, and continued to run the Iron Gate until 2010, when the restaurant closed for the first time since opening in 1924, making it one of the longest-running eateries in D.C. history. As of early 2013, noted chef Tony Chittum was working to renovate and reopen the Iron Gate Inn as a contemporary, artisan Italian restaurant.

The Iron Gate wasn't the only example of stables converted into a tearoom. In 1923, Mrs. Ruth Patillo opened the WHITE PEACOCK TEAROOM in the former stables at 812 Seventeenth Street Northwest, just a block north of the Lotos Lantern. Patrons followed an old brick path from the street back to the former stables, which were freshly painted in pea green shades that were very fashionable for tearooms. The tearoom sported accoutrements from the old White House stables, including a saddle said to have been owned by Dolley Madison, and like the Iron Gate featured horse stalls converted into dining booths. An *American Restaurant* magazine reviewer wrote in July 1926 of her experience at the White Peacock:

> *Shortly a maid comes in with a tray of the most delicious things to eat. She hands you a fringed bit of ecru that matches the fringed linen runner on the table. How you revel in the tall glass of Russian tea, iced and spiced with mint and such things, frozen fruit salad, hot biscuits and a parfait! Your check is presented on a seashell!*

In 1930, the tearoom was acquired by Marie Mount and her University of Maryland colleague Adele Stamp, and they rechristened it the TALLY-HO TAVERN AND TEA SHOP. A menu from 1942, advertising it was "For the Discriminating Diner," offered rather uninspiring fare: roast prime rib, grilled calves' liver with bacon, fried spring chicken, grilled club steak with butter sauce. The restaurant remained in business until 1959, when the structure was razed for an office building.

Before the Kennedy Center for the Performing Arts was built alongside the Potomac River in Foggy Bottom, several stables and horse-riding academies had buildings in that area, and at least two of them were converted into country inns. One at 2620 E Street Northwest (the Kennedy Center now covers the site) was the STABLES, operated by restaurateur Jean Richards in the 1940s. During World War II, when gas rationing limited automobile use, Richards faced a disadvantage in that her quaint and charming inn was out of the way for most downtown visitors. She responded by outfitting an elegant Victorian-era coach drawn by a pair of bay horses to serve as an evening hours' shuttle between downtown hotels and her restaurant. The coach rides generated great publicity and added to the restaurant's charm. Nevertheless, Richards was beleaguered by wartime rationing restrictions. Her inn was finally seized by the government and closed down in 1949 for failure to pay back taxes.

Close by the Stables was a much more enduring eatery, the WATER GATE INN, which operated from 1942 to 1966 at 2700 F Street Northwest, a site also now covered by the Kennedy Center. The restaurant was the creation of Marjory Hendricks (1896–1978), a highly successful restaurateur who carved a unique niche for her eatery.

Born in Seattle, Hendricks came to the D.C. area with her family in 1918. After a brief first marriage and early restaurant experience in Reno, Nevada, Hendricks traveled to France in 1929 to study cooking. On her return in 1931, she acquired a failing country club in Rockville, Maryland, which she turned into the NORMANDY FARM restaurant, an institution that remains in business today. Eleanor Roosevelt was among the Washingtonians who discovered the Normandy Farm, and she is said to have encouraged Hendricks to open a restaurant in D.C. In 1941, Hendricks bought the former Riverside Riding Academy on the Potomac River in Foggy Bottom as the site for her new restaurant. While wartime materials shortages kept her from opening the new place until August 1942, it soon became a hit with local diners.

Hendricks adopted a distinctive Pennsylvania Dutch motif for the décor of the Water Gate Inn, reflecting growing interest in the culture and its artifacts. Her sister, Genevieve Hendricks (1893–1976), a well-known interior designer, was in charge of decorating the new space with Pennsylvania antiques, including a number of old hobbyhorses, which became emblematic of the new restaurant. Large windows offered an enchanting view of the Potomac River, and the former stables' heavy wooden carpentry lent a cozy, rustic atmosphere to the restaurant.

For many of the authentic Pennsylvania Dutch dishes offered at the Water Gate, Hendricks relied on Flora G. Orr (1893–1953), a longtime friend and culinary consultant who developed recipes and trained the kitchen staff. Several Water Gate Inn dishes were consistently singled out by critics and customers alike as especially memorable, including the popovers, which had first been introduced at the Normandy Inn. The inn's menus would usually list a traditional dish, such as the unpronounceable "Sigh Flaysch Rick Mays El mit Rode Graut" (pork tenderloin cooked with red cabbage) or the popular "Shrimp Wiggle Esche Puddle" (shrimp and peas in cream sauce). Other dishes included traditional pork-and-sauerkraut recipes, layered dishes called Gumbis (shredded cabbage with layers of fruit and/or meat) and new recipes inspired by traditional Pennsylvania Dutch techniques. One dish, Chicken Barbara (battered chicken breasts with cream sauce), was so successful that Hendricks trademarked the name. The dish, she claimed, was an impromptu concoction invented for a finicky customer and named after his girlfriend.

In 1960, the restaurant was threatened by plans for the new National Cultural Center, which would become the Kennedy Center. While the inn was not directly in the footprint of the proposed center, architect Edward Durrell Stone felt that

---

WATER GATE INN
PENNSYLVANIA POPOVERS

2 eggs, beaten
2 cups milk
1 tablespoon butter, melted
1 teaspoon salt
Pinch of nutmeg
2 cups flour, sifted

Mix well-beaten eggs with milk, melted butter, salt and nutmeg. Sift flour over gradually, beating with strong rotary beater until the batter, while still thin, is smooth and has the appearance of heavy cream. Put batter in refrigerator to chill it thoroughly. Prepare oven so that it will be 450 degrees Fahrenheit. Grease custard cups with unsalted vegetable fat. Put greased cups in the oven so that they will be sizzling hot to receive the batter. Take hot, sizzling cups from oven. Fill each cup two-thirds full of the chilled batter. Pop immediately into the 450-degree oven. Bake for 15 minutes at 450 degrees and then lower heat to 350 degrees and bake for 20 to 25 minutes longer. It takes at least 35 minutes to bake popovers. Serve hot with butter.

additional green space was needed around the center, which would necessitate removal of the inn. Hendricks fought back, urging her patrons to write to their congressmen to protest the plan. "This product of private enterprise, the culmination of the owner's thirty years in the distinctive restaurant business, and means of livelihood of ninety employees, would be destroyed," she warned.

The restaurant stayed open until 1966, when Hendricks finally reached an agreement with the government on the sale of the property, reportedly for $650,000, significantly less than the $1 million she had hoped for. With bulldozers already rumbling all around it, the inn closed in May. "No more Dutch noodle soup, piping hot popovers with melting butter, rich Mennonite chicken, oven-baked loin of veal with Pennsylvania egg noodles, fresh yellow squash, bread-and-butter pickles and apple-tart pies," the *Evening Star*'s John Rosson lamented.

No discussion of teahouses and country inns would be complete without considering their urbanized cousins: department store tearooms. Department stores in Washington, as in other major cities, had gained enormous popularity in the early years of the twentieth century, transforming the way people purchased goods. They made every effort to provide comprehensive services that would keep female shoppers within their doors as long as possible. A natural amenity, despite its relatively low profitability, was a tearoom. Though rarely offering notable cuisine, department store tearooms were safe, comfortable, reasonably elegant and alcohol-free. Their faithful clientele often dearly loved them. Among D.C.'s department stores, Woodward & Lothrop and Garfinckel's were two that became renowned for their tearooms.

Woodward & Lothrop, or "Woodies" as everyone knew it, dominated Washington throughout the golden age of department stores. Walter Woodward (1848–1917) and Alvin Lothrop (1847–1912) were New Englanders who first opened their Boston Dry Goods House on Pennsylvania Avenue in 1880. Seven years later, they moved to the corner of Eleventh and F Streets Northwest, where the store, rechristened Woodward & Lothrop, would remain for another one hundred years.

The store attempted to provide everything shoppers could possibly want, including a large tearoom on the seventh floor that became a longtime favorite of many Woodies shoppers. Most famous for the elegant little sandwiches served there as light refreshments, the Woodies Tea Room also served full-course meals. *Washington Post* food critic Martha Ellyn visited in September 1941, just before America's entry into World War II, and found she had to wait in line at the busy tearoom for lunch one day. She was not disappointed with the results—baked red snapper stuffed with dressing and a side of broiled tomatoes, all washed down

THE
TEA ROOM
Seventh Floor
Woodward & Lothrop
Washington

A postcard view of the Woodies Tea Room. *Author's collection.*

with a refreshing glass of chilled loganberry juice. Peach pie was for dessert. It had been worth the wait.

Many clubs and charitable organizations held luncheons at the Woodies Tea Room. Groups as large as six hundred could be accommodated in the capacious seventh-floor space. There was even a separate area set aside for children, decorated with large toy rabbits.

A big draw was the restaurant's many fashion shows. A February 1955 show entitled "Today's Beautiful Bride" showcased the latest bridal fashions and included a talk by renowned etiquette expert Amy Vanderbilt (1908–1974). The six hundred anxious young women who attended heard Vanderbilt lecture them on how to avoid doing things that would irritate their new husbands. Then, to get them in the buying mood, they admired the latest bridal fashions on models who entered the room through cathedral-like church doors complete with stained-glass windows. One wonders how much attention they paid to their fancy tea sandwiches.

Woodies may have been innovative when it first opened, but by 1980 it was too set in its ways to keep up with the times. Deep-pocketed outsiders, like Bloomingdale's,

Nordstrom and Neiman-Marcus, began moving into the Washington area and aggressively taking over the retail market. But even as product sales dragged in the 1980s, the tearoom was often filled to capacity. The delicate tea sandwiches remained the tearoom's highlight, although "comfort" foods like chicken potpie loaded with large chicken and vegetable chunks also were popular. *Washington Post* food critic Tom Sietsema noted in 1986 that the crowds seemed not to mind the "dowdy and well-worn" décor of the aging eatery. The desserts were another highlight: "Don't miss the spice-redolent sweet potato pie or a slice of sweet-tart lemon meringue."

After Woodies declared bankruptcy in 1994, Federated Department Stores bought the chain's assets, converting some of its many branch stores to the Hecht's nameplate but abandoning others, including the original downtown location. In 1996, the Woodies building was bought at auction by the Washington Opera for $18 million, using money donated by Betty Brown Casey. The opera company hoped to convert the building for use as a theater, but the cost of doing so proved unaffordable, and the building was sold again, in 1999, to developer Douglas Jemal for $28.2 million. Jemal renovated the structure in 2002 to provide office space on the upper floors and retail space at ground level.

While Woodies was strictly middle of the road in its appeal, GARFINCKEL'S aimed at a higher economic stratum. Founded by Julius Garfinckle (1874–1936) in 1905 (he later changed his and the store's name to Garfinckel), the store carved out a unique, high-end niche and held on to it for eighty-five years, cultivating generations of dedicated shoppers who depended on the store for the trendiest and classiest apparel. Loyal customers came to revere Julius Garfinckel and defer to him without question in matters of fashion and taste, making him a rock star in D.C.'s small world of haute couture. Originally located at 1226 F Street Northwest, Garfinckel's moved to a grand, custom-built building on the northwest corner of Fourteenth and F Streets Northwest in 1930.

When the new Garfinckel's building opened—the last of the great department store buildings to be constructed downtown during their golden age—it surprisingly had no tearoom. Julius Garfinckel had hoped to have one constructed on the seventh floor but never got around to it. Instead, his corporate successors created the Greenbrier Garden, which opened on the fifth floor in 1940, four years after Garfinckel's death. In typical fashion, it was more elegant and sophisticated than any of the other department store tearooms. Designed by the New York firm of William and Harrell, specialists in department store tearoom planning, the new one-hundred-seat Greenbrier drew rave reviews. Its modernistic garden layout included a grass-green floor and blond furniture upholstered in a flowery variety of pastel chartreuse, rose, purple and peacock. A fancy trellis held potted flowers, and a large potted palm sat in the middle of the room.

The custom tables had shelves for pocketbooks and were fitted with trays at each setting so that it would be quick and easy for the waitresses to remove and replace the dishes. Customers paid a flat fee of sixty cents as they entered and were assigned to a numbered table where a trio of waitresses rapidly—but graciously!—served them. Even the waitresses were chosen to fit in with the design scheme: all were redheads, decked out in blue blouses and candy-striped peasant skirts.

Sixty cents bought a choice of five "salad entrées," a beverage and a cake or pastry from the dessert cart. During afternoon tea, the fee dropped to fifty cents and included a choice of sandwiches or "tea salads," beverage and pastry. At the eatery's press preview, a fashion show was held that included a chic Native American–inspired outfit complete with feather headdress and handmade jewelry from a western reservation. Supposedly, the feather headdress was "functional for keeping the wind from blowsy-ing your hair," according to Katherine Smith of the *Times-Herald*. No word on how well it sold.

The Greenbrier quickly became an exclusive Washington institution that continued for fifty years (until Garfinckel's closed), an extraordinary run for a Washington restaurant. Generations of Washington women traveled downtown once or more each week to have lunch at the Greenbrier and peruse the store's posh offerings. As a luncheon haven for well-to-do socialites, the tearoom had a distinctly conservative bent. In fact, when its concessionaire filed for a permit to serve alcohol in 1969, the Washington chapter of the Woman's Christian Temperance Union (WCTU) protested the move. Arguing that the Greenbrier was "just about the only place you can go for lunch in the downtown area and not be met with a rowdy crowd," the WCTU's local president argued that there was no need to taint the staid old tearoom with alcohol. She also threatened that her D.C. members would boycott Garfinckel's if alcohol were served at the Greenbrier, which she implied would be a substantial blow. Nevertheless, the Greenbrier got its permit—the first for a D.C. department store—and the *Evening Star* soon observed that remarkably "no unlady-like tipplers have had to be mopped up from the corner of 14th and F Streets." In fact, one in every four customers was ordering a drink, and in that heyday of cocktails, they were whiskey sours, Manhattans, martinis, old-fashioneds, pink ladies, sidecars and daiquiris—in that order of popularity. "Women are embarrassed to go where there are a lot of men," one patron remarked to the *Star*'s reporter, "but we like to be able to have a cocktail occasionally when we're downtown shopping."

By the 1970s, Garfinckel's was leasing the Greenbrier to Dutch-born restaurateur Robert van Linden, who had previously run an elegant French restaurant called CHEZ ROBERT, which operated for several years in the early 1970s at 1827 M Street

Northwest. *Washington Post* critic Donald Dresden found that his offerings at the Greenbrier in 1974 were as good as any fine restaurant in the city, an achievement no other department store tearoom could match.

The Greenbrier continued to operate until Garfinckel's finally closed in 1990, a victim of a complex web of corporate takeovers and financial deals that depleted the venerable old store of its assets and left it little room to adapt to changing times. Its passing was lamented by the many former customers who remembered its attentive, old-fashioned service and quality merchandise.

Chapter 6

PROHIBITION AND THE SUPPER CLUB ERA, 1920–1950

The Roaring Twenties were a time of accelerated change in the restaurant world. Dining out was no longer primarily an occasion for a public display of one's social status; instead, it was, like going to the movies, an integral part of the modern consumer society. People wanted to eat out for the sheer pleasure of doing so, and Washington's restaurants changed to meet the new demand.

Of course, most people wanted to drink when they went out, and the ban on the sale of alcoholic beverages, which went into effect on November 1, 1917, didn't stop them. Hundreds of clandestine speakeasies sprang up all over the city, and even many legitimate restaurants discreetly served liquor on the side, at least to some of their patrons, or turned a blind eye to customers who brought their own spirits. While the speakeasies emphasized drinking over dining, they generally offered music and dancing and helped to set new expectations for dinnertime entertainment. When Prohibition finally ended in 1933, the glamorous new supper clubs, many of which had been established in the 1920s, filled the void left by the speakeasies. Silken-voiced singers and lush orchestras offered people an escape from the hard economic realities of the Depression. Exotic décor heightened the sense that one was fleeing to another place and time, to some romantic and foreign place. These were the golden years of the supper clubs, a unique era when dining and entertainment were more closely linked than ever before or since.

How did D.C.'s old-line restaurants fare during Prohibition? Large numbers of them closed. Across the city, beloved watering holes—Gerstenberg's, Perreard's, Hancock's, Mades and Fritz Reuter's—all shuttered, ending a generation of Washington eateries.

A few managed to survive, although they often tangled with the liquor police. A prime example was HAMMEL'S, founded by Carl Hammel (1870–1952), a native of Baden, Germany. Hammel started out in 1904 with a lunch counter at Twenty-fifth and G Streets Northwest in Foggy Bottom and then moved to 922 Pennsylvania Avenue Northwest, where the headquarters of the Department of Justice is now located. Hammel offered sandwiches, deviled crabs and his signature dish, planked rock bass, to downtown office workers.

Hammel's was just one of many D.C. establishments that were raided by authorities trying to stem the illicit trade in alcoholic beverages after passage of the Sheppard Act in 1917. One raid on Hammel's took place on April 25, 1923, and it was captured on film. According to the *Evening Star*, Prohibition enforcement officers found 1,200 gallons of beer and red wine in the cellar of Hammel's as curious onlookers stood by. Hammel and his clerk were arrested, but they were soon back in business.

Hammel retired in 1929, leaving the restaurant to his son, Louis J. Hammel (1899–1990), and his son-in-law, Harry G. Kopel (1887–1964), a native of Austria who had previously served as headwaiter at the Willard Hotel. In 1931, after the government acquired their old building for the Federal Triangle project, Hammel and Kopel moved the restaurant a short distance to its final location, at 416 Tenth Street Northwest. It was here that Hammel's enjoyed its greatest success. As Phyllis Richman described it, "In the thirties and forties, if you were downtown at night, which was the fashionable place to be—social Washington took evening strolls around the Ellipse—you dined at Hammel's."

If the food didn't pull people in, there was also the "near beer," which was supposed to not have the alcohol content of real beer. In August 1932—less than two years before Prohibition was repealed—the police conducted another raid on Hammel's. This time, they meant business. As reported in the *Post*, they brought a chemist along to test the alcohol content of the seventy gallons of "alleged beer" that were found on the premises. They then proceeded to remove not only the restaurant's beverages but also virtually all of its fixtures, from its massive bar to the collection of autographed photos of celebrities that hung on the walls. Hammel, Kopel and two other staff members were arrested.

About a month later, a trial was held in police court, and the restaurant men were all acquitted. It seems that an undercover Prohibition agent had drunk a near beer at Hammel's and reported that it gave him a "glow"; the raid was then conducted on his word. They jury found that the agent had no sound basis to conclude that the beverage exceeded the allowable amount of alcohol (despite the fact that the chemist's on-site tests indicated an alcoholic content varying from 2.5 to 9.0 percent). Further, the jury also concluded that the police exceeded their authority in confiscating the restaurant's fixtures. Hammel and Kopel won their case by lining up a number of "civic leaders" to testify that they had eaten at the restaurant and had never known it to serve anything but near beer. The giant bar and autographed photos were returned to Hammel's—at the restaurant's expense, of course.

Despite its legal entanglements, Hammel's continued to thrive for several more decades. A *Post* review in 1968 called it a "handsome, comfortable restaurant with an air of graceful middle age." By then, Hammel's carried an extensive menu of mostly seafood and steaks, offering large portions with filling sides, such as potato pancakes and dumplings. Around the end of the decade, the restaurant moved from Tenth Street to a new location in Georgetown, but within a few years it closed for good.

The supper clubs that began in the 1920s were raided as well. Perhaps the most notable was LE PARADIS, at 1 Thomas Circle Northwest, opened in 1922 by the legendary bandleader Meyer Davis (1893–1976). The lavish club featured two floors of public and private dining rooms, as well as a rooftop lounge. Davis, who would later be dubbed the "Toscanini of society band leaders," offered dancing on the roof to the accompaniment of his orchestra. His club was very popular and soon drew the attention of federal agents. "The opening shot in a war on 'wet' roof gardens here was fired last night when a squad of prohibition agents raided the fashionable Le Paradis roof, opposite Thomas circle, and arrested five patrons on charges of possessing liquor and drinking in public," the *Washington Post* reported in 1924. Many on the crowded rooftop didn't even notice the arrests; the orchestra played on, and people danced through the entire event.

Le Paradis was a big and prominent supper club, and it continued to draw attention from the Prohibition authorities. Like other clubs, it would serve an inordinate amount of ginger ale and ice-filled glasses. What customers did with the glasses of cracked ice and ginger ale was their own business, in the restaurant owners' eyes. But in 1928, the authorities were able to convince the D.C. Supreme Court that Le Paradis had been illegally facilitating the consumption of alcohol and was therefore a "public nuisance." The U.S. marshal infamously padlocked Le Paradis in August for a period of one year, making a big splash in the news but failing to make any dent in the consumption of alcohol. Despite the loss of business, Davis and his associates waited out the year and then successfully reopened in 1929 with fresh stocks of ginger ale and cracked ice.

One of the most prominent and longest lasting of Washington's supper clubs was the RESTAURANT MADRILLON. Peter Borras (1888–1950), a Catalan native, opened the Madrillon in 1920 at 1304 G Street Northwest. He had come to America in 1910 and worked as a chef at the Plaza Hotel in New York City; he later cooked at the German

The Washington Building, where the Restaurant Madrillon was located, in 1930. *Author's collection.*

Embassy in Washington. His new restaurant served French and Spanish cuisine, and he boasted that it would satisfy both "world-traveled diplomats, used to the famous cuisines of continental hotels," as well as "the American man of culture and affairs who demands perfect service and perfect food."

Borras also made sure there was plenty of entertainment to go with the continental cuisine, adding a "Spanish Village" nightclub to the main dining room in 1925. Kate Smith (1907–1986) was among the singers who made early appearances at the club, where nightly dancing soon became popular. In 1927, Borras moved the Madrillon a few blocks west to the brand-new Washington Building on the southeast corner of Fifteenth Street and New York Avenue, where the solid concrete construction meant that the new eatery's dance floors would be "Charleston-proof."

The new Madrillon was one of Washington's earliest large, custom-designed supper club spaces, consisting of four spacious dining rooms—the Mayan Room, the Moorish Room, the Caliph's Room and a new Spanish Village—as well as an Aztec-themed entrance lobby. Patrons were immersed in the fantasy worlds that Borras had created for them. "Silk draped bazaars and cross-legged rug sellers" lined the "streets" of the

Moorish Room, and "veiled maidens in softly flowing, pantalooned transparencies" danced in the Caliph's Room. The Spanish Village was in a kind of inner sanctum, with tiny village *casas*, tiled tables and "streets" and a patio fountain that gurgled water through colored lights. The Madrillon would pave the way for many "themed" restaurants and supper clubs in D.C. that became wildly popular in the 1930s.

The Madrillon's floorshows were for many years a prime venue for a variety of vaudeville-style singers and dancers. The "orchidaceous" Betty MacDonald, formerly of the *Ziegfeld Follies*, performed in 1933. Six years later, she would portray Lady Godiva at the World's Fair. A certain Ada Winston was on tap in 1934, "an exponent of exotic choreography," as the *Post* explained. "Miss Winston is an artiste whose creations bear the stamp of distinctive originality—and some daring."

While the provocative entertainment set a tone of frivolity, more serious business was often afoot among the tables. Local bankers and lawyers, with their businesses centered on Fifteenth Street, often had power lunches at the Madrillon. The restaurant was also a favorite of Latin diplomats. Manuel Quezón (1878–1944) was said to have planned the creation of an independent Philippines with his "determined band of patriots" over the Madrillon's steaming *puchero*, while U.S.-backed Cuban exiles likewise plotted the overthrow of Gerardo Machado (1871–1939) while dining on the Madrillon's Spanish delicacies.

Post critic Kay Ware observed that "the thing that gets the patrons and brings them back" to the Madrillon was the excellent food, and H.L. Mencken (1880–1956) likewise was said to have called it "an oasis of good eating in a Washington desert lacking good eating places." Reflecting the prevailing views of his

MADRILLON BIZCOCHO BORRACHO

Cream 4 ounces butter and 4 ounces granulated sugar together for ten minutes. Add 2 whole eggs and 1 egg yolk one at a time until well creamed. To this add 4 ounces winter wheat flour and a pinch of salt, and flavor with vanilla. Place in a mold that has been buttered and powdered with flour. Bake for 30 minutes in a 300-degree oven.

Sauce: Melt two ounces granulated sugar with a little water and let caramelize slowly. When golden, remove from fire and add quickly and carefully one-half pint of sherry. Stir until dissolved. Pour sauce over cake when cooled so that it absorbs the liquid. Top with whipped cream as desired.

time, Peter Borras credited his sauces with his culinary success. "Sauce is to cooking what poetry is to literature," he told the *Post*. Affable Italian-born chef Gaicinto "Chinto" Maggia ruled the restaurant's kitchen, where he prepared Borras's Spanish recipes, as well as his own Italian ones—and everything in between. One classic Castilian recipe from the Madrillon was for a "drunken" pound cake. Borras died from a heart attack at age sixty in 1950. The Madrillon hung on for several more years but, like so many other clubs and restaurants, was never the same after its guiding light was gone. It closed in 1958.

Beginning in the late 1920s, the stretch of Fourteenth Street Northwest just above G Street—a block east of the Madrillon—emerged as one of downtown's hottest nightlife districts. Several large supper clubs sprang up, each drawing hundreds of customers. The soaring etched-glass tower of the Trans-Lux Theater, an elegant Art Deco movie house, stood at the center of the action, on the west side of the street just north of New York Avenue, beginning in 1936. The lights at night on Fourteenth Street were probably as close as Washington was going to get to Times Square.

Dick Gee Lam (1902–1993), a native of Taishan, China, opened one of the first supper clubs, the LOTUS RESTAURANT, at 727 Fourteenth Street Northwest, in 1928. The club, like many Chinese restaurants, was a partnership among several Chinese-American investors. "The Lotus has the distinction of being the first Cabaret Restaurant established in Washington," Lam's advertising proclaimed. "It presents three Stupendous Revues nightly. This feature coupled with its superb cuisine and its fascinating music played by the Lotus Orchestra undoubtedly constitutes it the outstanding place to Dine, Dance and enjoy a delightful Floor Show. There is no cover charge at any time."

Rowdy patrons posed problems from the start. In November 1928, a suit was filed against the restaurant's owners after a brawl injured several customers. The suit stated that a "melee began when a patron of the restaurant violated the rules of the place by requesting a dance with a woman guest without introduction to her." Curiously, the Lotus's strict rules on social conduct did not extend to other sensitive subjects, such as the possession of firearms. Two women dancing at the 1930 New Year's Eve party at the Lotus were injured when another partygoer wantonly fired a pistol during the celebration. Miss Evelyn Burke, a C&P Telephone Company employee, was wounded in the leg and her clothing burned. Mrs. Blanche Giesler was also shot in the leg and suffered severe burns; her husband even separately sued the Lotus for "loss of the services of his wife," according to the *Post*.

A wide variety of dancers and singers appeared at the Lotus in the 1930s—DeAngelo and Porter, Free and Freely, the Miller Sisters "just back from South America," the

Seidler Sisters, the Codanse Trio. Diane and Duval's "Indian adagio and veil of mists dances" was a big hit in 1937. Tap and acrobatic dancing were big, and the emphasis often was on "gals, gals, everywhere," as the *Post*'s enthusiastic reviewer Chanticleer described one show in 1935. "Soft shoe…tap…shim-sham…plenty of variety in fast footwork," Chanticleer mused. "Keep grandpa away from the ringside tables…unless he's still good for a little chin chucking…because the girls just will effervesce in one number…and muss the gentlemen's hair and talk baby-talk."

The Lotus was popular among military and government personnel during the war years. The *Washington Daily News* called it "sort of a poor man's Stork Club, where the average Joe can put on the dog without pulling more than a five-spot out of his billfold to settle the ante, dinner included." It probably achieved its greatest success in the 1940s and 1950s, when big name entertainers, including Johnny Mathis, Mel Torme, Dean Martin and Sammy Davis Jr., performed there. The restaurant occupied the top level of a two-story 1926 building that was purchased by Kass Realty and expanded into the modernistic twelve-story Kass Building (which still stands at 717 Fourteenth Street Northwest) in 1948. The renovated second-floor Lotus, seating six hundred and featuring eight master chefs and a ten-piece orchestra, was said to be one of the largest Chinese nightclubs in the country. Lam closed the nightspot in the early 1960s, reopening the Lotus as a traditional Chinese restaurant in Bethesda shortly thereafter. The Bethesda Lotus lasted into the 1980s.

Also opening in the late 1920s was another large Chinese supper club, the ASTER, at 1401 H Street Northwest. The restaurant featured Chinese and American cuisine and showcased fashionable entertainment in a large, second-story space where a sea of dinner tables surrounded an orchestra and dance floor. Colored lights from a central dome flooded the room with changing colors to simulate the various hours of day and night. Local radio station WRC included the Aster Orchestra in its regular music lineup.

The successful supper club changed hands, and names, several times in the early 1930s. Entrepreneur Lee Fong reopened it as the CAFÉ LA PAREE in 1933. Four years later, La Paree was replaced by the BAMBOO GARDENS, which the newspapers also said was popular but which lasted only three years. Finally, K.L. Yee's CASINO ROYAL—a supper club that was destined to be perhaps Fourteenth's Street's most prominent—superseded the Bamboo Gardens in 1940. The new restaurant advertised "elaborate Broadway revues presented 3 times nightly with dance music by the peppiest orchestra in town." A big draw was the orchestra's leader and star, the "irrepressible and unpredictable" Jivin' Jack Schafer (as *Post* nightlife commentator Marry Harris described him), a seemingly double-jointed swing master who "hit the

A postcard from the Casino Royal, circa 1941. *Author's collection.*

stratosphere with trumpet notes" and kept the place hopping with the latest boogie-woogie rhythms.

The parade of dance duos and all-girl groups continued at the Casino Royal throughout the 1940s with the likes of the Taft Titians, an all-redheaded dance troupe; comedians Ming and Ling; and the Betty Boopish Helen Lane and her steel guitar, all of whom had shows during the war years. In 1949, the restaurant featured a retro vaudeville act called Bourbon and Bane, with Miss Bane dancing a "Dixie Jive" number in high-buttoned shoes and pink-ruffled skirt. It was all good, clean fun.

Yee tried to make sure the food he served was as enjoyable as the entertainment. He reportedly traveled to China to study authentic food preparation, though his dishes were of course altered to suit American tastes. An example was the Pressed Duck, described as "young duckling, steamed with spices, then boned and pressed into cakes, which are crisp-fried and served with a special sauce and a sprinkling of Virginia ham."

Despite its success, the Casino Royal's entertainment became outmoded by the early 1950s, and the restaurant's popularity was waning when Leon B. Zeiger (1918–2002), a former government bureaucrat from Philadelphia, bought the place in early

1953 with his partner, Harry Snider. Zeiger set about thoroughly renovating the old club and injecting new life into it. While keeping the restaurant's traditional menu of Chinese and American offerings, Zeiger stepped up the entertainment bookings. Hollywood stars like Ann Sothern, Dorothy Lamour and even a young Andy Griffith made appearances, but the real headliners were the singers—Ella Fitzgerald, Count Basie, Sarah Vaughn, Peggy Lee and Bobby Darin, among many others. Rock-and-roll got a kick start at the Casino in 1956 with a group of early performers—Clyde McPhatter, LaVern Baker, the Jayhawks—that formed "a sort of definitive presentation of the new group of sounds that have sent teen-agers scurrying to the record stores."

The Casino had always featured a popular line of chorus girls, called the Royal Sapphires, and Zeiger made sure he ratcheted up the cheesecake along with the rest of the entertainment. In 1954, the famous burlesque dancer Gypsy Rose Lee (1911–1970) appeared at the Casino for an engagement timed to coincide with a large American Legion convention. The *Post*'s Paul Herron marveled that Lee was "the most fabulous night club and cabaret dancer of all" and could "probably sell out the house without the help of the visitors." The next year, the only other equally famous burlesque dancer, Lili St. Cyr (1918–1999), made an appearance and likewise packed the restaurant. "I don't really strip," St. Cyr helpfully explained to Herron. "I just dance nude."

One of the biggest names to star at the Casino was Mae West (1893–1980), who first appeared in February 1955. In the 1950s, after her movie career had ended, West put on a Las Vegas–style road show with a retinue of young male bodybuilders who would parade around the stage flexing their muscles as she sang about "what women want." The Casino reported that it was swamped with reservations for West's show, and it brought her back in June 1956 for an encore event. Herron observed that "Mae has fought a fine battle with Father Time and with the aid of her feathers and the Casino's darkest purple lights manages to present a creditable act." West impressed the *Post*'s Richard L. Coe with her seeming youthfulness, to which she replied, "Yes, I like fresh air. Between shows I always go for a drive. Rock Creek Park. The Public Buildings…"

West hoped to snare the latest Mr. Universe, about to be chosen at a contest in nearby Virginia Beach, for her chorus of strongmen. Instead, she found herself unable to keep the existing troupe of headstrong young men under control. At a press conference between shows at the Casino, a fight broke out between the former Mr. California, Chuck Krauser, and the former Mr. Universe, Mickey Hargitay (1926–2006). Hargitay, who was being dropped from West's entourage, apparently made some sort of gesture at Krauser, who responded by giving him a black eye and a cut lip. Krauser was charged with assault, and the three were in D.C. municipal court two days later to testify about the incident, gamely posing for photographers after the hearing was over. Hargitay even doffed his sunglasses to show off the shiner he had received. The back story to the incident was that Hargitay had become romantically involved with one of West's perceived rivals, Jayne Mansfield (1933–1967), which was why he was being dropped from West's show. Hargitay would marry Mansfield two years later and appear with her at the Casino in 1963.

In fact, it was Jayne Mansfield who starred in the Casino Royal's last live show, held in 1964. While acts like hers were certainly risqué, they were rather tame in comparison to the peep shows, burlesque clubs and adult bookstores that took over Fourteenth Street in the 1960s. The Casino remained in business throughout the 1960s but was mostly only open on the weekends for dancing. It was closed in 1972 for extensive health code violations and never reopened, although a large adult bookstore in the first-floor space beneath it stayed in business through the 1980s.

Lebanese-born Ameen David (1896–1982) opened another prominent supper club, the BLUE MIRROR CAFÉ, at 824 Fourteenth Street Northwest, in 1945. David had come to Washington in 1929 and run several small eateries, including the Crescent Café and several Owl Sandwich Shops. By 1945, he was ready to open a major nightspot, investing $100,000 in his elaborately decorated new club with its blue mirrors and bold two-toned red and white booths. Perched at the northern end of the same block as the Casino Royal, it even featured a revolving stage for the performers. David booked top-name entertainment at the Blue Mirror, including Louis Armstrong, Cab Calloway, Billie Holiday, Nat "King" Cole and Ella Fitzgerald.

In 1952, David decided to add a second Blue Mirror. The first was renamed the Blue Mirror Club, and the second, at 1304 F Street Northwest, became the BLUE MIRROR GRILL. Whereas the club emphasized entertainment, the grill concentrated on food. The grill's long, narrow space could accommodate 120 people, including dozens seated at the ninety-five-foot counter, which featured a two-way conveyor belt. While both establishments were successful, David focused his energies on the grill, adding a downstairs entertainment venue, called the Champagne Room, in the early 1960s, which also featured exotic dancers. He eventually sold his interest in the original Blue Mirror Café, which began a slow drift toward lower standards, beginning perhaps with the appearance of stripper Blaze Starr in 1958. It continued as a strip joint through the 1960s until its building was demolished in the early 1970s to make way for the McPherson Square Metrorail station. A concerted effort by local property owners in the 1980s gradually drove out all of Fourteenth Street's many X-rated businesses, including such memorable institutions as This Is It? and Benny's Home of the Porn Stars. Soon, gleaming new upscale office buildings replaced the former motley assortment of low-rise storefronts.

Interior of the Mayfair Restaurant. *Library of Congress.*

Other cafés of the supper club era included the MAYFAIR RESTAURANT, nicknamed the "Café of All Nations," which opened in 1935 at Thirteenth and F Streets Northwest. The stylish Art Deco dining room was decorated by *Ziegfeld Follies* artist Lillian Roland, who painted colorful murals of scenes from around the world, as well as a long row of the flags of every nation. Waitresses likewise were individually attired in the native garb of different nations, all carefully researched through the National Geographic Society. The poor waitress who was stuck with the Dutch costume even had to wear wooden shoes.

While the Mayfair's entertainment was less racy than that of the Fourteenth Street joints, it remained a perennial favorite. Supposedly, one day shortly after Pearl Harbor, a group of businessmen were lunching at the Mayfair when one of them exclaimed,

"Holy smoke! Look at that Jap flag!" Of course, the mural of flags of all nations included the Japanese flag. A black cloth was hurriedly hung over the flag, and plans were immediately set to paint the flag a pure white on the day the war ended. After the war, the Mayfair continued to be popular, but in time the "Café of All Nations" theme was deemphasized. A rechristened Mayfair Lounge featured jazz musicians and, later, Caribbean music. It closed in the early 1960s.

The CLUB TROIKA occupied perhaps the most elegant venue of any of Washington's popular supper clubs, the stately former mansion of "Boss" Alexander Shepherd at 1011 Connecticut Avenue Northwest, facing Farragut Square. The Washington landmark had been designed by famed architect Adolf Cluss (1825–1905) for the then-governor of the District of Columbia. Shepherd lived in the house for only a few years, but it was subsequently occupied by a succession of prominent officials and diplomats, including the Chinese and Russian legations. In 1932, the former mansion was converted into the SILVER SLIPPER supper club, complete with striking silver and black paint scheme. After only one year, the club was taken over by Leonard Hamilton, Max Heimoff and Max Nemiroff, who converted it into Club Troika. The new supper club offered "a little bit of old Russia, reflecting the glamour of the Czarist regime," including authentic dances and songs performed by Russian entertainers, as well as a variety of American performers. Dinner offerings were likewise a mix of standard dishes, as well as Russian delicacies such as *pirojok*, *syrniki*, Eels Ecossaise and Broiled Shashlick of Baby Lamb Caucasian.

The Troika was open seven days a week in the mid-1930s and managed to skirt blue laws prohibiting the sale of alcoholic beverages on Sundays by creating appealing cocktails with just a very small—and allowable—amount of alcohol. Upon the death of her husband, Helen Hamilton took over management of the Troika in 1936, and the supper club became a gathering place of diplomats and social leaders. "During the war years wealthy industrialists and high-ranking members of the Allied military could be seen there nightly," the *Times-Herald* remarked in 1946. In 1942, local fire department inspectors ordered removal of the silvery canopy covering the ceiling of the Troika's dining room, an embellishment that had been installed for the short-lived Silver Slipper. To everyone's amazement, removal of the false ceiling revealed the original hand-carved, gilt-leafed ceiling that had been built for the Shepherd mansion. Also removed at the time was paneling that hid the dining room's grand original fireplace. Ironically, the fire prevention move that revealed all this finery did not keep a serious fire in February 1946 from ruining the building's interior. The destruction was devastating, and Hamilton decided not to try to reopen the Troika.

Late-night entertainment at the Club Kavakos in 1950. *D.C. Public Library, Star Collection,* ©
Washington Post.

The glamorous supper club era saw many other popular Washington nightspots. Just
a block north of the Troika on Connecticut Avenue was the BALALAIKA, at Connecticut
Avenue and M Street Northwest, another Russian-themed cabaret and dinner club.
The NEPTUNE ROOM was in the same building as the Earle Theater at Thirteenth and
E Streets Northwest, and the Latin-themed EL PATIO was at 711 Thirteenth Street
Northwest. Many of the better hotels in the city also hosted supper clubs, such as
the Ambassador Hotel's HI-HAT LOUNGE and the Hamilton Hotel's RAINBOW ROOM,
located on opposite corners at Fourteenth and K Streets Northwest. Over at 727 H
Street Northeast, the CLUB KAVAKOS offered lively supper club entertainment in what
is now the H Street entertainment district. Charlie "Bird" Parker, the Bud Powell Trio
and Dizzy Gillespie all recorded songs with the Club Kavakos Orchestra.

On the Other Side of Town

All of these places, of course, were open strictly to whites. Virtually unknown to most of their oblivious patrons, the city also hosted an entirely separate nighttime entertainment district on U Street Northwest, the famous "Black Broadway." While less numerous than their white counterparts, the elite black supper clubs and nightclubs often hosted greater artistic talent, and white jazz aficionados would make their way to U Street to catch top acts that they rarely saw in the Fourteenth Street clubs.

One of the first of the U Street spots was the Republic Gardens café, a private club opened by William G. Tindel (1895–1988) in the early 1920s in his row house at 1355 U Street Northwest. Tindel's backyard served as a summer garden, one of the city's first. Pearl Bailey (1918–1990) sang at the Gardens when she was just a teenager. Nat "King" Cole, "Jelly Roll" Morton, Duke Ellington and Ray Charles all performed there as well, entertaining an audience of sophisticated African Americans who could afford and appreciate their talents.

Another early U Street landmark was the Night Club Bohemia, which opened in 1926 in the basement of the Davis Drugstore at the corner of Eleventh and U Streets Northwest. With its dark basement location, the club struggled at first, and its original owners sold it in 1931. New owner Dan Garrett hired New York nightclub architect Edward St. Cyr Barrington to redesign the place for greater success. Barrington came up with the idea of capitalizing on the club's subterranean setting by installing imitation cave-like walls and a ceiling hanging with stalactites. The remodeled café, opened on December 31, 1931, was called the Club Crystal Caverns, and it became a hit. Also known as the Club Caverns, the nightspot soon hosted many outstanding performers, including Willie Bryant, Duke Ellington and Pearl Bailey. Because it was officially a private club, the café was not constrained by local ordinances that prohibited the sale of alcohol after midnight, and the club became celebrated for its late-night jazz sessions. Musicians and entertainers, finishing up at other nearby spots such as the Howard Theater, would drop into the Caverns when they were done and provide impromptu late-night performances.

Ownership changed many times and included Blanche Calloway (1902–1978), sister of famed bandleader Cab Calloway, who took over the Club Caverns after retiring from leading her own orchestra in 1944. Calloway enjoyed promoting the next generation of jazz performers, and she discovered and became the manager of R&B singer Ruth Brown (1928–2006) while running the Club Caverns.

The club's third major change came in 1959, when promoter Tony Tayler (1927–1981), a native Washingtonian, purchased and transformed it into the Bohemian Caverns, a

Ella Fitzgerald cuts a cake in her honor at Club Bali in 1947. *D.C. Public Library, Washingtoniana Division.*

modern jazz club that hosted a new generation of performers, including Miles Davis, John Coltrane and Roberta Flack. The Bohemian Caverns was one of the top jazz spots in the country through the 1960s, until the riots in April 1968 forced it to close. After more than three decades of dormancy, the building was purchased by Iranian-born businessman Amir Afshar, who restored and reopened the nightclub in 2000. Since taking over in 2005, Omrao Brown has led it to become once again an important jazz venue.

One of the largest and most noteworthy of the elite U Street supper clubs was CLUB BALI, which opened in 1943 at 1901 Fourteenth Street Northwest, just a block south of U. This sophisticated supper club was the creation of Bennie C. Caldwell (1897–1967), a native of South Carolina who at the time also owned the Club Caverns. In keeping with the trend of evoking exotic fantasy locales, Caldwell choose a South Seas theme for Club Bali and served food that seemed equally exotic, prepared by his Korean chef, George Kim.

Advertised as the "Washington Home of the Stars," Club Bali featured the very best black performers of the day, including Louis Armstrong, Cab Calloway, Erol Garner and Dinah Washington, among many others. The *Baltimore Afro-American* reported that Sarah Vaughn (1924–1990), "juke box favorite from coast to coast and new singsation of the land," made her Washington supper club debut at Club Bali (then called the New Bali) in November 1947. Perhaps the most dramatic performances were those of the legendary Billie Holiday (1915–1959). *Washington Post* critic Georganne Williamson was deeply impressed by Holiday's singing at Club Bali in 1949: "There's a singular kind of repose about [her features]: Billie is earthy, but with complete good grace. More factual than suggestive, still she's got a wallop that has the bar sitters, around her in a semi-circle at her feet, supplying a chorus of adulation."

Caldwell ran into serious legal troubles in 1950 when he was charged with jury tampering in a case involving one of his customers at Club Bali. The restaurant closed that spring. In the 1950s and 1960s, a number of short-lived restaurants and clubs operated in the building, which was finally purchased by Arena Stage in 1984 and used for many years by its Living Stage Theatre Company. As a theatrical venue, it later also hosted the Washington Stage Guild. Most recently, the building was renovated in 2012 to house an artisanal pizza restaurant called Matchbox.

By the 1960s, the supper club business was nearly extinct. The era of big-name entertainers traveling from city to city was quickly drawing to a close, and the business of offering live entertainment at dinner was being severely eroded by rising expenses, changing lifestyles, the dominance of televised home entertainment and the decline of downtown nightlife. Nightclubs that made money primarily from alcohol sales and cover charges soon largely replaced supper clubs. The escapism of the Depression years that had fueled the growth of supper clubs had faded into the past.

Chapter 7

BLACK WASHINGTON'S RESTAURANTS

For generations, the heavy hand of racial segregation and discrimination kept Washington's fine restaurants, and even many of its lunchrooms and cafeterias, off limits to blacks, as James E. Churchman found out one Sunday evening in April 1890 when he stepped into the high-class Jersey Dairy Lunch Room at 1002 F Street Northwest and ordered a mug of milk and a slice of pie. He was refused service, and he had the gumption to take the matter to court, arguing that the city's civil rights law required that he be served (which was true). It was no use; his case was thrown out on a technicality. Though African Americans were served at some lunchrooms, the overall message was clear: they were not welcome in the best white establishments.

Being shut out of white restaurants, however, had the unintended benefit of spurring the creation of a wide range of African American eateries, from informal cafeterias hosted by local churches to full-service commercial restaurants, some aspiring to the same elegance as the most exclusive white eateries. As we have seen, African Americans played an important role in the D.C. restaurant scene. A black man, Beverly Snow, operated one of the first restaurants in the city. Later, the distinguished James Wormley ran one of D.C.'s finest nineteenth-century dining rooms. And the legendary performers at the famous U Street supper clubs of the early twentieth century consistently outclassed their counterparts on the other side of the city.

Outside the limelight, other less prominent eateries served blacks on a daily basis. The Delmo-Koonce Café, for example, operated in the 1890s on the ground floor of the Odd Fellows Hall at 1606 M Street Northwest, only a few blocks north of Wormley's hotel. Jesse S. Koonce, a young Alabama native who had come to Washington around

Jesse S. Koonce. *From the* Colored American, *April 9, 1898. Library of Congress.*

1890, ran the café, while his older brother, Morris, ran a separate confectionery and catering business on Fourteenth Street.

In 1899, a grand testimonial dinner was held at the Delmo-Koonce in honor of Robert H. Terrell (1857–1925), the prominent school administrator who would go on to become the first African American judge in the nation's capital and who was married to civil rights leader Mary Church Terrell (1863–1954). The dinner was held in the Delmo-Koonce's spacious dining room. "Mr. Koonce has the finest banquet hall in this section of the country for the accommodation of Afro Americans," the *Colored American* reported. When the café closed abruptly in August 1900, the *Colored American* called it a "race calamity." "Ministers, statesmen, editors, poets and lions of every social, professional and commercial degree have been wined and dined at Koonce's, and it had earned a national reputation," the newspaper lamented.

While the Delmo-Koonce catered to African Americans, other successful black-owned restaurants in the late nineteenth century continued the practice of serving primarily white customers, who were wealthier and more numerous. Members of D.C.'s "elite" black families opened establishments that exuded the air of elegance that upper-middle-class white Washingtonians expected, but African Americans naturally didn't take well to being excluded from black-owned businesses. In 1886, the *Washington Bee* reported, "Mr. John A. Gray has been a very liberal man in his times. He kept one of the finest [eating] houses in the city. He first opened it for white people and was having a success until the Negroes kept clamoring for a respectable place to go. He opened his house to the high toned colored people and [in] less than a year they broke him up." Gray's experience demonstrates how difficult it was for fine restaurants to try to cater to both races. With discrimination and segregation tightening in the 1880s and 1890s, moneyed whites were increasingly intolerant of blacks, and many blacks, chafing at the erosion of their civil rights, pushed back. Nevertheless, Gray, for one, managed to survive. He went on to jointly operate a successful dining room for African Americans, GRAY & COSTLEY, at 1313 E Street Northwest. Like many nineteenth-century D.C. restaurants, Gray & Costley featured a liquor store and cigar stand on the ground floor and a "ladies' and gentlemen's dining room" upstairs. Its bartender, Wash Wood, was one of the best mixologists in the city in 1900.

In 1901, the Union League of the District of Columbia, an organization founded by Andrew F. Hilyer (1858–1925) in the 1880s to promote black economic cooperation, tallied ninety-five black-operated "eating houses" in D.C., in addition to fifty-six confectionery shops, twenty-three dining rooms and nine saloons. Several had prominent downtown locations, including Gaskins & Gaines's ACADEMY RESTAURANT at 320 Eighth Street Northwest, Moore & Prioleau's SPARTA BUFFET at 1216 Pennsylvania Avenue Northwest and M.F. Carroll's PHILADELPHIA HOUSE at 348 Pennsylvania Avenue Northwest, all of which primarily served black customers.

Over the next several decades, black-owned businesses, including restaurants, cafés and lunchrooms, grew and thrived in the face of restrictions that kept them out of white communities. Retreating from downtown, they increasingly filled the U Street corridor, from Fourteenth Street to Fourth Street Northwest, which became the city's major focal point for black culture and commerce. The neighborhood now known as Shaw, originally populated by a mixture of whites and blacks, became almost entirely African American. Many lunchrooms, restaurants and other businesses lined the north–south streetcar routes of Seventh Street and Fourteenth Street.

One of the best-known and most successful restaurants was HARRISON'S CAFÉ, at 455 Florida Avenue Northwest, opened in 1923 by Robert Hilliard Harrison (1875–1959), a native Washingtonian who gained knowledge of the culinary arts at an early age. As a teenager, Harrison served as a butler in the household of an Ohio congressman, and later, from 1894 to 1898, he was the valet for a wealthy businessman who took him on extensive travels to Europe. Young Bob Harrison learned how to prepare a wide range of culinary delicacies and gained hospitality skills that would later serve him well. In 1910, while working as a government clerk, he started making Harrison's Old Fashioned Molasses Kisses at home and offering them for sale in city drugstores. After ten years, he had gained such a following that he decided to quit his government job and open a candy store at 467 Florida Avenue Northwest, featuring Harrison's Special Ice Cream, among other delicacies. Finally, in 1923, Harrison closed his candy store and, with the help of his wife, Lottie, opened Harrison's Café in the Victorian town house adjacent to their home. His goal was to offer a first-class dining experience for African Americans.

A fixture in the black community for almost forty years, Harrison's had few rivals. (Samuel Keys's restaurant, which opened in 1933 at 1853 Seventh Street Northwest, might have been the only one that came close.) The sign outside Harrison's proclaimed the café was "Open All Nite," and Harrison skirted the liquor curfew by allowing guests to retire to private upstairs dining rooms after midnight, where they could continue drinking into the wee hours of the morning. An elegant banquet hall, called the Gold Room, was the scene of countless formal dinners and special celebrations. After Harrison died in 1959, he left the café to his manager, Miss Nealy S. Boone, with whom he was said to be very close, and another employee. The two continued to operate the eatery until 1962.

While Harrison's embraced elegance, there were many humbler dining spots in the neighborhood as well. One of the most colorful was the Depression-era HAPPY NEWS CAFÉ, at 1727 Seventh Street Northwest, the work of the energetic and inspiring Elder Solomon Lightfoot Michaux (1884–1968). Michaux was a charismatic evangelist who did much to lift up the spirits of discouraged and destitute African Americans weathering the worst of the Great Depression. Born in Virginia, Michaux moved to Washington in 1928 and the following year started broadcasting his popular inspirational Sunday radio show on station WJSV. His theme song was the infectious gospel ballad "Happy Am I," and Michaux became known to millions of listeners as the Happy-Am-I preacher.

In 1933, Michaux began an active social agenda that included founding the Happy News Café in conjunction with the Bernarr MacFadden Foundation, a promoter of health and fitness. Advertising "vital foods at bargain prices," the café featured nourishing lunches for as little as a penny a plate. The homeless were given free meals in exchange for selling copies of the *Happy News* newspaper. The *Washington Post* called the café a "dietician restaurant for unemployed" in a brief article it ran about a nine-cent "banquet" held there for the unemployed. "Elder Michaux, who is giving all surplus foods each day for the benefit of worthy colored families was also in the party," the article noted.

The Happy News Café was likely in business for only a few years. Elder Michaux went on to become famous for leading massive baptisms at Griffith Stadium, featuring huge canvas tanks filled by the D.C. fire department. In 1946, he built the Mayfair Mansions housing project in Anacostia, providing 594 apartments for African Americans. The popularity of his ministry declined after he was accused of mishandling donations in the late 1930s, but he continued to have followers until his death, at Freedmen's Hospital, in 1968.

The crowd waits to be served at the Happy News Café, 1937. *Library of Congress.*

Just a few doors down from the Happy News Café, the SOUTHERN DINING ROOM, at 1707 Seventh Street Northwest, opened in 1938 with none of the evangelical flair of the Happy News Café or any of its health food pretentions. Owner Hettie T. Gross (1908–1968), a former hairdresser from Evergreen, Alabama, came to Washington in the midst of the Great Depression with her husband, Elijah. Working as a laundress, she earned a reputation among friends for her delicious cooking. She was encouraged to go into business and finally purchased an old lunch counter for what she claimed was "a day's grocery money," according to *Jet* magazine, and set up her new eatery. Working with her husband, Gross offered fifteen types of home-cooked dishes, most based on old family recipes, at "working man's prices."

Lunchers at the Southern Dining Room, August 1977. *D.C. Public Library, Star Collection,* ©
Washington Post.

The Southern Dining Room, which moved a block south to 1616 Seventh Street
Northwest in 1952, became renowned by the 1960s as the nation's first and most popular
soul food cafeteria, and Gross was known as the "Soul Food Queen" in the days when the
term was fashionable and the food trendy. "At any hour, you are likely to find construction
workers in their hard hats, Howard medical students in their white jackets, school children,
salesgirls, teachers, and just plain hungry people, all drawn by the servings of food that
Mrs. Gross made famous," the *Baltimore Afro-American* wrote in 1969. Shortly before she
died, Gross explained soul food to *Washington Post* writer Judith Martin: "Soul food is food
that will hold your body up. It's not chicken or fish—you can easily get hungry eating
that. Your meals can't come quick enough. With soul food, all you need is two meals a day
and maybe a little snack with some lemonade. Even one good meal a day, and you'd be
surprised at the weight you can gain." After her death, Gross's two daughters continued to
operate the Southern Dining Room into the 1980s.

SOUTHERN DINING ROOM
SWEET POTATO PIE

Peel, boil and mash two pounds of sweet potatoes. Add 2 beaten eggs and 2 cups of sugar, ¼ pound of butter, ½ can of evaporated milk and 1 teaspoon lemon extract. Spoon mixture into a large pastry dough piecrust. Bake in 375-degree oven for approximately 1 hour. Test for doneness.

Other African American women who established notable restaurants in the U Street corridor were the Penny sisters—Ann, Cecelia and Evelyn—who originally hailed from Pomonkey, Maryland, a small Charles County settlement thirty-five miles south of the city. In the early 1930s, the Penny family moved to Washington, and the girls attended the Armstrong High School on O Street. In 1953, Cecelia Penny Scott (1919–2004) opened CECELIA'S at 2002 Twelfth Street Northwest, in the heart of the U Street corridor. As Scott recalled in 1988, it was furnished with plush red velvet upholstery, a cloverleaf bar and oversized black leather stools. Located near the Lincoln Theater, which featured dancing in the basement, the restaurant attracted customers both before and after the dances. Scott offered home-style southern cooking, including beef stew, lima beans, ham hocks and chitterlings.

After five years, Scott moved to 618 T Street Northwest, adjacent to the Howard Theatre, while her sister Evelyn (1920–1996) converted Cecelia's old restaurant into EVELYN'S PASTEL ROOM. Sandra Butler-Truesdale, a native Washingtonian, recalls a great feeling of excitement upon walking into Cecelia's. The waitresses were dressed in crisp white blouses and black skirts, and performers from the next-door Howard Theatre could always be found there. Jackie Wilson, Redd Foxx, Dinah Washington and Billie Holiday were among Cecelia's frequent customers, as were James Brown, Sam Cooke and boxer Joe Louis. "Oh my goodness, what a great time we had," Butler-Truesdale recalls. "Oh man, we had lots of fun." Scott even ran a small boardinghouse with rooms available on the second floor above the restaurant, where many performers stayed while playing at the Howard.

Though U Street was in decline in the 1960s, both Cecelia's and Evelyn's did steady business and are still fondly recalled as lively, welcoming places offering excellent southern food. Scott presided over Cecelia's until 1969, and Evelyn ran her Pastel Room until the 1970s.

In 1953, the Supreme Court ruled that the District's Reconstruction-era anti-discrimination laws were still in effect, confirming that it was indeed illegal to segregate public places, including restaurants. African American activists led by Mary Church Terrell had precipitated the court case in 1950 by attempting to dine at Thompson's Cafeteria at 725 Fourteenth Street Northwest and, as expected, were refused service. The case marked a turning point for both white and black D.C. restaurants. The white restaurants could no longer refuse to seat blacks, and the black restaurants no longer had a captive clientele unable to dine elsewhere in the city.

The effects of desegregation on public dining were very gradual, as neither whites nor blacks were quick to change their old ways. Restaurants owned by and catering to African Americans continued to thrive in traditionally black neighborhoods for several decades after segregation officially ended. While African Americans could—and did—eat at restaurants from which they had previously been excluded, many still felt more comfortable in black-owned places.

Perhaps best known of the African American fine-dining spots in the post-segregation era was BILLY SIMPSON'S HOUSE OF SEAFOOD AND STEAKS, at 3815 Georgia Avenue Northwest in Petworth, which opened in 1956. Owner William W. "Billy" Simpson (1914–1975) was a native Washingtonian who attended Dunbar High School and worked at the Government Printing Office as a young man. By 1948, he had opened an informal club, called the Robin Hood Dell, in a house at 652 Newton Street Northwest. Like many such "after-hours spots" that would remain popular with African Americans for decades to come, Simpson's place served alcohol at all hours of the night but was also known for its food. Simpson's specialty was the "652" sandwich, made of spicy chopped sirloin on toast. When he was able to open Billy Simpson's on Georgia Avenue in 1956, Simpson kept the 652 on the menu, and it remained a perennial favorite.

Unlike his first place, Billy Simpson's restaurant on Georgia Avenue was an elegant eatery that offered a variety of seafood, steaks and sandwiches. The first-floor dining room was paneled in knotted pine, a fashionable finish in the 1950s, and the service could be as good as at any fine eatery on the other side of Rock Creek Park. Unlike other supper clubs, Simpson's did not offer live entertainment. "Why should I pay entertainers to draw people here?" Simpson asked a *Washington Post* reporter in 1971. "I got 'em coming through the portals after my steak and shrimp." The restaurant gained a national reputation, drawing comedians Redd Foxx and Dick Gregory, singer Ella Fitzgerald and actor Sidney Poitier.

Despite its popularity, Simpson's was most famous, not for its food, but as an elite meeting place for Washington's most influential African Americans, including diplomats, government officials and successful local politicians. On the second floor, an informal group of influential black leaders, called the Round Table, would frequently

Tending bar in the upstairs Ebony Table room at Billy Simpson's. *Ruth Simpson Redmond.*

meet. Also known as "Billy's friends" and the "Uptown Forum," the group mapped out the course of D.C. politics in the 1950s and 1960s, including organizing a key registration effort for the 1964 primary elections. Walter E. Washington, the city's first mayor in the twentieth century, and Reverend Walter E. Fauntroy, the District's first congressman, both held meetings at Billy Simpson's, and Jesse Jackson used it as his headquarters during the 1968 Poor People's Campaign.

While the restaurant's exterior had a Tudor-style finish, Simpson in 1962 remodeled the upstairs lounge as the Ebony Table to commemorate the many nations of Africa that were emerging from colonial rule. He paneled the walls in rich African mahogany, furnished the lounge with ebony tables and chairs and installed a raised map on the ceiling with lights showing the capitals of the continent's free countries. Representatives of eleven African nations attended the grand opening of the new space, and African diplomats became regular customers at Simpson's thereafter.

By the 1970s, Simpson's restaurant had become an established community institution, though after more than a decade it was no longer trendy. According to a

1971 *Washington Post* article, business was starting to decline as more people entertained at home or went downtown. In 1975, Simpson died suddenly from a heart attack while in Colorado Springs, to the great dismay of his many friends and admirers. His restaurant was shuttered several years later.

By the time Simpson's closed, several newer African American eateries in the Georgia Avenue corridor had made their mark, including ED MURPHY'S SUPPER CLUB, which opened in 1965 at 2271 Georgia Avenue Northwest. Born in Raleigh, North Carolina, Ed Murphy (1930–1997) moved as a child with his single mother to Washington, where he started his first retail business selling hosiery when he was just seventeen. Determined to get ahead, Murphy worked at a number of occupations until he was finally able to open his Georgia Avenue club.

Much like Billy Simpson, Murphy aimed to offer African Americans an elegant dining experience to rival anything they could find on K Street or Connecticut Avenue. Murphy offered the usual club cuisine of steaks, seafood and chicken but added soul food specialties as well. He also offered some of the best live entertainment since the golden years of the U Street clubs. Stevie Wonder, Roberta Flack and Redd Foxx all performed at Murphy's. At lunchtime, his club attracted many young professionals from nearby Howard University, Freedman's Hospital and Washington Hospital Center. While his patrons were mostly African American, "Murph's," as it was widely known, drew whites as well.

Murphy originally had a policy of requiring men to wear coats and ties, but as times changed, he found he had to change as well. By the early 1970s, the sign on the restaurant door said, "Gentlemen are expected to wear neckties, turtlenecks, ascots or dashikis."

Murphy was always ambitious, and the success of his supper club didn't stop him from wanting to move to the next big thing, which, for him, was to build a luxury hotel right on Georgia Avenue, where his restaurant stood. With the help of influential friends, he obtained federal government financing for a nine-story, 160-room hostelry, dubbed the Harambee House when it was completed in 1978. Unfortunately, the hotel was plagued with financial, management and other problems, and in 1981 the government sold the building to Howard University. It now houses offices and the Howard University bookstore.

Murphy's supper club closed in 1972 in anticipation of construction of the hotel. He opened a new club just up the street in 1974, but it had none of the magic of his first club and closed within a year. His last restaurant was MURPH'S SEAFOOD AND CUISINE, which opened in the new Reeves Municipal Center at Fourteenth and U Streets Northwest in 1989. However, it, too, faced financial problems and closed in 1992.

Murphy's bartender in the 1960s, when his club was at the height of its success, was the legendary Adolphus "Face" Wiggins (1921–1989). Wiggins, called a "freckle-faced, cherubic, genial restaurateur" by *New York Amsterdam News* columnist Cathy Connors, was one of those bartenders everybody knew and could confide in. In 1968, *Washingtonian* magazine named Wiggins one of the five best bartenders in the city. His nightspot, FACES, at 5626 Georgia Avenue Northwest, opened in 1972 as the culmination of a long career that had also included tending bar at JACQUES' ELEVATOR CLUB on G Street downtown. Originally just a small neighborhood bar, Faces gained fame and prominence over time. Ella Fitzgerald, Lena Horne and Mohammed Ali were a few of the luminaries who stopped by, and former mayor Marion Barry was a frequent customer.

Though Faces was said to be famous for its fried chicken, the warm and welcoming atmosphere and the chance to socialize were major draws. The restaurant was often called an "African American Cheers." Though Wiggins sold it in 1976, its second owner, Donzell Tate, kept it going until 1997, when the space was taken over by a drugstore.

While the elegant places were making their mark, many African Americans were spending their time and money at much humbler joints, such as the PIG 'N' PIT at Sixth Street and Florida Avenue Northwest, where the best barbecued ribs and pork sandwiches could be had, or WINGS 'N' THINGS at Fourteenth and U Streets Northwest, said to have been a favorite of Dr. Martin Luther King, as well as the originator in D.C. of the wildly popular "Mumbo Sauce" (the sauce actually was created and trademarked by Chicago-based Select Brands).

Many African Americans did little eating out at formal commercial establishments, however. A number of churches in the community offered cheap, home-style meals, usually in a cafeteria setting. Menu options were universally similar: rib, chicken or fish sandwiches; pigs' feet or chicken "dinners" (meaning it came with sides of collard greens, potatoes, mac and cheese, sweet potatoes or a corn muffin); and bean soups. The United House of Prayer for All People at Sixth and M Streets Northwest had one of the largest, offering full breakfast, lunch and dinner meals seven days a week. The Kelsey Temple Church of God in Christ at 1435 Park Road Northwest in Columbia Heights had one as well. Participants in the March on Washington for Jobs and Freedom congregated there on August 28, 1963, to eat breakfast. Many hoped to see Dr. Martin Luther King there for breakfast as well; that afternoon, he would deliver his famous "I Have a Dream" speech on the Mall.

On weekends, when commercial restaurants and clubs closed for the night, many African Americans frequented the numerous informal "after-hours spots" that were common in the U Street area, particularly on Seventh and Fourteenth

Streets. These were relatively small bars and dining rooms run by ordinary people out of their basements or ground floors, which they fitted up with tables, barstools, jukeboxes and even live entertainment. They went by names like "Turk's" or "14th Street Shorty's." Here, one could not only drink past the legal curfew but order a late meal as well. And many were open on Sundays, when the commercial places were closed. Over time, as the commercial places broadened their hours, the after-hours spots became less common.

While few of the formal supper clubs like Billy Simpson's, Murph's or Faces have survived into the twenty-first century, two celebrated restaurants with roots in the "old days" are still thriving today. One is the FLORIDA AVENUE GRILL, at 1100 Florida Avenue Northwest, opened in 1944 and still going strong after almost seven decades. The grill was founded by Lacey Carl Wilson (1913–1989), a native of Burlington, North Carolina, who scrimped and saved from his waiter's job until he had $5,000 to start out on his own. He purchased what had been a run-down corner food stand across Florida Avenue from the Central High School (now Cordozo Senior High School) and immediately fixed it up as the Florida Avenue Grill. In classic family restaurant fashion, Carl served as the front man, manning the cash register, while his wife, Bertha, cooked and waited on tables.

Some of the grill's best food was at breakfast time—eggs and grits, salmon cakes, fried apples, fresh biscuits. The grill would open as early as six o'clock in the morning and have plenty of customers. Carl Wilson put the word out among D.C. cabbies that this was the place to get a hearty, inexpensive meal. Soon, the small eatery was packed at all hours, with lines frequently extending down the block. As an added convenience, customers could get their cars washed in the adjoining lot while downing a satisfying meal at the grill.

The grill was a place that from its earliest days served people of all races and all walks of life. Cabbies, students from the school across the street, professors from Howard University, doctors and nurses from Garfield and Children's Hospitals—they all came to the grill. While the neighborhood surrounding it became dangerous, the grill was always a safe haven. The *Washington Post* reported in 1975 that the grill had been held up only twice. On one of those occasions, one of the grill's loyal regulars, an elderly man, threw a ketchup bottle at the villain, who ran out but was later caught by police. Should there ever be a note of rancor among the grill's customers, legendary head waitress Ophelia Jones, with her sonorous voice and commanding personality, would set things right and quickly have everybody smiling again. As the U Street corridor has gentrified in recent years, the grill's friendly atmosphere and filling meals have remained a mark of continuity for longtime customers and newcomers alike.

Ben's Chili Bowl in 1960. *Ben's Chili Bowl.*

The other venerable U Street corridor eatery, BEN's CHILI BOWL, at 1213 U Street Northwest, is probably the neighborhood's most famous. It was opened by Mahaboob Ben Ali (1927–2009) and his wife-to-be, Virginia Rollins, in 1958. Ali, a native of Trinidad in the West Indies, had come to the United States to pursue a higher education. He earned a bachelor's degree at Howard University and was enrolled in its College of Dentistry when he fell down an elevator shaft and injured his back, ending his plans to become a dentist. Once recovered from the fall, Ali moved into retail sales, including working the counter at ANN's HOT DOG GRILL, located at 1231 U Street Northwest next to the Lincoln Theater. Ann's, owned by Ann Penny, called itself the "home of the giant hot dog" and advertised, "The flavor is in the chili sauce!" Working at Ann's, which stayed open late, Ben quickly picked up the ins and outs of the business, and by 1958, he was ready to open his Chili Bowl, just on the other side of the theater.

To create Ben's Chili Bowl, the Alis converted an old pool hall that had originally been built as a movie theater in the early days of motion pictures. The new diner, with its grill in the front window and long Formica-topped counter, offered a simple, fast-food-style selection of chili, hot dogs, "half-smokes," cheeseburgers and milkshakes. Though not the first chili bowl restaurant on U Street, Ben's soon gained a loyal following. A young Bill Cosby, stationed as an army private near Washington, tried Ben's one day early in its history. It was the first time he'd had a chili half-smoke, and he instantly became a lifelong convert and one of Ben's most ardent supporters.

Though U Street in the 1960s was in a state of transition, many top African American performers and other celebrities could still be found in its clubs, theaters and nightspots. After the shows, they and their fans would often stop for chili dogs or cheeseburgers at Ben's. Soon, the humble neighborhood eatery's busiest times were between midnight and 4:00 a.m. on weekends.

But the 1968 riots changed everything, leading to severe hardships throughout the African American community and devastating the U Street corridor. As crime spiked, most of the old nightclubs and restaurants were forced to close. Ben's managed to hang on, at times the only business open on its block. In the late 1980s, Ben's struggled again as subway construction tore up the street directly in front for several years.

By the 1990s, Ben's was one of the few establishments on U Street that had been continuously in business since U Street's heyday, and it had gained a reputation as one of the best chili restaurants in the country. Along with loyal neighborhood regulars who had kept it going for decades, the Chili Bowl served a seemingly endless stream of celebrities. Scenes from a number of D.C.-centric movies and television shows were filmed there, and Ben and Virginia Ali earned awards for their many achievements.

When President-elect Barack Obama stopped by Ben's for a chili half-smoke shortly before his inauguration in 2009, the event was the culmination of the little diner's storybook career.

Like the Florida Avenue Grill—but perhaps even more so—Ben's Chili Bowl in the twenty-first century is a national institution and slick tourist destination. Its success is a credit to the Alis and a source of pride for the local community, even as the atmosphere of the once-humble neighborhood eatery has forever changed.

Regrettably few, if any, white-tablecloth restaurants in recent years have aimed primarily at African Americans. GEORGIA BROWN'S, for example, which opened in 1993 at 950 Fifteenth Street Northwest on McPherson Square, harkens back to African American roots in its home-style southern cooking but caters to a mixed, upscale clientele. The large investment required to open a classy new restaurant in the city makes it improbable that such places would aim narrowly at African Americans (or any other racial group).

Just as the term "soul food" has slipped from favor over the years, the fate of authentic D.C. African American eateries hangs in the balance. Are these homegrown favorites gone for good? The barriers, financial and otherwise, to opening new restaurants are formidable, and whether younger generations of D.C. residents will patronize them in the future remains an open question.

Chapter 8

ON THE WATERFRONT

After giving Alexandria County back to Virginia in 1846, the District of Columbia had two commercial waterfronts left, one in Georgetown and the other in Southwest. The Southwest waterfront offered the more direct connection with downtown Washington and served as a primary gateway for waterborne traffic. It was from these docks in 1848 that African Americans embarked on the schooner the *Pearl* in the largest recorded escape attempt by slaves in America. During the Civil War, these docks were the destination of countless hospital ships carrying wounded soldiers from battles in Virginia to the network of hospitals in Washington City. "In July [1862], the wounded poured in a great tide from the battles of the Seven Days. Crowds gathered at the Sixth and Seventh Street wharves to see the men carried from the ships and loaded on the ambulances," Margaret Leech recounts in *Reveille in Washington*.

Known to most Washingtonians as the Seventh Street wharves, the Southwest waterfront after the Civil War was a rather seedy place, a neighborhood of warehouses, factories, icehouses and saloons. A number of companies ran passenger service from the wharves to destinations up and down the East Coast. Commercial boats also docked here laden with food or building materials, and individual fishermen brought their catches. The wharves became a sprawling and untidy marketplace. Speaking to the Columbia Historical Society in 1922, Dr. Sarah Huddleson recollected:

> In the long ago it was no unusual sight to see 50 to 100 sailing vessels in the harbor at one time, and the hungry but jolly Jack Tars would rush ashore to John McKinney's old restaurant for chowder, beef, crabs and beer, or they would go farther up the street to the restaurants of Johnny Branson or Joe Gordon or John Kenny. Those were great

old days with wonderfully appetizing meals, served for a song, to as quaint a clientele as ever graced our city.

The blocks farther inland from the waterfront were densely populated with frame houses and other humble abodes largely housing African Americans and immigrants. These working-class families drew their limited incomes from jobs at the nearby Washington Arsenal (now Fort McNair) and the Navy Yard, as well as from the commercial business along the wharf.

Among the many waterfront saloons and cafés was HARRIGAN'S HARMONY HALL, founded by Irish immigrant Peter Harrigan in 1885 at Ninth and H Streets Southwest. For most of its existence, it was just another watering hole on a corner in Southwest. After it was taken over by Lithuanian immigrant Morris Engle (1901–1986) in 1942, the rechristened Harrigan's Bar and Grill offered a disorienting blend of Irish and Eastern European cuisine. Harrigan's suddenly came into the big time in 1959, when it started showing paintings by local artists. The D.C. alcoholic beverages control board ordered the paintings taken down, asserting that anyone selling alcohol couldn't engage in any other type of business. The resulting flap in the media generated great publicity for Harrigan's; the art was soon back up on the walls, and Harrigan's became a trendy place to hang out. Local reporters from the nearby *Evening Star* newspaper offices began frequenting the place, and soon VIPs from Capitol Hill and even the White House were making appearances. By the time urban renewal shut the restaurant down in 1968, everyone was lamenting the loss.

Another Southwest café started in 1885 was HALL'S RESTAURANT AND GARDEN, located for most of its career at Seventh and K Streets Southwest. In the rough-and-tumble world of the late nineteenth-century waterfront, Hall's was little more than a neighborhood saloon. Franklin Pierce Hall (d. 1925), a native of Virginia who founded the restaurant, repeatedly ran into trouble with the law in the mid-1890s for allegedly selling alcohol on Sunday. The infamous Anti-Saloon League pushed to shut down prosperous barkeepers like Hall, but the notoriety probably only increased Hall's business, and sympathetic juries saw to it that he never lost his liquor license. By the early 1900s, Hall had added his famous Summer Garden to the rear of the establishment, an open-air beer garden that did a booming business in the warmer months. Such beer gardens were very common in Washington in the early decades of the twentieth century, before Prohibition drove all the fun indoors. Hall's was one of the more notable ones. "It was a place where gentlemen took off their coats, stretched them over the backs of chairs, and went to the serious work of shelling Chesapeake Bay hard-shelled crabs, with foaming siedels on the side," wrote John J. Daly in the *Post* in 1933.

Brunch scene at Harrigan's Bar and Grill in 1947. *D.C. Public Library, Star Collection,* © Washington Post.

Hall's survived Prohibition, complete with its Summer Garden, which sold mildly alcoholic "near beer" during the dry years. By the 1950s, it had become a charming time capsule of the old Southwest as urban renewal threatened its demolition. Its main dining room still had an old-fashioned tile floor, pressed tin ceiling, gas-powered Welsbach lighting fixtures, cherry wood paneling and an immense Honduran mahogany bar with a trough of running water around its base—for spitting, of course. At one end of the bar was one of those highly decorated golden brass cash registers with the name "Frank P. Hall" proudly emblazoned on top. Behind the bar were beveled mirrors and a large nude painting of Adam and Eve. Eccentric as it sounds now, it was the sort of décor that had been commonplace in 1897, when cafés and saloons catered to an exclusively male clientele and cultivated a club-like ambience. An itinerant artist had done the Adam and Eve painting for a Norfolk hotel owner,

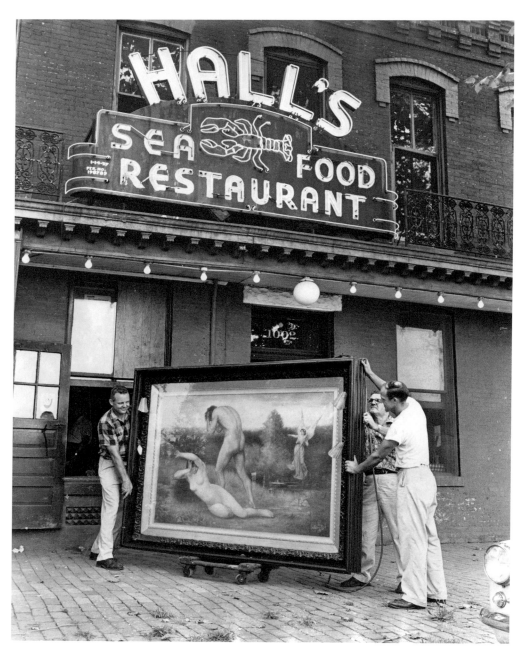

Moving the Adam and Eve painting out of Hall's in 1964. *D.C. Public Library, Star Collection,* © Washington Post.

who didn't like it, and he reportedly sold it to Frank Hall for fifty dollars one day when he dropped by Hall's for a drink. The *Evening Star*'s John Harry Shannon, aka the Rambler, called the painting "one of the most hideous nude paintings ever put on canvas," but apparently not everyone agreed.

When the restaurant was finally forced to close in 1964, the painting of Adam and Eve was carefully moved, along with the Honduran mahogany bar, to Hall's new location at First and V Streets Southwest, just to the east of Fort McNair at Buzzard Point on the Anacostia waterfront. A new Summer Garden was set up there facing the water, but the location was very isolated, and the restaurant remained in business for only seven more years. The property was redeveloped in 1971, dispersing the mahogany bar and the Adam and Eve painting to parts unknown.

Cleaning up the waterfront was a perennial social cause through the first half of the twentieth century, beginning with construction in 1916 of the Municipal Fish Market, designed by city architect Snowden Ashford (1866–1927), as a replacement for the "deplorable and unsanitary fish wharf along the Washington channel." Seafood-borne typhus was a perennial worry in those days, and the modern market house offered customers the assurance of food that was as healthy as it was fresh.

The market house was the home of a cluster of seafood restaurants that became popular in the first half of the twentieth century. One was HERZOG's, started by a Swiss couple, Charlie (1886–1929) and Henrietta "Yettie" (1882–1970) Herzog, in 1912. They moved into prime fish market space that featured a narrow second-floor iron balcony overlooking the water. The balcony at Herzog's became quite popular, especially in the summer months when the breeze from off the water provided exquisite relief from the sweltering heat. Herzog's boasted that all its seafood was bought "fresh off the boats as they come in from Chesapeake Bay." Although Yettie Herzog retired and sold the restaurant in 1938, it stayed in business and continued to offer its balcony seafood dining into the 1950s.

Another place that started at the fish market was NAYLOR's, located next door to Herzog's. Grover Cleveland Naylor (1884–1962), known to friends as Pop Naylor, opened his raw bar at number 20 in the market in 1929. It began as little more than a modest storefront selling smoked fish and other seafood, mostly to fellow watermen. According to the *Evening Star*, the men on the wharf asked Naylor why he didn't cook his seafood, and thus the full-fledged restaurant was born. In 1936, Naylor expanded by opening an additional, much larger restaurant on the other side of Maine Avenue, at Tenth Street Southwest, while keeping the original restaurant going in the fish market. Naylor's offered lavish seafood dinners at reasonable prices, specializing in a wide range of crab dishes. One notable special was the Naylor's Shore Platter, which included filet

On the balcony at Herzog's in July 1941. *Library of Congress.*

of fish, fried scallops, fried oysters, fried shrimp, crab cake, fish cake, sliced beets, French fries and coleslaw. Naylor expanded with additional restaurants on Capitol Hill and in Maryland but eventually became overextended. In 1957, his large Maine Avenue restaurant was sold at auction to pay back taxes. Naylor retired that same year.

The eatery that took over the sizable former Naylor's space at 951 Maine Avenue Southwest was the FLAGSHIP RESTAURANT, which, like Naylor's, had its origins in a fish market business. Daisy Carter Lanhardt (1903–1994) and her brother, Bill Carter, opened the Carter-Lanhardt wholesale seafood company at the fish market in 1928. The company owned its own boats, as well as its own Chesapeake Bay oyster beds. It expanded by opening the small Flagship Restaurant in the fish market. The business thrived, and after Carter died, his wife, Ethel, joined her sister-in-law in running the business. In time, Daisy and Ethel's popular eatery needed larger quarters, and sometime after Naylor's was closed in 1957, they took over that space, which seated five hundred.

Flagship was one of several Washington seafood restaurants that maintained the unique and much-loved practice of serving warm, sugary rum buns as appetizers before all meals (in addition to hush puppies, a more widely known staple of southern seafood restaurants). Rum buns are Danish-like pastries with dough swirled in cinnamon and raisins and drizzled with rum-flavored brown icing. To those not used to the concept, the idea of rum buns as an appetizer seems like eating dessert at the wrong end of the meal or eating a breakfast food at dinnertime. Yet the pastries were a fixture of many local seafood restaurants throughout the twentieth century, and customers often thought they were the best part of the meal. In 1969, the Flagship's manager, Stella Cauble, told *Washington Post* food critic Donald Dresden that she'd be out of business if she didn't include hush puppies and rum buns with every order.

The threat of redevelopment loomed over the new Flagship Restaurant from the start. Since World War II, momentum had been gaining for a large-scale urban renewal project that would replace the slums of Southwest with tasteful modernist residential complexes. Along with many blocks of houses, almost the entire waterfront was razed in the 1960s to be replaced with the broad, pedestrian-unfriendly streets and a massive concrete flood-protection deck that together define the waterfront today. The municipal fish market was torn down in 1960, over the sustained objections of its tenants. All the smaller restaurants and other businesses on the waterside of Maine Avenue had also been cleared away by that time. This left just two large eateries, Flagship and Hogate's, which were located on the other side of the street. Both were promised leases of space on the new concrete deck along the waterfront once it was completed.

The Flagship moved into its large, new, nine-room, 750-seat restaurant at 900 Water Street Southwest in late 1972. Donald Dresden, who had reviewed the previous incarnation of Flagship, visited the new place and was unimpressed. The kitchen apparently struggled to keep the food freshly cooked and warm for such a large number of tables. Still, the tradition of the venerable family-owned seafood restaurant on the waterfront was enough to keep customers happy.

The restaurant closed abruptly in October 1985, when Daisy and Ethel decided to retire and sold their business to the Phillips seafood chain, which renamed it Phillips Flagship. The Phillips restaurant remains in business to this day, awaiting the next waterfront redevelopment.

FLAGSHIP RUM BUNS

Mix a half-stick butter, ¼ cup sugar and 1½ teaspoons salt in a bowl. Add 1 cup scalded milk and let the mixture cool to lukewarm. Sprinkle 1 envelope of dry instant yeast over the mixture and beat until it is smooth. Add 1 beaten egg and 1½ teaspoons rum extract. Add 1¾ cups of sifted flour and beat until the mixture is smooth, then add an additional 1¾ cups of sifted flour and again beat until smooth. Cover the dough with a towel and let it rise in a warm place (over 80 degrees Fahrenheit) for about 2 hours, or until it has doubled in size. Punch down the dough and divide it into 2 equal pieces.

Next, roll out each piece of dough so that it is a rectangle approximately 12 inches long, 4 inches wide and ½ inch thick. Brush each piece of dough with 1 tablespoon melted butter and sprinkle 2 tablespoons of sugar and 2 tablespoons of chopped raisins over each piece. Roll the dough up jellyroll fashion, stretching it so that it is 15 inches long. Cut each roll into 18 pieces, each ¾ inch thick, and arrange them cut-side down in well-buttered 3-inch muffin tins.

Let the buns rise in a warm place for 1 hour, covered with a towel, or until they have doubled in size. Bake the buns in a preheated 400-degree oven for 15 to 20 minutes, or until they are golden brown. To make the icing, combine 1 cup of confectioner's sugar, 2 tablespoons hot water and 1 teaspoon of rum extract in a bowl. Spread the buns with the icing as soon as they come out of the oven. Cool the buns on a wire rack. Makes 36 buns.

One of the biggest names in waterfront seafood dining for most of the twentieth century was HOGATE'S, operated by twin brothers Watson Birdsalle Rulon (1904–1984) and Joseph Keen Rulon (1904–1999). The Rulons were born in Philadelphia and initially took very different career paths. Joseph earned a degree as a mechanical engineer and worked for twenty years in the X-ray film division of the DuPont chemical company, where he earned nine patents for technologies such as the bite-wing film strip universally used by dentists to X-ray teeth. His brother Watson was the one who first went into the seafood business, opening a small seafood stand in Ocean City, New Jersey, in 1928.

It was the family doctor, John Hogate Whiticar (1887–1969), who facilitated the Rulons' move to Washington and the Southwest waterfront. Whiticar had purchased a former iron foundry building at Ninth Street and Maine Avenue Southwest in the heart of the old industrial waterfront district. The sturdy old building had reportedly been built at the dawn of the Civil War as a foundry and stayed in operation as an iron and brass foundry for many years. Then from 1912 to 1915, it served as the factory for the Washington Aeroplane Company, one of the earliest aeronautical companies in the world. The factory produced Columbia monoplanes, biplanes and flying boats, which were conveniently launched out on the Potomac across the street from the factory.

After its brief stint as an airplane factory, the building resumed its old role once again as an iron foundry until Dr. Whiticar acquired it in 1935 and leased the space out as a restaurant called Beck's. Beck's was an Ocean City, New Jersey seafood eatery, and this became its Washington branch. But Beck's didn't last long; in 1938, Whiticar convinced Watson Rulon to take over the restaurant, which Rulon renamed Hogate's (the separately run Ocean City restaurant also was renamed Hogate's). Then, in 1946, brother Joseph left DuPont to join Watson in running what quickly became an established Washington landmark.

Hogate's liked to advertise that it was the second-largest restaurant in the country, seating as many as six hundred customers in the spacious former foundry building. In addition to offering great seafood, the restaurant put the Rulons' expert showmanship on display. The old building itself, with its sturdy, hand-hewn wooden beams, added quaintness and character to the dining experience. The huge upstairs dining room (seating was on two floors) included many windows. Along the west side, patrons had scenic views out over the boats docked at the wharf; along the east side of the room, another long row of large windows displayed Hogate's massive main kitchen, with the meticulously clean ovens arranged so as to be in full view. Customers could watch closely as their lobsters, crab cakes and rum buns were

A postcard view of Hogate's Restaurant. *Author's collection.*

being made. Dining out at Hogate's was a complete entertainment experience, and it was highly popular.

By 1947, the kitchen was producing over 2,500 meals a day and as many as 3,000 a day by the mid-1960s. The *Evening Star* reported in 1964 that Hogate's diners consumed 100,000 pounds of shrimp a year, 52,000 pounds of Maine lobster, 50,000 pounds of crabmeat and 200,000 pounds of Idaho potatoes. The restaurant's popular Mariner's Platter, a generous assortment of seafood delights, cost just $1.90 that year. And Hogate's, too, like Flagship, had those delectable rum buns as appetizers. Despite hundreds of seats on two floors, Hogate's got so many customers that they still had to line up around the block to get into the restaurant.

The Southwest urban renewal planning that began in 1954 included eradicating almost the entire former waterfront area, replacing the old industrial infrastructure with pristine new residential blocks. Almost all the old buildings along Maine Avenue were pegged for destruction, including the historic foundry building that housed Hogate's, which no one seemed interested in preserving. To replace it, a massive new nine-hundred-seat restaurant complex was constructed directly across Maine Avenue.

The old foundry building remained until shortly after the new restaurant opened in 1972. As businesses and organizations of all types shuffled around Southwest during redevelopment, sometimes strange accommodations had to be made. The old Hogate's, for example, served for a time as a church on Sundays for a local Episcopal congregation that was between buildings—the bar in the back of the main dining room was discreetly covered with drapery during services. The congregation affectionately referred to the eatery as St. Hogate's.

The boxy new $2 million Hogate's building along the water never had the same magic for Washington's longtime seafood lovers. The Rulons retired and turned over the restaurant's operations to the Marriott Corporation. Hordes of people waited in the huge lobby for their names to be announced over a public address system, after which they were escorted through what seemed like miles of tables before reaching their assigned spot. A *Washington Post* review in 1978 found the food of less than exceptional quality and no longer particularly inexpensive either: "Maybe the lobster served to my wife for $8.50 didn't like being sautéed, but you could call this dish Lobster Akron for its rubbery consistency. We now know what it's like to chew on a pair of galoshes."

While the big buses continued to bring in swarms of tourists, local patronage began to drop off as word of Hogate's uneven quality spread. It finally closed in 2001 after getting socked by the drop in tourism following the attacks of September 11. In 2004, the building was briefly reopened as a nightclub/restaurant called H20, but by 2010, it was slated for demolition as a second renewal of the waterfront was being planned.

OFF THE WATERFRONT

Opened by John Mandis (1918–1971) in January 1960, the MARKET INN at 200 E Street Southwest was away from the waterfront on the northern edge of the Southwest redevelopment area. Mandis had worked in the seafood business for many years, and his father, Greek immigrant William Mandis (1883–1971), had operated a lunchroom on Pennsylvania Avenue. Mandis was an early enthusiast for the Southwest redevelopment area, and he chose the site for his Market Inn because it was near the offices of key customers, as well as fresh seafood from the waterfront markets. With Capitol Hill close by, Mandis had a congressional quorum bell installed in his restaurant so that congressmen and senators would know when they needed to head up to the Capitol for a roll call vote. When the bell rang, Senator Claude Pepper of

Florida would ask to have his food kept warm in the kitchen while he took off for a quick vote, promptly returning to continue his seafood lunch.

Though the new building was a plain, brick, single-story structure, the interior was lavishly decorated with antiques and other curios, some of which Mandis had salvaged from the destroyed buildings of the old Southwest. The overhead gaslights and fruitwood paneling came from an old church, as did a pew that was supposedly used by Calvin Coolidge. The two massive bars were antiques brought in from old saloons, including Jimmy Lake's place on Ninth Street Northwest. There was also an 1850s corn grinder that relatives had dug up in a field in Manassas and, for Redskins fans, a football signed by Sammy Baugh. And, of course, there were large vintage paintings of nude women, just like at all the old bars of Southwest. In fact, Mandis claimed that one of Southwest's old saloons used to stand on the same site as the Market Inn.

The Market Inn grew to be a Southwest D.C. institution, despite the fact that it was tucked in a corner of E Street just south of the railroad tracks that was off the beaten path for many of its customers. After Mandis died of cancer in 1971, his son Carl carried on with the restaurant, which kept a loyal clientele for decades. The menu included the most comprehensive selection of seafood to be found in the District, and in later years, a popular Sunday champagne-jazz brunch was featured. By 2008, however, the neighborhood was changing again, and property owners wanted more in rent than the restaurant could afford. It finally closed at the end of the year, and the building was demolished in 2009.

One of the longest-surviving and best-known seafood restaurants in the city was ironically one that wasn't anywhere near the waterfront. Thomas A. O'Donnell (1890–1949), a native Washingtonian, founded O'DONNELL'S RESTAURANT, at 1207 E Street Northwest, in 1922. As a boy, O'Donnell dropped out of grade school to become an apprentice bricklayer for his father. He bounced around a number of early professions—decorating display windows for a department store, running an early movie theater and operating a battery service for automobiles—before opening his restaurant. In 1940, he added O'DONNELL'S SEA GRILL at 1221 E Street Northwest, just up the street from his original place, which remained in business.

O'Donnell loved seafood, and his restaurant stood out for both its cooking and its décor. O'Donnell's has often been credited with inventing the rum bun. While the exact origins of the famous pastry are not known, it could well have started at O'Donnell's, which was serving rum buns with every meal as early as the 1920s. The restaurant also developed a devoted following for its distinctive "Norfolk-style" seafood, which Tom O'Donnell supposedly invented while on a fishing trip with friends in

Left: Portrait of James Wormley by Henry Ulke. *Historical Society of Washington, D.C.*

Below: Postcard view of the café at the Ebbitt House, circa 1910. *Author's collection.*

New Ebbitt Cafe, Washington, D. C.

Contemporary view of one of the dining rooms in the Old Ebbitt Grill. *Photo by Ron Blunt.*

Dining room at the Occidental Restaurant, circa 1927. *Author's collection.*

View of Harvey's Restaurant on Pennsylvania Avenue, circa 1930. *Author's collection.*

The Monocle Restaurant. *Photo by the author.*

Above: Dining room of the Monocle in 1960. *The Monocle*.

Left: Menu from the Parrot Restaurant, 1948. *Author's collection*.

Postcard view of the Water Gate Inn's rustic interior. *Author's collection*.

Pennsylvania Popovers, based on a Water Gate Inn recipe. *Photo by Austin Cuttino*.

The Madrillon featured several exotically themed dining rooms. *Author's collection.*

A 1942 postcard from the Lotus Restaurant features colorful décor and exotic dancers. *Author's collection.*

Ben's Chili Bowl. *Photo by the author.*

Postcard view of diners at the Silver Fox restaurant, circa 1941. *Author's collection.*

The 14th Street Lunch was just one of many lunchrooms in early twentieth-century Washington. *Author's collection.*

A D.C. Little Tavern seen at dusk. *Photo by Michael Horsley.*

Early Hot Shoppes restaurants drew attention with their orange roofs. *Author's collection*.

A double-decker hamburger based on the Hot Shoppes Mighty Mo recipe. *Photo by Austin Cuttino*.

The Vitrolite-clad China Doll restaurant. *Photo by Michael Horsley.*

Postcard view of the lavish interior of Paul Young's Restaurant, designed by William Pahlmann. *Author's collection.*

月宮酒家

Moon Palace RESTAURANT
COCKTAIL LOUNGE
3308 Wisconsin Ave. N.W. Washington, D.C.

Menu from the Moon Palace. *Author's collection.*

Interior of the Sans Souci. *Author's collection.*

California Avocado and Lobster Parisienne at the Sans Souci. *Author's collection.*

Postcard from the Roma Restaurant. *Author's collection.*

Ricotta and Prosciutto Manicotti, based on a Roma recipe. *Photo by Austin Cuttino.*

The dining room of the Primi Piatti. *Photo by the author.*

Primi Piatti risotto with truffle butter and mushrooms. *Photo by the author.*

Nora Pouillon cuts herbs from the garden adjacent to her restaurant. *Photo by Matthew Rakola.*

Strawberry rhubarb pie from Restaurant Nora. *Photo by Scott Suchman.*

A photo by Esther Bubley of a woman sitting in O'Donnell's Sea Grill, April 1943. *Library of Congress.*

Virginia. Norfolk style meant sautéing the lobster, scallops or shrimp in butter, Old Bay seasoning and garlic and then bringing the results to the customer's table sizzling in a small aluminum pan. Customers loved it.

In the 1920s and 1930s, dramatic décor was increasingly one of the most important ways to draw people into a restaurant, and O'Donnell realized this. His original eatery featured a great Civil War–era oaken bar, which O'Donnell had purchased from a tavern on E Street that had been driven under by Prohibition. With the later Sea Grill, he went to great lengths to evoke a nautical atmosphere, despite its F Street location. "There's the 'Wharf' done in weathered 75-year-old shingles from the Maryland shore, and across the gangplank (over real running water) is the cozy captain's cabin. Upstairs is the Harbor Room in white waxed wood rubbed until the knots show through in natural color, the tavern, and the hunt club room," the *Post* reported. O'Donnell had hired a New England family of interior designers—Marshall B. Martin; his wife, Helen; and their daughter, Joyce—to give his new place its special appeal.

O'Donnell's gained a national reputation, and celebrities such as comedian Red Skelton and actress Jean Harlow were known to favor the restaurant. O'Donnell's was proud of the fact that it never closed. A 1937 notice in the *Post* advertised that its "Tang O' the Sea" lobsters were available any time, day or night, so you could have one for breakfast if you so desired. The practice was put to a stop by food rationing in World War II. Beginning in March 1943, the Sea Grill was closed in the mornings (from 4:00 a.m. to 11:00 a.m.) because of the limited food supply. No more breakfast lobsters until the war was won.

Tom O'Donnell had turned the restaurant over to his wife and daughters in 1942. Following the trend of the times, Mildred O'Donnell (1890–1973) decided to branch out to the suburbs in 1956, opening a new restaurant in the former Edgemoor Motor Building at 8301 Wisconsin Avenue in Bethesda, Maryland. The original O'Donnell's closed in 1962, but the Sea Grill on the same block continued in business undaunted by the difficult post-riot years. However, it, too, closed in 1980, as new office buildings engulfed the old F Street strip. The Bethesda location also lasted many years but likewise closed when redevelopment came to that neighborhood in 2001. The family opened yet another spot in Gaithersburg, Maryland, in 1997 but in 2013 finally announced that that site would close, too, bringing to an end the eatery's ninety-year legacy.

Chapter 9

LEGENDARY D.C. LUNCHROOMS AND DINERS

The lunchrooms and diners of the late nineteenth and early twentieth centuries marked a dramatic transformation in the eating habits of Washingtonians. Earlier generations usually had all their meals at home or with friends, consuming their dinners—the big meal of the day—about two or three o'clock in the afternoon. As the city grew and people lived farther away from downtown, it was increasingly impractical for workers to return home at midday for dinner. Work grew more regulated and demanding, forcing the main meal to be split into a light luncheon and a later dinner. The modern midday lunch meal gradually became standard, and lunchrooms sprang up to meet the emerging need.

Turn-of-the-century Washington was famous for its lunchrooms, almost universally called "dairy lunches." "The dairy lunch is peculiarly a Washington institution, and its popularity is ever on the increase," the *Washington Post* reported in 1897. "There is scarcely a street or avenue in the city that has not several of these places. The prices of all are cheap and some are cheaper than others." The term "dairy lunch" originally meant that these places served simple cold lunches—sandwiches and pies accompanied by milk (no alcohol)—though by the late 1890s, dairy lunchrooms sold a full range of hot and cold meals. "The main advantages now claimed [for the lunchrooms] are quicker service and cheaper prices," the *Post* explained. "A man with only 3 cents need not go hungry. For the three pennies he may get a ham, tongue, or cheese sandwich."

The man often credited with inventing the Washington dairy lunch was Frank K. Ward (1848–1893), a native of Yonkers, New York, who had served as a drummer boy in the Army Signal Corps during the Civil War and later came to Washington as a civilian employee of the corps. After being dismissed from his job in a downsizing move, Ward went into the dairy business, founding the ALDERNEY DAIRY in 1875 with a "forlorn, dilapidated wagon and a not over-prepossessing horse." Ward rapidly built up his business, bringing in fresh milk by rail from large country farms and distributing it to homes across the city from a fleet of twenty-one wagons. He fitted out his main dairy building at Third and D Streets Northwest with a "dairy" lunchroom, featuring fresh Alderney milk, and then expanded to six locations across the city. By the late 1880s, Ward was one of the best-known and most successful businessmen in Washington, and his dairy lunchrooms had set the standard for the city.

Sadly, Ward suffered a fall as precipitous as his rise. Much of his empire was bought with borrowed money, and he was plagued with financial problems. In February 1889, he was forced to sell his company to Kingsley Bros. Creamery. Despondent over his loss, Ward took to drinking, and one night in June, while intoxicated, he shot a certain Maurice Adler in the Marble Saloon at Ninth Street and Pennsylvania Avenue Northwest. Adler eventually died of his wounds, and Ward was tried for murder but acquitted, largely because he was well liked and everyone felt sorry that he had fallen on hard times. But by then, Ward was a severe alcoholic, and within three years, his wife sued for divorce. Several months after that, Ward, again heavily under the influence, fell—or possibly threw himself—in front of a streetcar and was instantly killed.

But the lunchrooms established by Ward and his many competitors grew and prospered. One of the best known was the FORD & GRAHAM DAIRY LUNCH at 609 Fifteenth Street Northwest, opposite the Treasury Department, which was started about 1886 by John M. Ford and Thomas Graham. The two had learned the dairy lunch business working for Ward, and they created an eatery with an ambience that was in many ways the equal of any formal restaurant. Government clerks would drop by, sometimes bringing their own sandwiches, and order mugs of coffee while settling into the café's comfortable wicker chairs. By the early 1900s, Ford and Graham had purchased their own dairy farm, called the Hermitage, in Garrett Park, Maryland, to supply their lunchroom with fresh milk, thought to be the foundation of any dairy lunchroom's success. Ford & Graham's was so refined that it even for a time adopted an honor-based pay system. "Patrons of the place, in the most crowded hours of the day, walked up to the counter, helped themselves to what they wanted or called for it, ate, drank, chatted a few minutes with friends, returned to the counter and paid according to their own figures," the *Washington Times* explained.

One suspects that the honor-pay system did not last long, but the emphasis on fresh food and clean, "sanitary" settings struck a chord with turn-of-the-century restaurant patrons who were increasingly sensitized to food safety concerns. The New York–based CHILDS RESTAURANT chain, discussed at more length in *Lost Washington, D.C.*, opened its first D.C. eatery in 1913 at 1423 Pennsylvania Avenue Northwest, just west of the Willard Hotel and only a block from Ford & Graham. Childs would become one of the most successful fast-food chains of the early twentieth century, its restaurants conveying an almost overwhelming sense of cleanliness with their white-tiled walls and floors, white marble tabletops and waitresses dressed in starched white uniforms. As *Washington Post* humorist H.I. Phillips summed it up in 1929, "The early Childs restaurants were so glaringly white it didn't seem right to enter them without a bath, shave and haircut. They were architecturally part laboratory, part squash court, part Roman pool, and part goldfish bowl."

White was the color of cleanliness, and in addition to white tiles, early diners and lunchrooms often had the word "White" in their titles. A year before Childs came to town, the WHITE PALACE LUNCH, dubbed the "handsomest lunch room south of New York," opened at 1417 G Street Northwest, around the corner from Ford & Graham. Greek immigrant Louis Mandes (1882–1954), who had come to Washington in the 1890s, was its founder. Mandes boasted in a large newspaper advertisement that, "to ensure the greatest sanitation, the walls of the White Palace Lunch are entirely covered and finished in Opalite, a new and costly finishing material. This is the only lunch room in the United States entirely finished in this up-to-date material." Even the tabletops were covered in glassy Opalite. The White Palace was a great success, and Mandes followed by opening additional branches on Ninth Street in 1914 and Pennsylvania Avenue in 1915. The Ninth Street store had French and Italian frescoes decorating the ceiling and featured an "open fire broiler, where orders of poultry, steaks, chops, fish, &c., are broiled before the customer's eyes." The popular lunchroom chain remained in business until the 1940s.

Perhaps the most famous of the "white" diners of the early twentieth century was the White Castle chain that began in Wichita, Kansas, in 1921. While there were never any White Castles in Washington, D.C., the company's pioneering techniques for preparing and selling hamburgers defined the fast-food industry for many decades. It grew dramatically in the Midwest in the 1920s, becoming the envy of wannabe fast-food restaurateurs across the country.

White Castle had many imitators, the best-known being WHITE TOWER, a Milwaukee-based chain that began in 1925 and opened about six outlets in Washington beginning in the 1930s. White Tower's founders, John E. Saxe and Thomas E. Saxe, meticulously copied the White Castle system, studying how the eateries were located, designed and operated and imitating them as closely as possible. White Castle sued

An advertisement for the White Palace Lunch. *From the* Washington Times, *May 27, 1912. Library of Congress.*

White Tower over the imitation and won court rulings that required White Tower to change the design of its restaurants, avoid direct competition and pay royalties. White Tower subsequently operated in different markets than White Castle and featured streamlined shops with Art Deco styling rather than mini castles.

In Washington, the most fondly recalled imitator of the White Castle system was the LITTLE TAVERN chain founded by Harry F. Duncan (1899–1992) in 1927 in Louisville, Kentucky. Within a year, Duncan moved to D.C. and opened the first Little Tavern here at 814 E Street Northwest in October 1928. Like the White Tower shops, Little Taverns were unapologetic knock-offs of White Castles. They offered nearly the same five-cent hamburgers—small one-and-a-half-ounce patties cooked with chopped onions to enhance the flavor—as well as the same white finishes to emphasize cleanliness and the same small stores with hot grills, counters and a few stools. Little Tavern's "Buy 'Em by the Bag" motto adroitly preserved both the gist and the alliteration of White Castle's "Sell 'Em by the Sack" slogan. To top it off, the first Little Taverns even had crenellated cornices that looked just like White Castle's.

But Little Taverns soon had a distinctive look. In the early 1930s, Duncan hired the team of George E. Stone and Charles Brooks of Baltimore's Stonebrook Corporation to develop Little Tavern's trademark green-and-white, Tudor cottage–style design, permanently distinguishing the chain from White Castle and other competitors. By 1939, twenty-one of the tiny porcelain-enameled eateries with their sloped green roofs and faux shingles had popped up around the city, offering customers their distinctive mix of inviting hominess and antiseptic cleanliness.

Little Taverns filled a unique niche in the city's fast-food market. They offered one of the most affordable meals in the city, they usually stayed open all night and they turned no one away. As late as the 1980s, the price of a Little Tavern hamburger was only forty-nine cents. Everyone from congressmen to high-priced lobbyists seemed to have a secret weakness for the chain's "death balls" (the greasy, cholesterol-laden hamburgers), and they could be seen ponied up to the counters late at night next to homeless people nursing cups of coffee and trying to stay warm. People fondly referred to Little Tavern as "Club LT" in sarcastic reference to its utter lack of pretense.

The chain reached its peak in the 1950s with more than fifty Little Taverns spread across the Baltimore-Washington area, but it began a gradual decline after that. Once known for their cleanliness, many of the little diners grew old and decrepit. By 1981, when the chain was down to thirty shops, Harry Duncan decided to retire and move to Florida. He sold the chain to Gerald Wedren, an enthusiastic LT fan who set about sprucing up the remaining shops. Wedren oversaw sympathetic restorations of several Little Taverns, instituted a new dress code to sharpen up the appearance of the greasy-spoon cooks and added new items to the menu. He even opened an upscale eatery downtown, officially called CLUB LT, at the Shops at National Place. It was all too little, too late, unfortunately, and the chain was sold again several more times as it continued to shrink. By the 1990s, there were no Little Taverns left in D.C.; the last one, located near Baltimore, Maryland, reportedly closed in 2008.

There were several other lunchroom/diner "systems" in Washington beginning in the 1930s, all small shops with limited menus, often open twenty-four hours a day and catering to a broad range of city dwellers. Another example of a White Castle knock-off was the BLUE BELL chain, started here in the early 1930s by James N. West (1898–1982). West also started the WAFFLE SHOP chain, which featured sleek, Streamlined Moderne–style eateries that reflected the influence of the stylish West Coast diners and drive-ins of the late 1940s and 1950s. The first D.C. Waffle Shop, opened in 1949 at 522 Tenth Street Northwest, stayed in business longer than any of the chain's other

five D.C. branches, finally closing in 2007. The eatery featured the classic assortment of sandwiches, burgers and all-day breakfast fare universally offered in diners and lunchrooms of its era.

One of the best-known independent lunchrooms was HODGE'S SANDWICH SHOP, which actually started as a tavern at 407 Ninth Street Northwest in 1898. Lower Ninth Street in those days was a warren of saloons and lunchrooms and became a mecca for early burlesque and motion picture houses. Hodge's was a typical saloon with a great wooden bar and sawdust to absorb the spills on the floorboards. It offered free roast beef sandwiches (as was the custom at the time) to those who bought drinks. In time, the roast beef sandwiches got the upper hand, and the saloon business was dropped, most likely during Prohibition. For decades after, Hodge's was famous for its juicy roast beef sandwiches, carved to order from a great steamship round of beef. Speaker of the House Sam Rayburn would send his chauffeur for them. Eventually moving to hole-in-the-wall digs at 616 New York Avenue Northwest, Hodge's survived until 2007.

One famous Washington diner that got into the restaurant business almost by accident was the REEVES BAKERY, founded in 1891 at 1209 F Street Northwest by Sewell A. Reeves (1865–1940). Born in Winchester, Virginia, Reeves worked as a young man in his father's Front Royal grain business and then got a position at N.A. Poole's large grocery business on Louisiana Avenue near the old Center Market. Later taking over Poole's business, Reeves learned to stock fine gourmet products, such as patented California "roller" flour and Fox River butter from Illinois. Reeves opened his own grocery business in the 1209 F Street building in about 1886, offering unique blends of coffee, roasted and ground on the premises, in addition to other gourmet foods. He soon added a confectionery on the second floor of the building, followed by a bakery on the third floor. In 1899, Reeves installed a row of twelve stools at the counter, where he had been showing off all his fine comestibles, and suddenly the bakery and confectionery shop was transformed into a café. By late 1902, Reeves had expanded the first-floor eatery at the rear and installed seating to accommodate two hundred customers.

Opposite, top: The Waffle Shop on Tenth Street, circa 1950. *Library of Congress*.

Opposite, bottom: Interior of Hodge's Sandwich Shop in 1963, shortly before it closed at this location. *Historical Society of Washington, D.C.*

A postcard of Reeves Bakery and Café, circa 1915. *Author's collection.*

Reeves's primary customers were the ladies who lunched—downtown department store shoppers looking for refined and delicate food for a midday repast, as well as perhaps a box of chocolates to take home. "Women love dainty things," the *Evening Star* observed in 1902. "It is this love for dainty food and dainty china that, in a measure at least, crowds Reeves establishment, 1209 F street, to its very doors every day in the week, in bad weather as well as good." While chocolates and bonbons were the biggest draw in the early days, the pies eventually won out, with Reeves's strawberry pie becoming the top favorite through virtually the entire twentieth century.

Reeves's distinctive turn-of-the-century décor—dark walnut paneling, beveled mirrors, warm but dim Tiffany lamps, brass ceiling fixtures and rows of leather-topped counter stools—remained in place for many decades. The fame of Reeves's pies and cakes drew celebrities like actress Helen Hayes, who wrote of stopping for lemonade at Reeves as a child before going to the movies to weep at the exploits of Mary Pickford. In later years, she was said to be partial to Reeves's chocolate sodas. Bess Truman, who sat at the counter, liked the famous strawberry pie. So did Pat Nixon. And Lady Bird Johnson came in for roast beef and an orange freeze.

Reeves's son, Algernon Poole Reeves, took over after his father's death, and his son, John W. Reeves, sold the place in 1965 to brothers George and Henry Abraham. The Abraham brothers ran Reeves for more than two decades and became as well known and liked as the original Reeves family. But when they took over, they misjudged the attachment of Washingtonians to the old coffee shop. In 1966, they announced plans to renovate and update the store, completely gutting it and redoing the façade in a contemporary "California-modern" style. The plan was met with howls of outrage. Virtually no one wanted the dark, antiquated coffee shop updated. Everyone loved its old-fashioned hominess. Even Senator Everett Dirksen wrote a letter urging that the café be preserved. The Abraham brothers relented, and instead of remodeling the place, they restored the exterior and preserved most of the interior.

The Abraham brothers kept Reeves running through the bleak years of the 1960s and 1970s when downtown was at its lowest ebb. They added heartier fare, such as chili and beef barbecue, to lure in male customers and featured blueberry doughnuts—a favorite from their previous doughnut shop—to supplement the famous pies. As other small-scale retail shops closed and were replaced with block-long office buildings, Reeves stuck it out.

Then, in 1984, tragedy struck. A faulty electrical cord in a pastry freezer caused a massive fire that gutted the old building. Almost all the beautiful old décor that had been so cherished was destroyed. Only some of the wooden counter stools survived. The Abrahams rebuilt the restaurant, redesigning the interior with a lighter, more modern look and reopening in 1985. But the following year, they sold their valuable property to a developer, and in 1988, Reeves closed and was torn down to make way for a new office building.

The restaurant opened again a block away on G Street in 1991 in a new office building. Though the setting had changed, the food was still the same. "Glorious Consistency" was the title and theme of Phyllis Richman's review of the new Reeves shop in 1992. The food was "as comforting as chicken soup." Still, a lot had changed over the years, and as time went by, the restaurant lost customers. It finally closed for good in 2007, after a run of more than one hundred years

One of the city's most popular and long-lasting fast-food chains was the HOT SHOPPES, an important innovator in the fast-food business in the 1930s and 1940s. The Hot Shoppes was at the vanguard of the transition from early downtown eateries, which provided cheap lunches for the "working man," to the more upscale eateries of mid-century, which aimed to serve commuters and suburbanites with drive-in service and more fetching entrées.

The original Hot Shoppe on Fourteenth Street in 1927. *Historic photographs collection, Marriott International Archives*.

The Marriott rags-to-riches story used to be one of the most oft told in the city. The son of a Utah sheep rancher, J. Willard "Bill" Marriott (1900–1985) was imbued at an early age with strong Mormon beliefs and an intense work ethic. With a partner from Utah, Marriott rented out a slim corner storefront at 3128 Fourteenth Street Northwest in 1927 to operate as an A&W root beer stand. Inside was a counter with nine stools. Offering frosted mugs of cold root beer for a nickel, Marriott did a booming business. Within a few months, he had gone out to Utah to marry his college sweetheart, Alice "Allie" Sheets (1907–2000); driven her back to D.C. in his rickety Model T; and opened his second root beer stand downtown at 606 Ninth Street Northwest, another resounding success.

Selling root beer was great in warm weather, but once the temperatures dropped, Marriott needed something else to keep his business going. By some accounts, it was Allie who came up with the scheme to sell Mexican food. Washington was no stranger to Mexican eateries, which typically featured hot tamales and chili con carne. The challenge was to get good recipes and find a source for quality ingredients. Bill recalled that the Mexican Embassy was located over on Sixteenth Street, just a couple blocks away from their shop. Allie, who had majored in Spanish in college, talked the embassy's chef into sharing recipes, as well as the name and address of a San Antonio supplier of Mexican foods. After that, all they needed was a name for the place. The story goes that a good friend asked, "Hey, Bill, when are you and Allie going to open this hot shop I've been hearing about?" And so, with a few letters added to dress it up, the Hot Shoppes were born.

What to do next? For his third Hot Shoppe, at Georgia Avenue and Gallatin Street Northwest, Marriott planned something new—a drive-in like those he had known in Utah. When it opened in 1928, it was one of the first such restaurants on the East Coast, offering curbside service to customers who could drive up, order a meal and eat it right in their cars off a tray propped on the door. The little building in the center of the parking lot became a model for future Hot Shoppes, topped as it was by a bright orange roof to draw the attention of passing motorists—like the shops in the Howard Johnson chain that were getting started at about the same time.

Publicity for the new place invariable focused on the "curbers," the young waiters who would run out to cars to take orders and run back with trays of food, all for whatever they could earn in tips. Marriott commissioned a graphic artist to design a logo for Hot Shoppes featuring one of these newly famous "Running Boys," who epitomized the Hot Shoppes' cheerful, automobile-friendly service.

The Georgia Avenue store was shrewdly located away from downtown competitors and on a major artery, where it could lure in commuters. The Marriotts took to staking out major roads and intersections around the city to try to pinpoint the best sites for future Hot Shoppes. The next to open would become the chain's flagship, at 4340 Connecticut Avenue Northwest, in the area now known as Van Ness. Opened in 1930, this was the fifth Hot Shoppe. When it opened, the shop had fifty curbers, forty girls and ten boys. It soon had to add fifty more. In the midst of the Depression, the jaunty Hot Shoppe, with its exuberant curbers, was among the city's trendiest destinations, particularly for high school and college kids looking for inexpensive eats.

By 1933, there were six Hot Shoppes across the city grossing $1 million annually, and more were being added all the time. The chain's Mexican cuisine, supplemented by barbecue, had quickly evolved into a classic lineup of what people now call comfort food—hamburgers, steak sandwiches, grilled cheese, ham and eggs. A wartime menu featured an assortment of sandwiches, some of which would be a hard sell today: peanut butter and lettuce, fried egg with grilled spiced meat loaf and liverwurst with lettuce and egg salad. Main entrées included creamed flaked tuna fish on toast and "crab meat and chopped egg in a tomato," among other items.

The chain took on a more up-to-date, fast-food profile in the 1950s, highlighting new inventions like the Mighty Mo, a tasty triple-decker hamburger named after the battleship USS *Missouri*, which had just been retired. The Mighty Mo competed with the Big Boy, a triple-decker burger offered by rival Bob's Big Boy (which Marriott Corporation would later buy). The Hot Shoppe was also known for its grilled ham sandwich, called the Teen Twist, as well as its breaded onion rings, a milkshake called the Orange Freeze and Pappy Parker's fried chicken.

By 1964, a total of seventy-three Hot Shoppe restaurants and cafeterias were operating in thirteen states and the District, including food service operations at hotels and other institutions, as well as highway rest stops. One of the largest fast-food chains in the country, the combined operation used more steaks than any other enterprise except the U.S. Army. Indeed, Hot Shoppes seemed to be on top of the world in those days, at least in the Washington area, but change was already in the air. In 1974, two years after he took over as CEO, Marriott's son, Bill Marriott Jr., announced that the company was planning to phase out its Hot Shoppe brand. Under his leadership, the company's energies increasingly were being focused on its hotels and away from the Hot Shoppes. The iconic eateries were too costly to run, he said, and at around 3 percent, their profit margin was too thin.

There were only twenty Hot Shoppes left that year (not including the various food service operations and other eateries like Jr. Hot Shoppes), and eight of those were slated to close, dropping the total to twelve. The remaining dozen, it was promised, would remain open as long as they were profitable. The flagship Connecticut Avenue

Family dining at Hot Shoppe, circa 1954. *Historic photographs collection, Marriott International Archives.*

Hot Shoppe was one of the locations closed that year. It was sold for $6.5 million to the National Bank of Washington, which razed the old eatery and replaced it with a five-story office building (the structure still stands today and is owned by the University of the District of Columbia). Another remained open nearby at 4110 Wisconsin Avenue Northwest, but it, too, closed three years later.

One by one, the remaining twelve eventually closed as their leases expired and weren't renewed. The newspapers ran stories about people who had been going to Hot Shoppes for twenty, thirty or forty years. "This was where I met my husband," one old-timer told the *Washington Post* in 1995 when the Bethesda Hot Shoppe was closing. Gene Kelley, another longtime patron, summed it up: "For my generation, this was it. I hate to see the change. I think it's very sad. It's progress, but I don't want to be here for it." The very last Hot Shoppe to close was the one in the Marlow Heights Shopping Center in Temple Hills, Maryland, which was shuttered in November 1999. With that, the chain became extinct, although every now and then glimmers of the past have been known to surface. It's said you can order a Mighty Mo, even though it's not on the menu, at certain Marriott hotels, and they'll serve it to you on a Hot Shoppe plate. The legend, quaint as it may be, lives on.

Through much of the twentieth century, cafeterias, including Hot Shoppes and other chains, competed directly with diners and lunchrooms for casual budget-conscious customers. The first American eatery to be called a cafeteria opened at the 1893 Columbian Exposition in Chicago, and it instantly filled an unmet need for fast, efficient public eating. Perhaps the best known in Washington was SHOLL'S CAFETERIA AND DINING ROOM, first opened by Evan A. Sholl (1899–1983) in 1928 at Connecticut Avenue and L Street Northwest. Sholl, the second youngest of thirteen children born to a Pottsville, Pennsylvania farmer, started out earning a hardscrabble living at an assortment of odd jobs, just as J.W. Marriott was doing at about the same time. At age twenty, he opened his first restaurant, which quickly bankrupted him. After that, he went to work for the Kresge retail chain, which transferred him to its Washington store at Seventh and E Streets Northwest in 1927. After regaining his financial footing, and with more experience under his belt, he set out on his own again with Sholl's Cafeteria, and this time it worked.

A write-up in the 1930 *Book of Washington* noted Sholl's basic credo: well-prepared food served at a moderate price in a "spacious, well-lighted" place. The low prices in particular resonated with Depression-era customers. Sholl's offered self-service breakfast and lunch and a "four-course dinner, served by efficient maids, for 65 cents." In 1929, Sholl opened his second eatery at 3027 Fourteenth Street Northwest, just a block south of the first Hot Shoppe in Columbia Heights, and it was also a great success. Thousands of hearty home-cooked meals were served up to Washingtonians on a daily basis, and Sholl's chain rapidly expanded to eight locations across the city by the end of the 1930s.

Around 1940, Evan Sholl's business trajectory parted from Bill Marriott's. While Hot Shoppes continued to multiply and expand into new types of food service, Sholl's Cafeterias contracted. "One morning, I got up and as I was putting on my shoes, I decided to quit, get rid of almost all of it," Sholl later told the *Washington Star*. "I [didn't] have time for my wife or anything. It [wasn't] worth it." Health issues may have also dictated the shift. Over the next several years, Sholl sold off all but the original Connecticut Avenue shop, which he renovated and which continued to have lines out the door at lunchtime.

Behind the counter at Sholl's Georgian Cafeteria, 3027 Fourteenth Street Northwest, in 1946. *Library of Congress.*

Sholl's wife, the former Gertrude Fleishell, was a devout Catholic, and in time she influenced Sholl to become a fervently religious man. Like his decision to cut back and focus on just one cafeteria, Sholl's religious conversion was a sea change that he said occurred suddenly one day in 1949. As he later explained it to the *Washington Post*, "All of a sudden, holy mackerel, tears came to my eyes, I started smelling roses, and I began yelling, 'I'm going to be a Catholic!'" Sholl called all his staff together for a meeting and told them that the cafeteria would be run differently; religion and patriotism were to be the new watchwords. While a few staff and patrons were turned off by the change, most stayed with Sholl and appreciated his drive and passion for giving. Soon, little cards were placed on the tables with suggested texts for prayers of thanksgiving before meals. A framed prayer of St. Francis hung on the wall. And Sholl vowed to take only as much profit from the business as he needed for a living. He even deeded over his home to a Franciscan order.

People loved Sholl's, either because of its religious orientation or in spite of it, and the cafeteria was always busy. In 1950, Sholl's New Cafeteria opened at Vermont Avenue and K Street Northwest, and it was also a great success. Sholl's two cafeterias were famous for their liver and onions, fresh doughnuts and cherry and rhubarb pies. Like the city's best diners and lunchrooms, Sholl's welcomed all comers, ranging from celebrated VIPs to street people who couldn't pay for their food. (Sholl gave away many meals to the poor.) Texas billionaire H.L. Hunt, known to be frugal, enjoyed eating at Sholl's and loved the rhubarb pie. Presidents Harry S Truman, Richard Nixon and Jimmy Carter dined at Sholl's, as did the city's top judges, lawyers, lobbyists and other business leaders, as well as many busloads of tourists hungry for fast, inexpensive, home-style meals.

After Sholl passed away in 1983, his nephews Eddie Scholl and George along with Joe Fajfar Fleishell took over and kept the cafeterias running for almost twenty more years, despite the fact that the format and home-style cuisine were falling out of favor by this time. The low-priced eateries with their slim profit margins also found it hard to compete as downtown property values began to soar. In 1979, the original Sholl's on Connecticut Avenue was forced to move when its home, the LaSalle Building (which also hosted Duke Zeibert's restaurant), was slated to be torn down. The legendary cafeteria took up new quarters in basement space at Twentieth and K Streets Northwest. Then, in 1984, the other Sholl's café—the "Sholl's New Cafeteria"—was likewise pushed out of its long-standing location by extensive building renovations. After hosting former president Jimmy Carter and wife, Rosalyn, for a luncheon in September, the New Cafeteria moved to Rosslyn, Virginia, where it lasted only a few more years.

Meanwhile, the original Sholl's, transplanted to Twentieth and K, eventually faced the same financial pressures in its new location as it had in its original spot. After it was threatened with a massive rent increase in 1999, a group of loyal supporters organized a "Save Our Sholl's" campaign to keep the eatery going. The property owner relented, and Sholl's won a temporary reprieve. Nevertheless, times were changing. As had happened with the last surviving Hot Shoppes, Sholl's most loyal supporters were older Washingtonians who had been patrons for years. Younger generations found the cafeteria format antiquated and the offerings unappealing. Tour buses grew less and less likely to book a stop at Sholl's. Finally, after the attacks on September 11, 2001, patronage plummeted, and Sholl's was forced to shut down for good.

Of all the much-loved diners and cafeterias that D.C. hosted in the twentieth century, perhaps the most difficult to explain to the uninitiated was the enduring popularity of

SHERRILL'S RESTAURANT AND BAKERY at 233 Pennsylvania Avenue Southeast. Opened by William Sherrill in 1922 in a converted shoe store, Sherrill's was a simple Capitol Hill spot, one on a strip of inexpensive eateries that catered to congressional staff and Hill residents. It was noted particularly for its pastries and other baked goods. In 1941, Sherrill retired to his apartment above the store and turned the restaurant over to his close friends Sam and Lola Revis. Samuel Revis (1895–1975), born in Corinth, Greece, had previously managed nearby Louie's Bar and Grill, where he met his wife, Lola Marnakos Revis (1909–2001). Born in Pittsburgh to Greek immigrant parents, Lola had grown up in D.C. and attended the old Central High School. Together, the two of them amplified Sherrill's reputation as the best place for no-frills, down-home diner cooking on Capitol Hill.

The Revises kept not only the Sherrill's name but also many of the original furnishings, including the high-back wooden booths. As Sherrill's continued to draw in crowds of appreciative customers year after year, it became a veritable time capsule of another world. Even its decorative updates—such as the gold-flecked plastic upholstery added to the booths sometime in mid-century—ended up over time becoming charmingly quaint relics of the past.

Sherrill's offered the usual breakfast-heavy, diner-style comfort food, but under the Revises it continued to be best known for its baked goods. In 1957, the Revises' master baker Chris Christopoulos, creator of numerous birthday and wedding cakes, offered a special pumpkin layer cake for Thanksgiving. Other specialties included gingerbread cookies, baked in a specially designed brick oven, and doughnuts.

But Sherrill's greatest claim to fame, perhaps, was the brusqueness of its wait staff, a New York–style impatience that could easily descend into absolute meanness. Lola Revis, who took over the eatery after her husband's death in 1975, seems to have set the tone for the rest of the staff. Famous for being short-tempered on the one hand and generous on the other, Revis ruled Sherrill's with a benevolent iron hand. She believed that everybody deserved a good home-cooked meal, even on holidays (when Sherrill's remained open), but she also wouldn't tolerate any whining. She so impressed documentary filmmaker David Petersen when he came in one day that he decided to do a film about Sherrill's, called *Fine Food, Fine Pastries—Open 6 to 9*, which debuted in 1988 and was nominated for an Oscar the following year.

Some waitresses occasionally slammed patrons' dishes down on their tables hard enough to make the plates rattle. If you complained at the counter that your food was too slow in coming, you'd be told to sit down and shut up. A *Washington Times* profile of the restaurant in 1988 included several examples of such hostility. "A group was having Sunday breakfast in a booth and one of them, a first-time patron from out of town, shyly asked for coffee," the *Times* reported. "'We'll see about it,' snarled the waitress." On one famous occasion, Lola Revis got into an argument with a pregnant customer who was picking up a cake that was apparently not what she had ordered. After a testy exchange, the customer heaved the massive cake in Revis's face, knocking her over. As Revis screamed for someone to call the police, the customer ran out, and for a few moments no one did anything. Startled as they may have been, the Sherrill's patrons were probably not surprised that Revis had finally gotten a cake thrown at her.

After Revis retired, her daughters, Dorothy Polito and Kathyleen Milton, took over the restaurant and kept it going through the 1990s. But running such a popular eatery is hard work and demands long hours, and eventually the sisters wanted to retire as well. They finally sold their famous "eggs and insults" restaurant in 2000.

One by one, almost all of the classic diners and lunchrooms of the twentieth century had disappeared from the D.C. restaurant scene by the first decade of the twenty-first century. The industry had split markedly between national fast-food chains, which dominated the low end of the market, and sophisticated neighborhood cafés offering lattes, biscotti and blueberry croissants. For all intents and purposes, an entire category of restaurants, once wildly popular, had become extinct.

Chapter 10

POWER LUNCHES AND DINNERS

One of the most difficult things to predict in D.C. is which restaurant is going to be chosen by the city's "elite" movers and shakers as their next favorite haunt. Throughout the city's history, VIPs have gravitated to certain eateries—often steakhouses—and avoided others. While some of the chosen places have flaunted their elite status, others have not. All rely first and foremost on the warmth and discretion of their hosts to make guests feel relaxed and at ease. Yes, the food also needs to be good, but it's rarely the driving factor.

ON THE HILL

Of course, a convenient location is also paramount. In the nineteenth century, the restaurants in the U.S. Capitol were the city's dining power center. As early as the 1830s, a "refectory" run by local caterers was in operation in basement rooms near the center of the building, offering oysters cooked in a variety of styles, as well as beef, veal, venison, mutton, pork and green turtle soup. This early eatery served more as a food court for the convenience of busy congressmen than a formal dining room. In 1858, after the new south wing of the Capitol had been completed, Speaker of the House James Orr reserved a room in the basement to provide "wholesome refreshments" for House members, the first real restaurant on the House side. With several expansions, the space has served as the House Members' Dining Room ever since. After the Senate wing was completed, the Senate likewise established its own Capitol restaurant on the north side of the building.

An 1869 guidebook found the House restaurant to be "handsomely fitted up" and "one of the best restaurants in the Union." High praise was given to proprietor GEORGE T. DOWNING (1819–1903), who "has decidedly the most elegant manners to be seen in the Capital." What's more, "his bill of fare contains every delicacy of the season, and his dishes are served in a style which would not shame Delmonico himself."

Downing was already a successful restaurateur when he took over the House dining room shortly after the Civil War. He had previously run his father's celebrated oyster house in New York City and had branched out with his own restaurant (1846) and elegant hotel (1855) in posh Newport, Rhode Island, where New York City's wealthiest scions spent their summers. Like Beverly Snow and James Wormley, Downing was a socially gifted African American who found that the restaurant business gave him entrée into the highest levels of white society. A highly respected black community leader, Downing used his connections to further the causes he believed in. Having been an active participant in the Underground Railroad before emancipation, he vigorously promoted the cause of newly freed African Americans in the Reconstruction years with the many influential friends he made at the House restaurant.

Choosing who would run the House restaurant during each congressional term came to be a major contest in the 1880s after Downing left. In 1892, the House gave the concession to colorful THOMAS J. "TERRAPIN TOM" MURREY (1844–1900) of New York, one of the best-known gourmets of his day. A former journalist, Murrey had written extensively about cooking and had been a chef in New York City. He was famous for his terrapins, of course, but was also skilled at whipping up special impromptu creations to satisfy the whims of his patrons. He supposedly kept elaborate notes about which dishes leading congressmen ordered at his restaurant with the intention of writing a book about the effect of food on legislation, but nothing was ever published. Of course, his—or anyone else's—culinary prowess could never be as important as his political connections, and in 1896, Murrey, who had been supported by Democrats, lost the contest to keep the restaurant to Morgan D. Lewis of the Willard Hotel, a Republican favorite. Murrey returned to New York City, where eventually he fell ill and committed suicide in 1900.

Politics has always played an outsized role in the operations of both the House and Senate restaurants. As early as 1903, the sale of alcoholic beverages was prohibited in Capitol restaurants. The ban continued for thirty years, through Prohibition, and was not dropped without a fight, despite the fact that alcohol was known to be freely available on Capitol Hill from bootlegger George Cassiday, known as the "Man in the Green Hat."

A drawing of the Capitol restaurant that appeared in *Harper's Weekly* in 1899. *Collection of the U.S. House of Representatives.*

The year 1903 was an important one for Capitol restaurants. Not only did liquor leave the restaurants' tables, but bean soup also arrived, at least on the Senate side, and would remain on the menu every day until the present time—the only dish to gain this distinction. Made exclusively from Michigan navy beans, the soup is too ordinary to appear on many restaurant menus, and its popularity—other than as a novelty for visitors—is questionable. Yet it seems to have come to symbolize congressional commitment to the heartland of America. A waiter in the Senate restaurant in 1943 remarked to a newspaper reporter that he reckoned serving bean soup in Capitol restaurants was compulsory under the Constitution.

It's unclear how the tradition began. On the Senate side, Fred Dubois of Idaho is said to have pushed through a resolution putting the soup permanently on the menu, but there is no such resolution in the record. Perhaps Knute Nelson of Minnesota got it instated. Not to be outdone, the House restaurant also adopted bean soup as a permanent offering, with the exact impetus and timing equally shrouded in mystery.

SENATE BEAN SOUP

Take 2 pounds of small navy pea beans, wash and run through hot water until the beans are white again. Put on the fire with 4 quarts of hot water. Then take 1½ pounds of smoked ham hocks and boil slowly approximately 3 hours in a covered pot. Braise 1 onion, chopped, in a little butter, and when light brown put in bean soup. Season with salt and pepper and then serve. Do not add salt until ready to serve. Serves 8.

The story goes that powerful Speaker of the House Joseph Cannon (1836–1926) tried to order the soup one day in 1904, only to discover it was unavailable. "Thunderation!" he supposedly yelled with characteristic bluster. "I had my mouth set for bean soup. From now on, hot or cold, rain, snow or shine, I want it on the menu every day." And so it has been.

Over the years, the Capitol restaurants have remained steadfastly unchanged. A Senate lunch menu from 1953 offered four specials: roast round of beef au jus, lamb stew Irish style en casserole, fried goujons (breaded strips) of sole with crab cake and braised half-smoked sausages. The corresponding menu from 2012 is not dissimilar, also with four "main courses": Greek salad with grilled shrimp or chicken, chicken and dumpling, chili-glazed shrimp with grits and grilled salmon with poached baby potatoes.

A convenient modern alternative to the Capitol restaurants is the MONOCLE at 107 D Street Northeast on Capitol Hill, which has been doing a thriving business for over fifty years. Constantine "Connie" Valanos (1918–2012) and his wife, Helen (1925–2005), opened the restaurant in October 1960, right in the thick of the Kennedy-Nixon presidential race. They chose a historic circa 1885 building that had long served as a casual restaurant—most recently the Station View Spaghetti House—and they turned it into one of Capitol Hill's first "white tablecloth" eateries, serving well-prepared, traditional American fare within easy walking distance of Senate office buildings and the Capitol. Owner Connie Valanos was the son of Greek immigrants and a native Washingtonian who had attended the old Central High School. His stylish wife, Helen, served as bookkeeper but would also regularly make the rounds of the restaurant meeting and greeting their guests. The Monocle soon became a popular stop for senators, congressmen, Supreme Court justices and Capitol Hill residents in general.

Senator Hattie Caraway, the first female senator, lunches with Kate Smith, the "Songbird of the South," in the Senate dining room in 1938. *Library of Congress.*

Senator John F. Kennedy, who liked the roast beef sandwiches, would sit with his wife, Jackie, at the corner table in the front bay window. After gaining the presidency, he would occasionally have meals brought to the White House from the Monocle. Nixon frequented the Monocle as well, preferring the chopped steak stuffed with Roquefort cheese. Lyndon B. Johnson once came by in his vice-presidential days only to discover that no tables were available. He had Valanos ask over the public address system whether anyone was willing to give up his table for the vice president. There were no volunteers, and Johnson stormed out in a huff, never to return.

As originally designed, the wood-paneled Monocle dining room was decorated with chandeliers bought from an old casino, framed old newspaper front pages and a long *trompe l'oeil* mural along the left side wall by artist David Waters that gave the

Edward R. Murrow offers Connie Valanos a light at the Monocle. *Monocle Restaurant.*

impression of walking along a busy old-time Washington street filled with important personalities. Prominent near the center were both Kennedy and Nixon, dressed in period attire, appearing to be chatting amiably.

House and Senate clerks regularly call the Monocle to announce that votes are underway, knowing they are likely to find members there. This service was very important in the days before personal devices when there was no other practical way to reach members. The Valanoses' son, John, who took over the restaurant after his parents retired in the late 1980s, recalls that the vote announcements usually got congressmen moving, but not always. Once Valanos informed a certain senator that a key vote was going on but noticed that the senator didn't leave. A second phone call came in asking that the senator be urgently reminded to come and vote, and Valanos passed the message

> ### MONOCLE STUFFED SHRIMP
>
> *Mix 1 pound crabmeat, 1 tablespoon mayonnaise, ½ teaspoon dry mustard, 1 teaspoon chopped capers and 1 tablespoon sherry until well blended. Mound the mixture onto 12 jumbo butterflied shrimp. Next, mix 1 cup mayonnaise and 2 egg yolks and use to coat the shrimp. Bake or broil until lightly browned. Serves 3.*

on. The senator thanked Valanos and then explained why he wasn't moving: "Half my constituents will hate me if I vote for this bill, and the other half will hate me if I vote against it. But if I don't vote at all, they'll just think I'm lazy."

The eatery expanded within a few years of its opening to take over the next-door building. It has been remodeled over the years but still retains a comfortable, club-like atmosphere. Longtime maître d' Nick Selimos knows everybody on Capitol Hill and welcomes them all warmly. John Valanos has the unenviable job of maintaining the collection of framed portraits on the dining room's far wall, adding new photos when appropriate, changing the order and retiring older shots, all without wounding anybody's ego. He is apparently as successful at that as at maintaining the restaurant's reputation for good service and food.

JOINING THE CLUB

While the Monocle tries to be low key, Washington's most famous roost for power brokers, the OCCIDENTAL RESTAURANT at 1411 Pennsylvania Avenue Northwest, next door to the Willard Hotel, has quite the opposite tradition. Henry Willard, founder of the Willard Hotel, bought the adjoining property in the nineteenth century for use as a hotel after his brother Joseph gained control of the original Willard. In 1906, he built the Occidental Hotel on that spot, and in 1912 he leased it to Gustav Buchholz (1874–1925), a German immigrant who had been a popular headwaiter at the Willard. Buchholz remodeled the small hotel into the New Occidental Hotel and opened the Occidental Restaurant as part of it.

Conceived from the start as an elite restaurant, the Occidental featured an "electric grillroom" where food was prepared in full view of guests on the city's first commercial electric stove. "Elite" in 1912 also apparently meant men only; a notice in the *Washington Post* observed, "There will be no ladies' dining room in the new hotel, as Mr. Buchholz plans to cater to officialdom." Such was power dining at the beginning of the twentieth century. The Occidental's marble floors and columns, potted ferns and mahogany wainscoting imbued it with a clubby Edwardian atmosphere that fit its role as a den for wheeling and dealing.

The males-only Occidental lasted only three years. In 1915, Buchholz opened an "annex" next door with a dining room designated for both men and women. Whereas the original dining room was filled with framed and signed photographs of numerous statesmen and diplomats, the new one was hung with portraits of President Wilson and his two predecessors. From the start, Buchholz had made it known that he wanted to display the signed photographs of his most prominent patrons, and the VIPs of the day, their egos flattered, were quick to send him their pictures. The photographs became one of the restaurant's signature features, and in succeeding decades, thousands would be accumulated and would cover the restaurant's walls.

The success of the Occidental, like that of virtually all Washington's power restaurants, was due in no small part to Buchholz's exceptional talents as a maître d'. Buchholz knew everyone who was anyone, remembered their likes and dislikes and always had a table for them that they liked. When Buchholz died in 1925, his funeral was attended by hundreds of well-wishers "from every station of life," ranging from the waiters and bellhops of the Occidental to the city's most powerful bankers, lawyers and politicians.

Buchholz's son Fred and other family members oversaw restaurant operations for several decades before selling to brothers Danny and Sonny Price, experienced restaurateurs from New York. When the Prices gained control of the restaurant in 1956, they adopted the motto "Where Statesmen Dine," which seemed emblematic of the eatery's pretensions. They kept all of the restaurant's antique furnishings, including the huge original electric stove and the thousands of photographs. Manager Arthur Riback discovered heaps of old photographs in the restaurant's attic, including many of notable Washington sportsmen. It seems the Washington Nationals had held a celebratory banquet at the Occidental after winning the 1924 World Series, and their photo was in the pile in the attic. The best sports pictures were brought down and hung on the walls. In 1964, the restaurant acquired the presidential seal that had graced John F. Kennedy's inaugural pavilion in 1960 and mounted it on the dining room ceiling.

Throughout the 1950s and 1960s, the eatery rested on its laurels as a classic Washington steakhouse. Its most notable dish was its London broil. By 1971, the building was deteriorating and in need of expensive renovations. It was temporarily closed for health code violations that summer and then shut down for good in the fall, swamped with debt. In early 1972, an auction was held where all the restaurant's assets, including cookware, furnishings and thousands of photographs, were sold off to help pay down the extensive debt. Finally, once all had been liquidated, the building itself was demolished, signaling its complete demise.

But the Occidental was destined for reincarnation. As part of the extensive restoration of the Willard Hotel that took place in the 1980s, a modern extension was added to the hotel, and a new Occidental restaurant was opened almost on the same spot the old one had occupied. The Oliver Carr Company, developers of the new Willard, negotiated with the Columbia Historical Society to borrow some of the old photographs, nine hundred of which it had acquired, to be reinstalled in the new eatery.

The rejuvenated Occidental opened in 1986 as a sophisticated and updated heir to its venerable predecessor. After an extensive renovation in 2007, the restaurant continues in operation today under the supervision of executive chef Rodney Scruggs.

POWER LUNCHING IN THE "NEW" DOWNTOWN

In the twentieth century, steakhouses defined the cuisine of almost every power lunch spot. One of the pioneers of D.C.'s steakhouse culture was actually entrepreneur Ulysses "Blackie" Auger (1921–2004), who aimed to serve good steaks not to the rich and powerful but to the masses. With his wife, Lulu, Auger opened BLACKIE'S HOUSE OF BEEF at 1217 Twenty-second Street Northwest in the West End in 1953. The son of Greek immigrants, Auger began with a glorified hot dog stand called the Minute Grille before starting Blackie's. After years of shortages and rationing, steaks were finally becoming easily available in the mid-1950s, and Auger offered prime cuts at the lowest possible price. Over the years, Auger built up a large and loyal following, expanding his restaurant to meet increasing demand from those who wanted the experience of fine restaurant dining at an affordable price. He also invested in nearby real estate and eventually opened over twenty more restaurants, though none was as large or as long-lived as Blackie's. The highly successful restaurant finally closed in 2005.

Like Blackie's, not all of D.C.'s true power-dining spots have been formal or pretentious. One of the best known in the mid-twentieth century was the decidedly low-brow DUKE ZEIBERT'S, which opened in 1950 on the southwest corner of Connecticut Avenue and L Street Northwest. David "Duke" Zeibert (1910–1997),

a native of Troy, New York, grew up a poor Jewish boy stalking the downtown pool halls of his industrial hometown. He learned the restaurant business working at a resort in upstate New York and then moved to Miami, Florida, where he became a headwaiter at Fan and Bill's Restaurant. When the government took the place over in 1942, Fan and Bill's moved to Washington, and Zeibert came along to serve as maître d'. Located directly across the street from the Mayflower at 1132 Connecticut Avenue Northwest, FAN AND BILL'S, which remained in operation until 1962, was a popular steakhouse in the days when lower Connecticut Avenue was the heart of the downtown dining district. The flamboyant Zeibert developed a loyal following while he was at the restaurant, and with financial assistance from several supporters, he was able to open his own place just a block to the south in 1950. It was an instant success.

Soon, everyone was coming to Duke Zeibert's. President Truman dined there, as did every president through Bill Clinton. Senators, congressmen, lawyers and lobbyists had their lunches at Duke's, as did Vince Lombardi, George Allen, Joe Gibbs and Jack Kent Cooke. An inveterate sports fan, Zeibert decorated his dining room with giant caricatures of himself as various types of sports players.

The restaurant's steakhouse-style food was largely copied from the old Fan and Bill's, where Zeibert had worked. Every table was set with a signature dish of garlic-infused kosher dill pickles, which filled the dining room with their aroma. The lengthy menu featured primarily seafood and thick-cut prime steaks, but desserts prepared by pastry chef Al Sanders, such as the rum pie and coconut cake, were also popular. In 1966, *New York Times* food critic Craig Claiborne included Duke's on his list of a dozen restaurants in D.C. worth patronizing. While dismissing the décor as "gauche modern," Claiborne praised the pickled herring in sour cream and the chicken-in-a-pot with matzoh balls and thin noodles. Likewise, in 1971, the *Evening Star*'s John Rosson found the broiled Maine lobster "impossibly good."

Nevertheless, it eventually became accepted lore that the food was actually not very good and that people kept coming despite the mediocre cuisine. The sheer force of Zeibert's personality was the bigger draw. Duke styled himself as a Washington version of his friend Toots Shor (1903–1977), the legendary New York saloonkeeper. Like Shor, Zeibert developed a freewheeling, boozy camaraderie with his celebrity

Opposite, top: A postcard view of Blackie's House of Beef. *Author's collection.*

Opposite, bottom: A postcard from Duke Zeibert's displays the host's typical bravado. *Author's collection.*

patrons—the men, that is—and often greeted them by exchanging insults. Known to be warm-hearted, Zeibert enjoyed making a show of abrasiveness, and the customers seemed to like it. His waiters were also famous for their New York–style surliness. "The place has the charm of a tomb," the *Washington Post*'s Donald Dresden wrote in 1969.

Duke Zeibert's was essentially a throwback to the old men's clubs, like Gerstenberg's, the Mayflower Men's Lounge or the Occidental. It was this atmosphere that the VIPs of the day appeared to be seeking out as much as the thick but ultimately ordinary steaks. "It was so wonderful to have Duke meet and greet you," sports publicist Charles Brotman later recalled. "He made everybody feel important. It was something very special. He almost always sat at everybody's table. He'd tell you the latest gossip, and you'd tell him the latest gossip. Everybody knew what was going on around town because they heard it first at Duke Zeibert's."

The eatery was located in the old LaSalle office building, which was slated for demolition in 1979. When word came out, there was much speculation about what would happen to the restaurant. Zeibert ruminated long and hard about moving to another nearby location, but he couldn't find anything that was right. Finally, he decided to simply close. A celebration was held on the eatery's last day in 1980, with a wreath on the bar marked "Rest in Peace" and a marine playing taps. Zeibert, laughing and crying at the same time, shook the hands of hundreds of well-wishers before shutting down his fabled restaurant for good.

Or so it seemed. There was still another chapter of the story to be played out. Zeibert had already announced that he was passing the baton to his maître d', Mel Krupin, who would be opening a new restaurant just up the street. Mel Krupin's, at 1120 Connecticut Avenue Northwest, featured many of the staff who had worked at Duke's and nearly an identical menu. Soon, the old clientele was coming to Mel's as well, savoring the boiled beef or chicken-in-a-pot with matzoh balls and grousing that the new place was a little too comfortable and clean. The *Evening Star*'s Charles McCollum declared in early 1981 that Mel's was the hottest restaurant in town and Krupin the hottest restaurateur. Krupin wisely toned down the macho sports club atmosphere and succeeded in attracting more women, and he was virtually Zeibert's equal in making the power lunch crowd feel welcome and important. Krupin even had his own insult-laden shtick; if Zeibert had been like Toots Shor, Krupin saw himself like Don Rickles.

All would have gone well from that point on had Zeibert not decided that he didn't like being retired. In 1983, he reopened his restaurant in lavish new quarters on the mezzanine of the elegant Washington Square building, designed by Chloethiel Woodard Smith (1910–1992), that had taken the place of the old LaSalle structure. Zeibert proceeded to hire back many of his former employees from Mel Krupin's, gutting Krupin's staff while simultaneously offering serious and unexpected competition a block away from his former close associate. The two became bitter opponents, and the rivalry forced Mel Krupin's to close in 1988. Meanwhile, the new Duke Zeibert's hung on until Zeibert retired for the second time in 1994. Whatever the outcome of their battle royal, both restaurants had become dinosaurs by the late 1980s, their sexism and elitism off-putting to too many people. Washington still hosts a number of clubby steakhouses, but none has attempted to repeat the eccentric formula that worked so well for Duke Zeibert and Mel Krupin.

Krupin occupied the space that had previously housed PAUL YOUNG'S, another popular power dining spot in the 1960s and 1970s. Opened in 1960 by Paul Young (1911–1989) and his brother, David Young (1920–2004), the restaurant was one of Zeibert's biggest competitors and featured all the rich steakhouse-style food that people savored in those days, including steak Diane and lobster bisque with Cognac.

The Young brothers had had plenty of experience in D.C. restaurants before opening Paul Young's. They had come to Washington with their mother, Eva, in 1935 and bought an old florist's shop at the corner of Thirteenth and H Streets Northwest downtown, which they converted into the ROUMANIAN INN. Paul and David were the front men, while "Mama" Young cooked authentic Eastern European dishes like shashlik, kasha soup and borscht. Four years later, they added a supper club on the second floor above the inn, which they called Paul Young's Romany Room. "Big floor shows in the New York manner and modernistic dance music. The food is both delicious and unusual," was the *Washington Post*'s edict in 1941.

After twenty-five years in the old place, the Youngs decided to create a posh, upscale restaurant in their new digs on Connecticut Avenue. They hired celebrated New York designer William Pahlmann (1900–1987), who had just finished collaborating with modernist architect Philip Johnson (1906–2005) on the lavish Four Seasons restaurant in New York City. For Paul Young's, Pahlmann created a sleekly modernist yet plush—and very red—interior, with thick red carpeting and waiters in red livery. The "modern English" décor included heavy chandeliers and dark wood wainscoting with decorative china on the walls. Reaching the basement-level dining room required descending the grand staircase, which hovered over and spilled into the center of the room, inviting guests to make a grand entrance on every visit.

The elegant new restaurant was the talk of the town in 1960, and it scored a major coup early the following year when the Kennedys decided to hold their private party for 350 people there on the evening of John F. Kennedy's inauguration. After that, Paul Young's was a certified power restaurant. Johnson, Nixon, Ford and Carter all dined there, Carter celebrating his fifty-fifth birthday with a luncheon at Young's. VIPs who wanted a change of pace from Duke Zeibert's all came to Paul Young's.

Like other such eateries, Paul Young's began with a reputation for excellent food ("Mama" Young was still at work supervising the kitchen in the restaurant's early years). In 1963, in addition to the standard assortment of steaks and lobster tails, the restaurant featured such delicacies as Long Island duckling with Montmorency cherries, small Everglades frog legs sautéed à la Provençale and filet of Florida Pompano stuffed with lump crabmeat. Paul Young's was one of the thirteen restaurants to make *New York Times* critic Craig Claiborne's 1966 list of notable Washington eateries, Claiborne observing that "the menu is lengthy and uncomplicated with simple, well-prepared dishes." Over time, reviews were more mixed. In 1974, the *Post* concluded that the cooking at Paul Young's was merely "competent."

Whatever the verdict, after twenty years, the Youngs decided to retire. "Honey, next birthday I'll be 69 years old," Paul Young told *Post* reporter Myra MacPherson in 1980. "What do I need with this forever?" Young professed to be happy turning his place over to Mel Krupin and even planned to help Krupin set it up for himself. "It's like teaching a kid to ride a two-wheeler," he said. Young passed away nine years later.

ECHOES OF NEW YORK CITY

Sophisticated French restaurants like the Rive Gauche and Sans Souci (see later chapter) also served as important power dining spots in the mid-twentieth century. One of the most elegant and exclusive of that era was the JOCKEY CLUB, located in the Fairfax Hotel at 2100 Massachusetts Avenue Northwest near Dupont Circle. Like Paul Young's, the Jockey Club was one of a spate of elegant restaurants that reenergized fine dining in Washington around the time Kennedy became president. In fact, the Jockey Club opened just a week before JFK's inauguration in 1961. Modeled on New York City's famed 21 Club, it featured a dark wood-paneled dining room with intimate lantern lighting, pictures of horses on the walls and seating arranged in the same red leather semicircular banquettes that were going into all the best restaurants at the time. The Jockey Club deliberately aimed at the familiar rather than the new, its concept taken from the 21 Club and its name from numerous other Jockey Clubs around the world.

The "Club"—it was a public restaurant, not a club—was an instant hit. Owners Louise Gore and her brother Jimmy (cousins of Al Gore) shrewdly hired Paris-born Jacques Vivien (1925–2010) as their maître d'. Vivien, who had trained at the prestigious Paris Ritz and Crillon Hotels, was a classically graceful and discreet host, charming his important guests and always remembering exactly which tables they preferred. Vivien was given complete control of the restaurant's operation, and he hired Claude Bouchet (1924–1978), the talented former head chef of the French Embassy, as his chef. Under Bouchet, the Jockey Club produced some of the finest French cooking in Washington.

The rich and famous soon became regulars at the Jockey Club. The Kennedys, of course, dined there, and in 1964 Jackie made headlines when she had lunch at the Jockey Club with actor Marlon Brando. In the days afterward, the restaurant was filled to capacity and had to turn down hundreds of would-be guests. In addition to Washington's politicos, the Jockey Club hosted a number of other Hollywood legends, including Lauren Bacall, Frank Sinatra and Kirk Douglas. Jack Lemmon and Walter Matthau dined there together and shared an order of crab cakes.

Unlike Duke Zeibert's man cave, the Jockey Club was a cozy and inviting place that embraced traditional social graces. Women enjoyed lunching there, Nancy Reagan being one of its most famous regulars. Over its five-decade tenure, it was the home of distinguished chefs (Robert Greault, Jean-Claude Galan and Hidemasa Yamamoto), as well as distinguished maître d's (Jacques Scarella and Martin Garbisu). Garbisu served as the Jockey Club's genial public face from 1978 to 1993.

As much of a Washington institution as the Jockey Club had become over the years, it began to lose its footing during the Clinton administration. As Nancy Reagan's favorite spot, it began to seem old-fashioned, its appeal narrowing as time wore on. Several renovations were undertaken to attempt to inject new life, but no one dared change very much of what Phyllis Richman called the "look of relaxed money": the dark wood, the soft lighting, the horse pictures. With an ever-dwindling clientele of customers who remembered its older days, the Jockey Club closed in 2001. In 2008, it reopened after another massive renovation, hoping to attract a new generation of VIPs, but by then it was too late. The renovated eatery closed for good in 2011.

Echoes of the power restaurants of the past live on, in muted form, in several of today's steakhouses. A good example is the PALM, which has been around since 1972, when Duke Zeibert, the Youngs and the Jockey Club were all still going strong. Located at 1225 Nineteenth Street Northwest, the Palm is a branch of the famous New York City steakhouse founded by two Italian immigrants in 1926. The Washington eatery was opened partly at the suggestion of George Bush Sr., who was ambassador to the United Nations in 1972, and it quickly became a Washington fixture. Like its New York cousin, the Palm aimed for a relaxed atmosphere and offered classic American fare, like steaks and lobster. "The look is politico-macho. The service is tough-guy-with-heart-of-gold. The food is straightforward gargantuan portions of aged beef and lobster," the *Washington Post* observed in 1978. In keeping with the tradition of the New York eatery, the Palm's walls were (and still are) covered with cartoon caricatures of famous people who have eaten there. The Palm's amiable manager, Tommy Jacomo, came down from New York to open the Washington restaurant and has remained in charge of it ever since.

As long as Washington is the nation's capital, it will have its power dining spots, and they will be dominated by talented and likable maître d's and offer comfortable food and surroundings. Now that can't be so hard, can it?

Chapter 11
Chinatown and Chinese Restaurants

Chinese culture in the nineteenth century was profoundly strange to Americans, and Chinese cuisine, now so familiar, was one of its most exotic aspects. The first Chinese restaurants in Washington in the late nineteenth century were seen by wary Anglo Americans as dangerous places frequented by society's outsiders. But by the early 1900s, the nationwide fad for chop suey had changed all that, and Chinese restaurants were fast on their way to becoming a mainstay of the city's dining experience.

Chinese immigrants began arriving in the United States in significant numbers in the 1850s, when poor farmers and laborers from China's Pearl River Delta region sailed to San Francisco to join in the California gold rush. The poor Cantonese farmers, of course, brought their own cuisine with them, including a stew of various meats and vegetables that developed into the dish known as chop suey in the United States. While other Chinese dishes remained too strange for most Anglos, the rather bland stew of chopped meats and vegetables became wildly popular.

Chinese immigrants—almost all of them men—faced violence and hostility in California, where they were seen as competition for scarce jobs, and they began moving east to the larger cities, including a small number who came to Washington. According to sociologist Esther Ngan-ling Chow, the first Chinese resident of Washington was a man named Chiang Kai, who settled on Pennsylvania Avenue in 1851. D.C.'s Chinatown, or "Little China," as it was originally called, was little more than a block long and began to develop in the 1880s just south of Pennsylvania at Fourth Street Northwest, along the stretch of road that now separates the National Gallery of Art's east and west buildings. By the late 1890s, it was a small self-contained community.

For the city's better-off white residents, this became a place to go slumming. According to a *Post* article, Chinatown had but one restaurant in 1897, an exotic place that was abandoned during the day but teeming with life at night: "The savory odors of chop sui and rice, the crackling of Lichee gum nuts, the bubble and sparkle of cold tea and the ceaseless hum of strange, guttural conversation, beguile the senses."

After the visit of the great Chinese statesman Li Hongzhang (1823–1901) to Washington in 1896, excursions into Chinatown grew increasingly popular. The *Washington Times* noted in 1903 that

> *Chinese dishes have become a fad among the smart set, and a visit to a Chinese restaurant is looked upon as an excursion into Bohemia, a taste of slumming, as it were. In Washington there is hardly a night that the Chinese restaurants are not patronized at some hour of the night by fashionably dressed women with escorts in evening attire…The guests are required to take their places along with any other persons who may be in the room, some of whom are not far removed from the hobo class.*

Chow mein was a cheap and often-ordered dish, but among the slummers, the favorite was chop suey. The name comes from the Cantonese *zap tsui*, meaning "mixed pieces." Here is an early recipe for the dish from a popular Chinese-American cookbook:

CHICKEN CHOP SUEY WITH GREEN GINGER

Have a teaspoonful each of olive oil and peanut oil hot in the kettle. Put in first a half pound of lean young pig pork cut in long thin strips and brown carefully. When done add one pound cooked chicken meat both dark and white. Add one cupful bamboo shoots cut fine, one cup white mushroom tops, one-half ounce green ginger root and pour around dish one cup chicken stock. Cook for ten minutes and add one cup bean sprouts. Cook six minutes longer, no more, or bean sprouts cook too long. One teaspoon of each sauce with one teaspoon rice flour for thickening. Add six drops sesame oil just before serving. Cut bamboo shoots and mushroom tops very fine.

A postcard view of the interior of the Port Arthur restaurant, early 1900s. *Author's collection.*

Most of the early chop suey eateries were along the south side of Pennsylvania Avenue between the Capitol and the Treasury Department. Ung Wah, one of Washington's early successful Chinese entrepreneurs, began by co-owning a café on Pennsylvania Avenue in the 1890s. Wah then opened the PORT ARTHUR CHINESE RESTAURANT AND CATERING COMPANY at 515 Ninth Street Northwest in 1905. Wah designed his restaurant to appeal to the tastes of the Americans who had liked to go slumming in Chinatown. The building he took over, which was in the budding Ninth Street entertainment district rather than in Chinatown, was a former Methodist church originally constructed in 1835 and enlarged in 1879. According to Wah's advertisement, his new restaurant was "gorgeously furnished with teakwood tables, inlaid with pearl." A rare postcard view of the interior of the building shows the Gothic windows and sharply peaked ceiling of the former church complemented by a large, intricately carved Chinese screen, hiding the kitchen area, and tables likewise sporting elaborate Chinese carving and inlay.

The Port Arthur was very successful, staying in business into the 1920s. The location proved to be excellent, as the eatery was surrounded by stage and movie theaters whose patrons filled the Port Arthur late into the night. In the 1920s, it offered live dance music by a three-piece ensemble to accompany dinner, but by the early 1930s, it had closed.

Well into the 1930s, the city's Chinese restaurants all sold primarily chop suey and chow mein (which was essentially the same dish with noodles added), as well as egg foo young, wonton soup and egg rolls. These Americanized dishes largely reflected the Cantonese heritage of the early Chinese immigrants. More exotic offerings (like shark fins and bird's nest soup) were occasionally listed on the menus but rarely ordered, and most Chinese eateries also offered American dishes. Typically, Chinese restaurants served tea with their meals but no alcoholic beverages, which positioned them well to weather the Prohibition era, which drove many other eateries out of business. In the 1920s, Chinese restaurants began to offer music and dancing, as the Port Arthur did, and some eventually became lively nightspots.

Nevertheless, by the time of World War II, the city's numerous chop suey joints had become distinctly old-fashioned. The days of fashionable slumming in Chinatown were long gone. In fact, the whole of Chinatown had been displaced in the 1930s, a victim of the massive beautification efforts initiated by the McMillan Plan of 1902. Along with other landmark restaurants on the south side of Pennsylvania Avenue like Hancock's, Harvey's and Mades', all of the long-standing Chinese restaurants, laundries, apartment houses and other businesses were cleared away in the early 1930s. By then, Chinatown had also extended to the block of Four and a Half Street Northwest just north of the avenue, and that area was leveled as well. With municipal blessing, a new Chinatown was established along H Street Northwest between Fifth and Seventh Streets, a neighborhood previously populated by German, Jewish and Italian immigrants. It was in this neighborhood that a new generation of Chinese restaurants emerged.

One of the first was the China Inn, which Sing Sha Moy (1888–1944) opened in 1937 at 631 H Street Northwest. Moy had previously operated the restaurant, along with a Chinese imported goods store, on Pennsylvania Avenue in the old Chinatown. Irene Moy Yee (1923–1978) took over the China Inn after her father's death and cemented the eatery's enduring popularity. After she passed away, her husband, William Donald Yee (1920–1998), kept it going until 1997, by which time it was the oldest continuously operating restaurant in Chinatown.

Another early eatery was the China Doll, which would also become a long-running Chinatown favorite. Located at 627 H Street Northwest, in the heart of the new Chinatown, it was opened in the late 1930s by Jimmy Dere (1905–1975), a prominent Chinatown businessman. When completed, the China Doll represented

A postcard advertising the China Doll, circa 1940. *Author's collection.*

the height of fashionable art moderne styling; Dere transformed a vintage storefront into a shining new restaurant that served as a great example of how old buildings could be "renovized" into new ones. The restaurant's façade was solidly covered with glossy Vitrolite (a decorative glass tiling) that gave it an elegant jet-black finish bordered in a deep jade-like aquamarine. The mirrored surface was punctuated by distinctively Chinese octagonal windows and signs, topped with a giant neon "China Doll" marquee in flowing Palmer cursive letters, a sign that stood as a Chinatown landmark for the rest of the twentieth century. Inside, the décor was equally sleek and trendy. The main dining room featured tidy booths, recessed overhead lighting and a shiny Formica-topped bar, all hallmarks of 1930s restaurant design. Under Dere, the China Doll became a well-known Chinatown meeting place for those who appreciated good Chinese-American cuisine.

The wartime opening of the Washington branch of the well-known RUBY FOO'S chain made a big splash in the local entertainment world. Ruby Foo Wong (1904–1950) had opened her first Ruby Foo's Den in Boston in the late 1920s to great acclaim. More sprang up in New York City before Wong's brother opened the Washington restaurant at 728 Thirteenth Street Northwest in 1942. More a supper club than just a restaurant, Ruby Foo's featured dining on the first floor, dancing and entertainment on the second and "exotic" Chinese décor throughout. Upscale dishes were offered, including lobster Cantonese, *woo hip har* (jumbo shrimp wrapped in bacon and served in tomato sauce) and *guy kew* (chicken sautéed with water chestnuts and Chinese vegetables). In 1943, the second floor was remodeled as a Tahitian Room featuring Hawaiian dancers and jungle greenery. The restaurant suffered a setback in 1950, when cases of colorful Ruby Foo's matchbooks caught fire in the rear, starting a blaze that resulted in injuries to thirteen firemen. The club closed in the late 1950s.

After World War II, the ban on Chinese immigration was lifted, and a new generation of Chinese began arriving in Washington, bringing fresh styles of cooking that supplemented the Cantonese fare traditionally offered in Chinese restaurants. Noteworthy was the PEKING RESTAURANT, at 5522 Connecticut Avenue Northwest in Chevy Chase, which opened in 1947 and was one of the first of the new wave of Chinese eateries. The Peking was founded by Chuon Ming Lo (1918–1980), a Cantonese native who came to Washington in 1941 as a chef at the Chinese Embassy, and four friends. Lo offered "Peking-style" dishes, including moo shu pork and Peking duck, which quickly gained a following among diplomats and local connoisseurs. Other exotic novelties included 00 Soup, eight precious rice and something called *tsa sang shang*. For special occasions, the Peking would serve a unique ten-course meal centered on Peking duck that won for the restaurant the Washington Winers and Diners Club award for excellence in authenticity, taste and service in 1954. In succeeding years, the *New York Times* and *Holiday* magazine, among others, would rank the Peking as one of the city's best restaurants. After ten years of success, in 1957, Lo opened a downtown branch, at 711 Thirteenth Street Northwest, which had a distinguished twenty-year career of its own. As Lo told the *Star* in 1977, the Kennedy White House would sometimes order sizable late-night takeout meals from the downtown Peking. In the meantime, Lo added two more Peking branches.

The Peking's success inevitably inspired imitators, most notably the PEKING PALACE, which opened in 1955 just down the street from the Peking at 3524 Connecticut Avenue Northwest in Cleveland Park. The Peking Palace took over the building of an older restaurant known as the Seafare, which had opened in 1945 and had been created by combining two 1920s storefronts into one building. The Seafare was another small business that had been "renovized" with a shiny pale-green Vitrolite façade framed in black. The mirror-like Vitrolite became an enduring landmark on upper Connecticut Avenue, sometimes attracting unwelcome attention from passersby. In 1953, the Seafare's owner commented to the *Post* about gangs of young "hoodlums" that would frequent the neighborhood, claiming they would "daily preen themselves in the glassy surfaces of the tile covering the front of his restaurant. 'They all have long wavy hair—they call it duck-tails,' he said, 'and wear blue jeans and T-shirts or sweat shirts.'"

Whether the hoodlums were still coiffing their hair on the sidewalk two years later when the Seafare became the Peking Palace isn't known, but the Chinese restaurant soon found itself in new trouble. S. Van Lung (1926–1991), the founder of the Peking Palace, had previously worked at the Peking Restaurant, as had his business manager, twenty-three-year-old Paul Dietrich. Lung, the son of a top Nationalist Chinese army general in World War II, copied many aspects of the groundbreaking restaurant he had previously worked in, including the extensive menu of exotic dishes that went well beyond the then-accepted repertoire of Chinese eateries. So much so that the Peking Restaurant filed suit against Lung for unfair competition, arguing that both the name and the similarity of the new restaurant's menu unfairly implied a connection between the restaurants that didn't exist. The Peking Palace reportedly distributed misleading flyers urging customers to "visit our new place" to the south on Connecticut Avenue. And it allegedly appropriated the Peking's signature 00 Soup. However, the *Post* reported that Dietrich had written a letter arguing that the northern Chinese broth was in the public domain. He offered the following recipe:

00 ("ZERO-ZERO") SOUP

¾ cup lean pork, finely shredded
4 cups chicken stock
4 pieces Chinese bean cake
2 eggs
1 teaspoon soy sauce
Less than 1 teaspoon cornstarch
1 to 1½ teaspoons sesame oil
Green scallions, chopped

Fry shredded pork lightly. Put into boiling pot of chicken broth. Cut bean cake (which comes in squares) into long, thin shreds. Add to broth. Beat eggs and drop into broth, stirring vigorously. (For lighter mixture, use only egg whites.) Add soy sauce, starch and sesame oil last. Put mixture in serving bowl and sprinkle chopped scallions on top for garnish. Serves 3 to 4.

The legal tiff, well documented in the newspapers, probably provided valuable publicity for both restaurants. Legally, the newer one lost the battle and was forced not only to drop 00 Soup from its menu but also to change its name. However, as the YENCHING PALACE, it gained a loyal following. Already in 1956, it was adverting that it "entertained more diplomats daily than the White House." In 1958, a red twenty-foot neon sign was installed across the building's façade, festively proclaiming the new "Yenching Palace" name with an odd capital "Y" that looked like a backward "4." From this point on, the restaurant's fame eclipsed even that of the Peking. Celebrities known to have eaten at the Yenching Palace over the years—in addition to the diplomats from the Chinese and other embassies—included Mick Jagger, Danny Kaye, Henry Kissinger, I.M. Pei, advice columnist Ann Landers and many others.

The restaurant gained a unique spot in history as one of the "secret" sites where ABC News reporter John A. Scali (1918–1995) met with Soviet emissary Aleksandr Feklisov (1914–2007) to negotiate the terms for a peaceful resolution to the Cuban Missile Crisis in October 1962. The fashionable Yenching Palace, already well known as a rendezvous for statesmen and diplomats, was a natural spot to meet. Secretary of State Henry Kissinger met Chinese representatives there in 1971 to discuss reestablishing diplomatic relations. In keeping with its Cold War legacy, there were even suggestions that at least one of its booths was fitted with secret listening devices—although which side was supposedly doing the listening remains a mystery.

The restaurant remained popular through the 1960s and 1970s and continued in business for several more decades. After Lung died in 1991, it was taken over by his nephew, Larry Lung, who then retired in 2007. The building recently has been renovated as a Walgreens pharmacy, and what remained of the original Vitrolite façade was destroyed and replaced with a replica of the old Seafare front.

Meanwhile, Sam Gin Wong (1918–1984), who had run Ruby Foo's in the 1950s, created what would become another upper Northwest dining institution when he opened the MOON PALACE restaurant at 3308 Wisconsin Avenue Northwest in 1957, just two years after the Peking Palace debuted. The Moon Palace's menu featured such delicacies as *choung far har* ("selected jumbo shrimp split open, stuffed with minced pork, mushrooms and water chestnuts and sautéed in barbecue sauce") and *fong gone longhar* ("by popular request, fresh lobster meat, chicken liver sautéed with imported Chinese mushrooms and assorted vegetables") but tellingly also included an extensive list of old-fashioned chow mein, chop suey and egg foo young for less adventuresome customers, as well as plenty of ordinary American steaks and sandwiches for the truly uninspired. Like the Yenching Palace, the Moon Palace was very fashionable and successful in the 1960s and 1970s.

As the old downtown began to decline in the late 1950s and 1960s, the eateries in Chinatown struggled to keep their customers. A *Washington Post* article in 1958 told of how most of the city's 110 Chinese restaurants were joint ventures among many small-time investors who struggled to turn a profit and keep their businesses fresh and exciting for jaded customers who had eaten in Chinese restaurants all their lives. By that time, the Art Deco–inspired storefronts from the 1930s were out of date. "A Chinese restaurant should have pleasant Chinese surroundings—not chrome and neon and juke boxes," Kwang Lien Lee, a Chinatown leader, told the *Post* in an implicit rebuke of places like the China Doll.

The evolution of the China Doll reflected the changes in Chinatown. In 1969, Davis Lee, a successful Chinatown merchant, purchased the aging eatery and, with his wife, Tom-Lin Lee, ran it in the 1970s and 1980s. But in 1988, Lee's children, who had inherited the business, decided they needed to remodel their landmark eatery. It was difficult getting people to come down to Chinatown in those days, and the Vitrolite façade of the China Doll seemed outdated, a pointer to the quaint chop suey houses of yore. So they tore off the distinctive façade and replaced it with a blank, tan brick façade, keeping only the giant neon sign. "It's a sad story, but we had to keep up with the times," Dr. Toon Lee, one of the owners, told the *Post*. When the restaurant reopened as the China Doll Gourmet, it featured upscale gourmet dishes from Japan, Thailand and Hawaii, in addition to standard Chinese fare. It continued as a Chinatown fixture until 2006, when the family decided to retire and accept an offer from one of the developers who had been hounding them. The building was torn down soon thereafter.

Other landmark Chinatown restaurants of the late twentieth century included the Golden Palace, at 720 Seventh Street Northwest, and the Tai Tung at 622 H Street Northwest, both of which flourished in the 1970s and 1980s under the supervision of restaurateur Nelson Lee. After President Nixon visited China in 1972, spicy Szechuan and Hunan cuisines began to compete with the traditional Cantonese menus, and restaurants like the Szechuan at 615 I Street Northwest (opened in 1977) and the Hunan Gourmet at 726 Seventh Street Northwest (opened in 1981) became popular. The construction of the Washington Convention Center a few blocks away in 1980 brought new customers and new restaurants to Chinatown, carrying it along until the arrival of the MCI Center (now the Verizon Center) in 1997, which jumpstarted the neighborhood's current era of prosperity. While many observers feared that Chinatown would disappear completely as new businesses flooded in, it has managed to survive—at least for the time being.

Chapter 12

The Twentieth-Century Transformation of Haute Cuisine

French cuisine in the nineteenth century had been the undisputed paragon of culinary excellence. All the best restaurants had French chefs, French menus, dishes heavy with rich French sauces. In the early twentieth century, that strict regimen began to break down as the burgeoning middle classes sought more relaxed and varied dining experiences, although traditional fine restaurants and French caterers didn't disappear. In 1939, elegant French dining rooms saw a resurgence when the legendary Henri Soulé (1903–1966) took the 1939 New York World's Fair by storm as maître d' of the Restaurant du Pavillon de France. Thousands of visitors were in awe of the elegant décor, impeccable French wait service and exquisitely prepared dishes, including duck consommé, lamb medallions with chicken mousseline and lobster in shellfish cream sauce. Soulé subsequently opened his famous Le Pavillon restaurant in New York City, reestablishing the primacy of haute cuisine in America.

Nevertheless, many Americans remained wary of the pretenses of formal French dining, favoring simpler and more eclectic alternatives. By 1959, *New York Times* critic Craig Claiborne famously lamented, "Two time-honored symbols of the good life—great cuisine in the French tradition and elegant table service—are passing from the American scene." Claiborne worried that great European chefs were no longer immigrating to America and that America was not producing great chefs of its own. Time would make it clear that sophisticated restaurants were not really becoming extinct at all but being transformed by new standards of culinary excellence. The scene was set for a variety of nouvelle cuisine and other revolutionary cooking styles to come to D.C. and redefine fine dining for modern tastes.

A menu from the Café Parisienne, dated October 15, 1944. *Author's collection.*

Several D.C. firms continued the tradition of French confectioners and caterers that also offered full-service dining rooms, in the tradition of Boulanger and Gautier. The MAISON RAUSCHER, opened in 1892 at 1110 Connecticut Avenue Northwest, was a notable example. Born in the French border province of Alsace, Charles Rauscher (1854–1917) was a traditional confectioner-caterer. His restaurant featured a commodious upstairs ballroom that was the scene of numerous formal dinners, dances and other elegant receptions. According to the *Evening Star*, Rauscher's came to be known as the "Delmonico's of Washington" for its central role in so many Washington social functions. It closed in 1918 after Rauscher's death.

In its heyday, AVIGNONE FRÈRES (1920–1986), at 1777 Columbia Road Northwest in Adams Morgan, was celebrated for its sophisticated, exquisitely made pastries and its elegant dining room. It opened in 1920 on Eighteenth Street and then moved its *salon des epicures* to the Columbia Road address in 1928. The French-style catering establishment was actually founded by Italians. Pietro Orcino (1908–1984), who bought it in 1945, was a longtime proprietor who made Avignone Frères a Washington institution. Its closing in 1986 marked the end of the tradition of confectioner-caterers in Washington.

In the 1930s and 1940s, white-tablecloth French restaurants in D.C. were few. They included the CAFÉ PARISIENNE at 1120 Connecticut Avenue Northwest, across the street from the Mayflower Hotel, and LA SALLE DU BOIS, nearby at 1800 M Street Northwest. The Café Parisienne offered traditional delicacies including sautéed frog legs and palmetto squab, as well as lobster Thermidor and oysters Rockefeller. La Salle du Bois, which opened in December 1941, at the dawn of American involvement in World War II, was an outpost of a New York City restaurant of the same name that capitalized on the success of Soulé's Le Pavillon. The new restaurant was decorated in a "patriotic modern" style of rose, white and blue, with Colonial revival wallpaper and soft pink lighting. Chef Robert, from French Louisiana stock, produced an assortment of unique dishes, including pheasant with foie gras and truffles, pompano en papillotte and venison with sweet and sour sauce. The *Post* termed the Salle du Bois "swanky but gayly informal" at its opening: "a river of silver fox, ermine and mink wraps poured through the entrance, flash bulbs popped, Robert Montgomery looked handsomer in his naval uniform than he does in the movies…"

Throughout the war years, La Salle du Bois served as one of Washington's few power lunch spots for diplomats and military officers. The wartime Office of Price Administration rationed meats and processed foods and set limits on what restaurants could charge for most types of food, meaning that even a swank spot like La Salle had to apportion servings judiciously. Lavish eating, once a sign of refinement, became distinctly unpatriotic. After the war, the Salle du Bois continued to wear the mantle in D.C. for elegant dining, gaining a reputation for being pretentious. *Holiday* magazine observed in 1950 that it served "a mean crêpe Suzette." It survived into the 1960s but had closed by the end of that decade.

The 1940s and early 1950s marked a particularly low ebb for fine dining in the District, which had been hit by a triple punch in the early twentieth century: first Prohibition, then the Depression and finally World War II. Though alcohol was available again after the war ended, it remained rather scarce, and many of the OPA's limits continued until the early 1950s. Most people splurged no further than eating out occasionally at their humble neighborhood cafés.

Nevertheless, the seeds for a resurgence of haute cuisine were being sown. One of the best French chefs to come to Washington after the war was François Haeringer (1919–2010), a native of the French province of Alsace, who opened the popular CHEZ FRANÇOIS restaurant at 818 Connecticut Avenue Northwest in 1954. Haeringer knew from a young age that he wanted to be a cook and at age sixteen took on a tough apprenticeship in the kitchen of an Alsatian hotel. He then served as a cook in the French army during World War II and was captured by the Germans, who made him prepare meals at the Four Seasons Hotel in Munich. Coming to Washington in 1947 to work at his brother's cafeteria, he soon became chef at Les Trois Mousquetaires, which he bought in 1954 and renamed Chez François. In April 1962, Haeringer opened a sidewalk café in front of his restaurant, only the second in the city. Haeringer said he had always wanted to bring sidewalk dining to Washington, and his café became a perennial lunchtime favorite.

Chez François, decorated in quaint Alsatian style, was always crowded, and the food was consistently good. You could get calves' brains, tripe, Basque-style shellfish and cooked apples for dessert. Though the fare could be exotic, Haeringer made sure the prices stayed affordable. The popular eatery lasted for twenty-one years. As time went by, Haeringer expanded and added decorative touches such as Alsatian tiles and craftwork to make his restaurant cozier and more like a country inn. Ever low key, the "old school" chef Haeringer stayed in the kitchen most of the time. A distinguished-looking elderly gentleman with a curled moustache greeted customers in the early 1970s, and many thought he was Haeringer, but he was actually family friend Claude Jarret.

Chez François was located in a hotel building, which was sold in 1975, to be razed and replaced by an office box. Haeringer moved his eatery to Great Falls, Virginia, where he opened L'AUBERGE CHEZ FRANÇOIS in 1976, an even more authentic Alsatian-style country inn. Though Haeringer kept to his low-key ways, he also maintained exacting standards of quality, and his restaurant was often solidly booked as far in advance as reservations were allowed. Haeringer supervised the kitchen there until his death at age ninety-one in 2010. The restaurant continues under the direction of his sons.

Meanwhile, other restaurateurs were beginning to vie for celebrity status in Washington's still-emerging market for fine dining. None would be more influential than Blaise Gherardi de Parata (1909–1978), a native of Corsica, who came to the United States in 1949. Gherardi's opening in 1956 of RIVE GAUCHE, at 1310 Wisconsin Avenue Northwest in the heart of Georgetown, marked a sea change in the city's restaurant culture. With the arrival of Rive Gauche, austerity and restraint were passé; fine dining was back in style.

Gherardi enjoyed playing the part of the flamboyant, high-profile restaurant owner who was forever fighting with his temperamental chefs. Not a chef himself—he would later tell a *Post* reporter that he never cooked anything in his life except to "open a can of Campbell's soup on Sundays"—Gherardi was instead a shrewd businessman who hired the best young chefs and wait staff from France. Gherardi's original chef was Eugène Batisse (1910–2003), whom he had brought from Paris in 1953 to work at his first restaurant, the Place Vendôme. When Batisse left in 1959 to work at Le Bistro, a new downtown competitor, Gherardi brought the celebrated Jean-Pierre Goyenvalle from France, establishing a pattern that would continue for years to come. Gherardi would go on scouting trips to France and bring back promising young chefs to the Rive Gauche, where they would make a name for themselves and subsequently set out on their own ventures, often after having been fired by the temperamental Gherardi. Goyenvalle would go on to great fame as the chef of two very sophisticated and successful restaurants, Jean-Pierre at 1835 K Street Northwest (from 1971 to 1976) and Le Lion d'Or at 1150 Connecticut Avenue Northwest (from 1976 to 1997). Another find, Paul Delisle, would leave to become maître d' at the renowned Sans Souci restaurant on Seventeenth Street. And chef Camille Richaudeau would go on to run the exquisite Chez Camille at 1403 L Street Northwest (from 1965 to 1983). So many successful careers were launched from the Rive Gauche that Gherardi came to be known as the father of the modern French restaurant in Washington.

Chef Goyenvalle's tenure in particular seems to have really put Rive Gauche on the map. It fortuitously coincided with the arrival of President John F. Kennedy in 1961. Kennedy, who famously spurred the renewal of Pennsylvania Avenue after noticing how run down it looked during his inauguration, also sparked a renewed interest in fine dining. He and Jacqueline Kennedy took a liking to Rive Gauche, and soon everybody important was vying to dine there or, more importantly, to be seen dining there. Jackie, who lived nearby in Georgetown, continued to frequent Rive Gauche after Kennedy's death. With Defense Secretary Robert S. McNamara at her side, she had dinner there in March 1964, feasting on Goyenvalle's baked oysters, duck pâté and veal chops.

The Rive Gauche was an expensive, top-drawer French restaurant, furnished in quilted burgundy-colored leather banquettes, a mammoth crystal chandelier and gilt-framed oil paintings. *Evening Star* critic John Rosson noted that his dinner check came to a hefty $15.87 in November 1968, more than many of his readers could afford, but that it was well worth it. He ate *quenelles de mantua*, "the most delicate of poached French dumplings topped with tiny, tender shrimp in a rich shrimp sauce," and thought that chef Goyenvalle could not have done better.

Staff of the *Rive Gauche* assemble on the restaurant's twentieth anniversary in 1977. *D.C. Public Library, Star Collection,* © Washington Post.

The restaurant's hostess for many years, Polish-born Jeannine Cusson (1930–2009), became as much a fixture as any of the restaurant's colorful chefs. A strong personality, Cusson had ardent admirers, who frequented the restaurant because of her gracious hospitality, as well as severe critics. The *Post*'s Sally Quinn, writing in 1973, called Cusson a "blonde Gallic terror" who "was feared for years by everyone in town who had a distinguished palate or a need to be seen, for she had her likes and dislikes and turned away the powerful and rich the way Blaise [Gherardi] turned away employees." At the time of Quinn's writing, Gherardi had just fired Cusson after nearly twenty years of service.

Business slipped after Cusson was let go, and later that same year Gherardi decided to retire and sell the restaurant. It moved up Wisconsin Avenue in 1981 but closed soon thereafter.

The SANS SOUCI, at 726 Seventeenth Street Northwest, near the White House, opened in January 1963, just in time to gain a little patronage from the short-lived

Kennedy administration. It was an immediate hit, soon rivaling the Rive Gauche as a fashionable spot to meet and be seen. Located so close to the seat of power, the Sans Souci drew countless Washington power lunches, and soon all of the government's important decisions were supposedly being made there.

The elegant décor, in retrospect, was strikingly similar to the Rive Gauche's. The dining room featured tufted green leather banquettes and French carpeting, with mahogany high-back chairs upholstered in black leather. A grand crystal chandelier commanded the center of the room, and gilt-framed paintings hung on the gold brocade walls. The *Evening Star*'s John Rosson called the place "a chic little number with Versailles-like appointments which undoubtedly will become one of THE places to dine out in the Nation's Capital, if it hasn't already." It had, indeed, already, and it would remain so for more than a decade.

Much of the restaurant's success was due to the skill and charm of maître d' Paul DeLisle (1928–1983), who had previously worked at the Rive Gauche and the British Embassy. DeLisle was born in Marseilles, France, and came to Washington in 1954. Like all great hosts, he had an uncanny ability to understand his guests and their needs, to orchestrate exactly who should be seated near—or away from—whom and to be utterly discreet about everything. Humorist Art Buchwald would frequently write about the Sans Souci in his syndicated column, "Capitol Punishment," and when the upheaval of Watergate and the Nixon resignation was finally over, Buchwald interjected a typically sly bit of commentary about DeLisle: "One of Gerald Ford's first acts as President was to ask Paul DeLisle to stay on as maître d' of the Sans Souci Restaurant," he joked. "We don't know President Ford," Washington's many ambassadors supposedly told him, "but we do know Paul and we can deal with him."

Chef Gus Diamant offered an extensive menu of traditional fine French cuisine, including foie gras, Chateaubriand with Béarnaise sauce, bouillabaisse Marseillaise and canard à l'orange flambé au Cointreau, among many other choices. Classic desserts included mousse au chocolat, crêpes Suzette and profiteroles. Under succeeding chefs, the food at Sans Souci, though conservative, remained consistently good.

By the time of the Carter administration, the Sans Souci's preeminence began to fade. The vogue turned to casual dining, and many people began to feel less of a need to be seen at the Sans. The restaurant's fortunes turned decidedly for the worse when Paul DeLisle left in 1979 to work at the rival Jockey Club. Many customers followed him there. In the same year, a McDonald's restaurant opened next door to the Sans, eliciting wisecracks and undoubtedly further tarnishing the Sans Souci brand. The restaurant filed for bankruptcy and closed in 1981.

Paul DeLisle entertains diplomats from the Israeli Embassy in 1967. *D.C. Public Library, Star Collection*, © Washington Post.

By the 1970s, competition among high-class eateries was intensifying, and French restaurants became decidedly more adventuresome in their menus. Perhaps the most famous of these was DOMINIQUE'S, at 1921 Pennsylvania Avenue Northwest. Dominique's was the creation of Dominique D'Ermo (1927–2002). Born in Lyons, France, D'Ermo had fought with the French Resistance during World War II and afterward became a pastry chef, learning the culinary arts at restaurants and hotels in France and England. He came to Washington in 1962 to be food and beverage director at the Shoreham Hotel and then opened Dominique's in 1974.

The restaurant began as a largely traditional French restaurant, occupying the cozy former space of several modest earlier eateries (Le Pigalle and Jacqueline's). D'Ermo even kept the traditional French-themed décor that he inherited. One night, Willie Morris, a columnist for the *Washington Star*, came by for dinner, and D'Ermo brought a bottle of cognac to the table and joined him for a drink, regaling the journalist with colorful stories of his days in La Résistance. Morris was so taken with the experience that he wrote glowingly in the *Star* of how Dominique's was to him just like the romantic Parisian café where Rick and Ilsa had last met before fleeing the invading Germans in the movie *Casablanca*, "a joyous little place with Impressionists on the walls and food and wine good enough to bring your favorite girl and say to her, 'Here's looking at you, kid.'" Droves of customers soon followed. D'Ermo's magical touch had transformed an ordinary restaurant into an overnight sensation.

But D'Ermo knew he had to constantly find new ways to stay in the public spotlight. In 1975, he began a lasting tradition of hosting a grand annual Waiter's Race on Pennsylvania Avenue to commemorate Bastille Day. Such races had been held in European cities for many years, but this was one of Washington's first. D'Ermo was able to get the block of Pennsylvania Avenue in front of his restaurant closed for the day, and waiters from a variety of local restaurants would race while balancing trays of champagne and glasses on outstretched hands. The Bastille Day race was a hit and has continued, under varying sponsorship, to this day.

Meanwhile, the original restaurant setting was a little too snug and conventional for D'Ermo, and in 1977 he moved across the street to larger quarters on the ground floor of a Pennsylvania Avenue office building. The traditional décor was gone, replaced by eccentric touches—a row of gilded cow heads, oriental carpets, celebrity photographs and stained-glass windows. Phyllis Richman summed up the new place: "Handsomely eccentric setting, annoyingly eccentric service." The food, moreover, was excellent.

D'Ermo enjoyed hunting big game—he'd tell customers about hunting for polar bears in the Arctic—and this pastime prompted his most notorious innovation: the addition of a wide variety of exotic game to the menu, including alligator, lion, hippopotamus, mountain goat and Pennsylvania timber rattlesnake. The extraordinary dishes piqued both the curiosity of diners and the ire of conservationists, who often raised questions about the legality of obtaining certain types of animals. In one widely reported incident in 1979, Dr. C. Kenneth Dodd, a reptile expert with the Interior Department's Fish and Wildlife Service, wrote a letter to Dominique's, requesting that the Pennsylvania timber rattlesnake be taken off the menu because the species was nearing extinction. D'Ermo immediately agreed, substituting Texas diamondback rattlesnake, which he said was not endangered. However, the matter didn't end there.

Dodd's letter was reported in the *Star* and came to the attention of Interior Secretary Cecil D. Andrus, who happened to be a big fan of Dominique's. Andrus apologized to D'Ermo on his next visit to the restaurant, and Dodd was summarily fired. The firing—even more widely reported in the press—elicited much sympathy for the hapless Dodd. "He seemed like a very nice gentleman," D'Ermo observed to the *Post*. "Eet eez too bad he fell in love with zee snakes." Under broad pressure from powerful senators and congressmen, as well as conservation groups, the Interior Department within days rescinded its decision and reinstated Dodd. And D'Ermo, of course, got a massive dose of free publicity.

By the late 1980s, despite D'Ermo's colorful antics, Dominique's began to be outclassed by newer, trendier eateries. D'Ermo sold the business in 1987 to move on to other ventures. Without his presence, the restaurant rapidly fell out of favor, declaring bankruptcy in 1991 and closing in 1994.

Washington hosted many more French restaurants in the later part of the twentieth century, ranging from the quirky LA NIÇOISE at 1721 Wisconsin Avenue Northwest in Georgetown (1969–93), where the waiters dashed around on roller skates, and the homey LA CHAUMIÈRE at 2813 M Street Northwest, also in Georgetown, decorated with barnyard tools and a warm country fireplace (1976–present), to chef Yannick Cam's prestigious LE PAVILLON at 1820 K Street Northwest (1977–90), a pioneer of nouvelle cuisine in the District.

Nouvelle cuisine, a term coined by French food critics Henri Gault and Christian Millau in 1973, represented a revolution in French cooking that overthrew the old heavy, conventional dishes and their rich sauces with inventive, colorful, beautifully plated fare based on the freshest available ingredients and simplified cooking techniques. Perhaps the most famous D.C. exponent of the new wave in French cooking was Jean-Louis Palladin (1946–2001), an energetic young chef who opened JEAN-LOUIS AT THE WATERGATE at 2650 Virginia Avenue Northwest in 1979. Phyllis Richman called Palladin "perhaps the most famous French chef in America," and the *Post* called his restaurant "perhaps the most acclaimed establishment of its kind in the city." Few others could compare.

Palladin, a native of Gascony, France, had achieved extraordinary success even before he came to Washington at age thirty-three. He was the youngest chef to ever receive a coveted two-star Michelin rating. In 1979, this "hero of the nouvelle cuisine," as the *Post* described him, accepted an offer from the Watergate to come to Washington to open a small forty-seat restaurant in the space at the hotel formerly occupied by the Democratic Club. The Watergate had been hoping to better associate itself with fine dining, and it succeeded grandly. "Never before—in the memory of contemporary observers—has a French chef of such stature come to the United States to direct a restaurant," the *Post* observed.

An intense culinary artist full of seemingly endless energy, Palladin immediately set about creating exceptional dishes the same way he had in France, relying on the freshest ingredients he could find and varying his menu as different items became available throughout the year. "For me nouvelle cuisine is the cooking of liberty," Palladin told the *Post*. "It has given me freedom in the products I choose and in the methods I use." Palladin later described these methods, which were revolutionary at the time, in his landmark book, *Jean-Louis: Cooking with the Seasons* (1989).

The small Jean-Louis dining room was strikingly modern, with mirrors hanging on orange silk–covered wall panels. It was not clear at first whether nouvelle cuisine, simple as it was in concept and yet very expensive, would find acceptance in Washington. Not all initial reviews were favorable, but the restaurant soon gained a reputation for being Washington's finest. "This is subtle food, and beautiful, with color and texture as carefully orchestrated as is flavor," Phyllis Richman wrote in 1984. Meanwhile, the frenetic Palladin was known to frequently often utter French expletives as he tried to orchestrate all the delicate operations in the kitchen, and the police were even called in once to settle a dispute. A food critic who had written a negative review of the restaurant had come in for dinner, and Palladin yelled at him and refused to serve him. The critic called the police, who arrived and apparently told Palladin he had to serve all customers. Chef and critic were ultimately reconciled.

The restaurant won many honors over its seventeen-year run, but it was hugely expensive to operate, with a large staff and very limited seating capacity. Palladin spent $25,000 on Limoges china in 1984 and $88,000 for a custom-made sixteen-burner, eight-oven La Cornue stove in 1993. Acquiring the rarest and freshest ingredients, largely locally grown, was not inexpensive either, and food preparation was laborious. Despite charging extremely expensive prices, the eatery generally did little better than break even. When the hotel's new owners refused to renovate the dining room in 1996, Palladin decided to quit. He subsequently was involved in restaurant ventures in Las Vegas and New York that were less successful. Having served as an inspiration and mentor for a generation of chefs throughout the United States, Palladin died in 2001 at the age of fifty-five, from lung cancer.

Another mentor to many D.C. chefs and a former colleague of Palladin is Michel Richard, who first came to Washington in 1993 to open CITRONELLE, a highly regarded "California-French" eatery at 3000 M Street Northwest in Georgetown. A native of Brittany, Richard began as a pastry chef in France before moving to New York, Santa Fe and then Los Angeles, where he opened his first restaurant, Citrus, in 1987. Embracing

Chef Michel Richard at the counter of Michel Richard Citronelle. *Photo by Stacy Zarin-Goldberg.*

the nouvelle cuisine philosophy, Richard told the *Washington Post* in 1993 that his cooking was based on "very clean and simple flavors, no butter or cream, and a lot of texture, a lot of crunch." Richard enjoyed adding surprising, unbilled ingredients to his creations and ensuring they were playfully pleasing. When he added the Georgetown Citronelle in 1993, it was just one of several far-flung restaurants. That changed in 1998, when Richard moved to Washington to concentrate on helping turn D.C. into a culinary destination with his D.C. eatery, which he renovated and rechristened MICHEL RICHARD CITRONELLE. The restaurant, which featured an open kitchen, immediately rose to the top tier of Washington culinary institutions and has been consistently praised by critics ever since. Richard's verve and creativity have influenced many rising D.C chefs, going a long way to improving D.C.'s reputation for fine dining. While a flood damaged the restaurant in 2012 and resulted in its temporary closure, it was slated to reopen in late 2013.

Though nouvelle cuisine was a French invention, the basic tenets of nouvelle cooking, including an emphasis on fresh, locally obtained ingredients, eventually came to pervade a broad range of the city's best restaurants. An important pioneer in the "hyper-local" food movement was Nora Pouillon, a native of Austria who, in 1979, opened RESTAURANT NORA at 2132 Florida Avenue Northwest in Dupont Circle. Pouillon previously had been a food writer and an owner of the Tabard Inn. When she opened her namesake restaurant in 1979, it filled a niche for organic and locally grown food that had been previously overlooked, despite heightened awareness of environmental issues in the 1970s. Phyllis Richman called it "more than a restaurant…a culinary statement of radical chic." Nora's made its own soups, its own bread, even its own mayonnaise. Herbs were (and still are) grown in a garden outside the restaurant.

Though it quickly drew a following, the eatery did not really take off until the 1990s, during the years of the Clinton administration, when health-conscious dining became fashionable in Washington. A typical vegetarian delicacy from 1993 was grilled portobello mushrooms with red lentil dal, goat cheese and *mizuna* (Japanese greens). "It's a cliché, but Democrats have always been more concerned about the food they eat and the impact on the environment," Pouillon told the *Washington Post* that year. "I think the restaurant is right for the time." In 1999, Nora's became the first restaurant in the country to be certified organic, cementing Pouillon's status as a celebrity chef. The designation required that the restaurant obtain at least 95 percent of its ingredients from producers who themselves were certified organic—a formidable undertaking. The restaurant's prestige has continued to increase in recent years as environmental concerns have become even more prominent.

Nora's Strawberry-Rhubarb Pie

6 cups rhubarb (6 medium stalks), cut into ¼-inch slices
1¼ cups sugar
2 pints strawberries, washed and hulled
2 tablespoons arrowroot or cornstarch
1 tablespoon grated orange rind or orange liqueur
Pie shell and strips, chilled

Preheat the oven to 375° Fahrenheit. Put the rhubarb into a bowl, add the sugar and toss to combine. Steep the rhubarb for at least 40 minutes until it releases its juices. Drain in a colander and set aside. Cut the strawberries in halves or quarters, depending on their size, and add them to the rhubarb. Sprinkle the fruit mixture with the arrowroot and grated orange peel and toss to combine.

Remove the pie shell and strips from the freezer or refrigerator. Fill the pie shell with the strawberry-rhubarb mixture. Place 5 or 6 strips of dough over the filling. Interweave the remaining strips under and over these strips to form a lattice and trim the ends. Roll the overhanging dough up and over the rim of the pie pan to form a thick rolled border. Crimp to form an attractive edge.

Brush the pie with egg wash. Bake for 45 minutes or until the fruit is bubbling and the crust is golden. Allow the pie to cool for about 10 minutes before slicing.

Chef Jeffrey Buben. *Bistro Bis Restaurant.*

Since the 1990s, other celebrity chefs, like Pouillon, have demonstrated how far fine dining has come since the days of French haute cuisine. Chef Jeffrey Buben is an example. Buben first made a name for himself at the Mayflower Hotel's Nicholas Restaurant, producing inventive dishes in a nouvelle American style, and then moved to the prestigious Occidental Grill when it reopened in 1986. With his wife, Sallie, Buben in 1993 opened VIDALIA at 1990 M Street Northwest, a distinctly southern-themed restaurant reflecting Sallie Buben's heritage. His second restaurant, BISTRO BIS, opened in 1998 at 15 E Street Northwest on Capitol Hill. Bistro Bis, said to be one of Hillary Clinton's favorite restaurants, features dishes based on French country-style cooking traditions but presents them in a distinctly upscale setting descended from the haute tradition. Like other sophisticated contemporary eateries, it demonstrates that fine dining can successfully embrace any cuisine or combination of cuisines, as long as it can be pulled off with skill and style.

Chapter 13
ITALIAN RESTAURANTS IN WASHINGTON

From Macaroni to Alta Cucina

Unlike the Irish, Germans and Chinese, Italian immigrants never settled in Washington in numbers large enough to create their own enclave, a "Little Italy," as other cities had. Nevertheless, skilled Italians were working here since Civil War days, when Constantino Brumidi (1805–1880) painted many of the Capitol's beautiful murals and frescos. Many of the Italian newcomers were artisans and stonecutters, but others became restaurateurs.

Late nineteenth-century Italian restaurants offered a pleasant diversion from the oysters, stews and game found at other local eateries. The COLUMBUS DINING ROOMS, for example, in business at 1117 G Street Northwest in the 1880s, advertised itself as "the only genuine Italian dining rooms in the city." Another pioneer was Giuseppe Marinelli (1849–1923), an immigrant from the south of Italy, who ran MARINELLI & MASINO'S, a restaurant at 335 Pennsylvania Avenue Northwest, in the 1890s. Marinelli's adjoining store sold a variety of "exotic" Italian and other imported foods, including "Italian Maccaroni, 11c per lb; Genoa Vermicelli; French Compounds for Soups; Foreign Cheese of every description" and more. According to the *Evening Star*, however, the most popular Italian eatery at the turn of the century was AMERIGO "HAPPY" GUIDOTTI's restaurant on New York Avenue at Seventeenth Street Northwest, opposite the Corcoran Gallery of Art: "Behind the shabby old front lay one of the few truly Bohemian places Washington has ever possessed. Happy's wine was of the best and his cooking irreproachable."

Like other ethnic eating houses, Italian restaurants were looked down on by many locals, regardless of how popular they were. They did not offer fine dining, and they did

Inside the "New Italian-American Restaurant" at 918 Seventeenth Street Northwest, circa 1934. *Author's collection.*

not seem very American. A 1901 *Washington Post* article scorned an unnamed Italian restaurant located "in the very heart of the city, down a dingy pair of steps," where Italians "eat great bowls of their beloved spaghetti…[T]he proprietor willingly serves the visitor with one of the coarse bowls of slippery spaghetti. Other Italian dishes may be had, all cooked in oil and heavy with herbs and garlic." Fair or otherwise, the reporter's perceptions reflected common attitudes about what food critics would later deride as "red sauce joints."

Italian cuisine in America was largely invented in late nineteenth-century New York City, where more Italians lived than in much of Italy itself. None of the cooks in the early restaurants had any professional training; they were poor people, most from southern Italy, who were simply looking for a way to make a living. Like Chinese and other immigrants, they adapted cooking traditions from their native land to available ingredients and the tastes of the local population, inventing a new cuisine that travelers from the mother country would scarcely recognize. Spices were played down, and meat was added. No one in Italy would have served meatballs with spaghetti, nor would they find the many veal dishes recognizable.

Bobby Abbo lifts grape maiden Karen Stewart into the barrel in 1980. *D.C. Public Library, Star Collection,* © Washington Post.

By the early twentieth century, larger numbers of Italians began arriving in D.C., lured by construction jobs on projects such as the massive Union Station complex, which opened in 1907, and more Italian eateries began to open. One of the best known of Washington's early Italian restaurants was the legendary ROMA RESTAURANT, founded in 1920 at 707 Twelfth Street Northwest, by Frank Abbo (1890–1970), a Genovese immigrant. Abbo arrived in the United States as a penniless youth in 1908 and first earned a living as a Pennsylvania coal miner. He served as a cook in World War I and afterward worked at the Willard Hotel until he had saved up enough money to open his first restaurant. In the 1920s, he had two Roma restaurants downtown, as well as a dance hall out on Rockville Pike, but was hit by the Depression and had to close them all. In 1932, he reopened the Roma at 3419 Connecticut Avenue Northwest in Cleveland Park, where it remained for another sixty-five years.

Though he generally spent long hours at the Roma, Abbo liked to go big-game hunting and mounted a stuffed Bengal tiger near the entrance of the Roma, as well as a polar bear in one of the dining rooms. The Roma was famous for its traditional Italian fare, including its signature homemade manicotti stuffed with prosciutto and ricotta, which might be served three or four hundred times on a busy day. In addition to the restaurant's spacious dining

---

ROMA RESTAURANT RICOTTA AND PROSCIUTTO MANICOTTI

Combine 1 pound (4 cups) flour with 4 eggs and 1 teaspoon salt; knead until it becomes a paste. Put dough in a cloth and let stand in a cool place for 1 hour. When ready to make manicotti, separate dough into 4 equal parts and roll into long sheets as thin as possible with a rolling pin. Cut sheets of dough into 3- by 4-inch pieces and cook in boiling water for half a minute. Set aside to dry. Meanwhile, make filling.

Filling: Mix 1½ pounds ricotta cheese, 2 ounces (2 tablespoons) grated parmesan cheese, 3 ounces chopped prosciutto, 2 eggs, 1 tablespoon chopped parsley, ½ teaspoon salt and ½ teaspoon white pepper. Blend into a firm filling; spread filling on dough sheets and roll. Place manicotti on a buttered 1-inch-deep pan and bake in 350-degree oven for 20 minutes. Serve with tomato, meat or mushroom sauce. Makes 6 servings.

rooms, a terrace garden in the rear offered pleasant al fresco dining in good weather. It was in this garden, lined with lush grapevines hanging from groaning trellises, that the annual grape harvest festival, known as "La Vendemmia," took place, complete with "beautiful girls in native dress," strolling musicians and the traditional stomping of the grapes in a large vat. Customers of course were welcome to join in, and young Bobby Abbo, Frank Abbo's son, was more than willing to help attractive young females step into the purple ooze.

Within months of celebrating the Roma's fiftieth anniversary, Abbo was struck by an automobile and killed while crossing Connecticut Avenue in front of his restaurant. Abbo's wife, Anna (1915–1995), had already been responsible for much of the restaurant's operations, and she continued to run it with her son Robert until her death. By that time, the Roma was declining, and two years later, in 1997, Robert decided it should close.

Another popular early Italian restaurateur was Ciro Gallotti (1883–1948), who opened GALLOTTI'S ITALIAN-AMERICAN RESTAURANT in 1922 at 404 Twelfth Street Northwest. He later moved to 1304 G Street Northwest, where his eatery was called CIRO'S ITALIAN VILLAGE RESTAURANT and later CIRO'S FAMOUS VILLAGE. Gallotti advertised that "here is found one of the most realistic reproductions of an Italian Village on this side of the ocean," complete with puffy clouds painted on the sky blue ceiling, tile-roofed wooden canopies and stuccoed walls. Ciro's was one of the first restaurants in Washington to serve pizza. A *Post* article in 1941 made it sound like something strange and exotic: "Pizza Neapolitan, served in Ciro's Famous Village, looks like the most beautiful pie you ever saw. But it's made of creamy yellow cheese, baked fresh tomatoes, and the proper Italian sauces." A simple peasant food from the streets of Naples, pizza was brought to America by poor Neapolitan immigrants. While the first American pizzeria, G. Lombardi's, opened in 1905 in New York City, when it was first offered at a D.C. restaurant is unrecorded.

Neapolitan-born Gallotti was an effusively outgoing individual ("one high-strung and ever exciting chum," according to the *Post*) and thus well suited to the role of restaurateur. Passionate about Italy and deeply disturbed by the Italian government's disastrous alliance with Hitler during World War II, Gallotti was ecstatic when Benito Mussolini went into hiding in 1943. On being handed a paper with news of the ouster one evening, Gallotti shouted into an entertainer's microphone, "Muss quit the fuss!" and started handing out free beers (which were scarce and subject to strict rationing) to startled patrons. After playing on his favorite French horn for his patrons (he had been a professional musician as a young man), he called his wife to the stage for many hugs and kisses, much to her embarrassment. Two months later, the surrender of the

A postcard from Ciro's Italian Village, circa 1932. *Author's collection.*

fascist government to Allied invaders was reason for Gallotti to hand out thousands more free glasses of beer.

Gallotti's chef in the 1940s was Augusto Vasaio (1908–1982), who moved on to found the somewhat eccentric but much-loved A.V. RISTORANTE ITALIANO at 607 New York Avenue Northwest in 1949 with his wife, Asunta (1923–2005). Brother Franco Vasaio (1910–1980) joined them the following year and became their chef. A.V.'s was a neighborhood place, where the owner was friendly but at times brusque and the wait service surly and painfully slow but the food delicious and comforting. "Informality and indifference characterize the restaurant's ambience," *Post* food critic Donald Dresden wrote in 1975. "Empty wine bottles are the main decoration...A large mirror has remained hanging cockeyed for several days at this writing, but no one seems to mind this or an accumulation of cigarette butts and ashes on a window sill." Patrons grew fond of the eccentric décor that never changed—a five-foot alabaster model of the leaning Tower of Pisa, a huge blowfish over the cash register, a jukebox with Italian opera, a dusty suit of armor and, of course, red-checked tablecloths.

A.V.'s featured many seafood dishes, but its specialty was a "white" pizza, made with garlic, oregano and Fontina cheese but no tomato sauce. A perennial favorite, diehards took it without the cheese. Other treats included Spaghetti Caruso, Calamari alla Genovese and Porchetta al Forno. Just as the Roma lasted only a couple of years after Anna Abbo died, so A.V.'s came to an end in 2007, shortly after Asunta Vasaio passed away. By that time, the property—on a stretch of New York Avenue that once was undesirable—had become a hot piece of real estate.

Other traditional Italian restaurants included FIO'S in the Woodner Apartment building at 3636 Sixteenth Street Northwest, which was run by Franco Vasaio's son Fiorenzo and featured the same kind of traditional Italian food but with 1950s décor, including a pink Formica-topped bar. GUSTI'S, founded in 1949, the same year as A.V.'s, was located at 1837 M Street Northwest in the city's unofficial restaurant district of the postwar years. Gusti's was the creation of Agostino Buttinelli (1914–1978) and, like A.V.'s, offered classic Italian-American food at reasonable prices. Buttinelli sold Gusti's in the early 1960s and moved on to other restaurant ventures but sadly committed suicide at age sixty-four. His namesake restaurant continued on, prospering in the 1980s because of its location at Nineteenth and M Streets Northwest, a center of nightlife. It finally closed in 1998. Just half a block away was LUIGI'S, at 1132 Nineteenth Street Northwest, opened in 1943 by Luigi Tito Calvi (1889–1963), a Genovese immigrant who had originally run an Italian restaurant called Lido at 1208 Eighteenth Street Northwest and who had also worked at Ciro's Italian Village. Luigi's, still operating at its Nineteenth Street address, is perhaps the oldest pizzeria in existence in Washington.

Despite the enduring popularity of these "red sauce joints," Italian dining in Washington was destined to rise above the level of the neighborhood trattorias. The turning point came in 1968, when Joseph Muran de Assereto (1929–1999) opened the CANTINA D'ITALIA at 1214-A Eighteenth Street Northwest in Dupont Circle. The sophisticated Cantina represented a sea change from earlier home-style Italian restaurants. De Assereto, an American of Genovese-French extraction, ran his eatery like a high-class French restaurant, featuring nearly illegible handwritten menus and the best recipes he could find from the north of Italy. Despite the inscrutability of the menu, de Assereto graciously catered to his customers' fondest desires and won over many a loyal fan. One veal dish, Tomaxelle alla Genovese, consisted of thinly sliced veal rolls filled with ground veal sweetbreads, pine nuts and garlic, cooked in a white wine sauce laced with mushrooms. Donald Dresden tried it in 1970 and thought it excellent. "The Cantina d'Italia is among Washington's finest restaurants," he wrote.

Still, the Cantina offered traditional Italian fare as well, de Assereto being unsure whether alta cucina would work. One of the restaurant's specialties, for example, was a very tasty veal scaloppini, and it also offered fettuccine Alfredo, which had been invented back in 1914 by a Roman restaurateur and made famous in America when Douglas Fairbanks and Mary Pickford enjoyed it on their 1927 honeymoon. What distinguished the Cantina's version was the care taken to use the best available ingredients, including fettuccine cut and cooked to order. The extra care was reflected in prices that were considerably higher than typical for an Italian restaurant. Food critic Phyllis Richman, writing in 1988, thought the Cantina's food a bit heavy but remained fond of what she termed the "first truly Italian expense-account restaurant" in D.C. The eatery was twenty years old at that point, and de Assereto had recently retired. Without his guiding hand, it soon closed.

Once the Cantina had opened the door to alta cucina—proving that Washingtonians were willing to pay premium prices for Italian food—elegant new Italian eateries soon began blossoming everywhere. The next, TIBERIO, at 1915 K Street Northwest, opened in 1975. Run by brothers Giulio and Michele Santillo, Tiberio had a French maître d' to emphasize its classiness. Its menu was entirely in Italian, emulating the French tradition. While the Cantina d'Italia huddled in a cramped Dupont Circle basement, Tiberio was "delightfully airy and light, with white walls and ceilings resembling fine stucco, arches that suggest a series of rooms, and modern painting that enliven the ambience," according to Donald Dresden. Dresden sampled the house specialty, Vitello Tiberio, consisting of thin slices of Parma ham and Fontina cheese sandwiched between slices of premium veal, dipped in a light egg batter and sautéed in clarified butter until golden. The dish was topped with tomato, demi-glace and truffles, and Dresden pronounced it "ambrosial." Tiberio continued in business until 1994.

Another exceptional Italian restaurant that opened in the 1980s was OBELISK at 2029 P Street Northwest, run by chef Peter Pastan. Located in a small, unassuming walk-up in Dupont Circle and accommodating only thirty at a time for prix fixe dinners, Obelisk concentrated on fine ingredients and authentic Italian cooking. It soon gained a reputation for offering a dining experience that was straightforward but nevertheless exceptional. Staying true to its original concept, Obelisk remains one of Washington's best restaurants to this day.

The dominance of Italian dining in the 1980s reached a crescendo with the opening of GALILEO, originally at 2014 P Street Northwest across from Obelisk, in 1984. Galileo was the creation of Savino Recine and Roberto Donna. Recine, a native of Rome, was an experienced restaurant manager who served as Galileo's maître d'. Donna, born in Turin, was a young and talented chef with extensive experience in European kitchens who had been in the United States for only five years.

Their new restaurant was instantly popular, its fame sealed by a fortuitous turn of events when Vice President George Bush's staff attempted to make a reservation for him soon after the small fifty-four-seat eatery opened. Galileo was overbooked, and Recine was in a spot. While it seemed unthinkable to turn the vice president down, it was likewise unthinkable to take a table away from someone who already had a reservation. Recine tried but could get no one with a reservation to cancel. He shrewdly decided to contact a friend of his, prominent newsman John Scali, to let him know of his dilemma. The news of the vice president being unable to book a table at the upstart little restaurant soon made headlines around the world. Recine's mother even called him from Italy. "What's the matter with you?" she wanted to know. Bush ultimately got his Galileo dinner at a later date—on the house, of course—while the notoriety compounded the allure of the new restaurant.

Galileo took sophisticated Italian dining to a new level. As John F. Mariani has said, Donna's "highly personalized, authentic cucina italiana immediately made the Northern Italian menus and staid décor at established places such as Cantina d'Italia and Tiberio look dated." Critics raved about the food. "Several other Italian restaurants make their own rolls and focaccia; none matches Donna's, particularly his olive focaccia," wrote Phyllis Richman. "Galileo's pastas are supple and thin enough to read through, its sauces both delicate and distinctive." The restaurant moved to more spacious quarters at 1110 Twenty-first Street Northwest in 1990, and Donna became involved in numerous additional restaurant ventures. As time went by, Galileo won many awards, including being named one of the ten best Italian restaurants in America by *Wine Spectator* in 1997 and one of the twenty finest Italian restaurants in the world by the president of Italy in 1996. In recent years, Donna's restaurants have experienced financial problems; the original Galileo declared bankruptcy and closed in 2006.

I RICCHI, at 1220 Nineteenth Street Northwest, opened in January 1989 and soon cemented its spot as the closest rival to Galileo, though perhaps it was not quite as flashy. In February 1989, President Bush was able to get a table without any trouble, despite the fact that i Ricchi was as big a hit as Galileo had been when it opened. The restaurant was the work of Francesco Ricchi and his American-born wife, Christianne, who had previously run the family's Trattoria i Ricchi in Italy. For their Washington venture, the couple offered fresh, authentic Tuscan cuisine, often using recipes from their old trattoria. They were helped in the 1990s by the fad for Tuscan food sparked by the 1996 publication of Frances Mayes's bestselling memoir, *Under the Tuscan Sun*. While Francesco Ricchi moved on to other ventures, Christianne continued at the head of i Ricchi, which remains open to this day.

Savino Recine prepares risotto with truffle butter and mushrooms in a wheel of Parmesan cheese at Primi Piatti. *Photo by the author.*

Just as enduring as i Ricchi is PRIMI PIATTI, which opened in 1987 at 2013 I Street Northwest near Pennsylvania Avenue and also continues to do a thriving business. Savino Recine and Roberto Donna decided to open this popular eatery as a second, moderately priced alternative to Galileo, and it was an immediate hit. "The smells of the restaurant are Italian, and the spirit and energy are the best Italy can offer," Phyllis Richman gleefully declared soon after Primi Piatti opened. People waiting to get in were "lined up to the end of the block every single night," Recine recalls. The restaurant offered a broader range of fare than Galileo and, according to Recine, featured the first authentic wood-burning pizza oven in the city, brought here from Italy, as well as a light, modern atmosphere. "This is food for purists, for people who like Italian food for its fresh, simple character, its lack of flossiness," Phyllis Richman commented. "It was totally different than what Washington was used to before," Recine declares.

After Primi Piatti's success was ensured, its two owners decided to part ways, with Recine taking over Primi Piatti exclusively, serving as both manager and executive chef, while Donna stayed at Galileo. While Primi Piatti began as a strictly casual eatery, over time its menu broadened, evolving as the restaurant-going public in Washington evolved. Like many contemporary eateries, it now straddles the casual and sophisticated camps, offering a few high-end dishes in addition to casual favorites such as the wood-fired pizza and maintaining an elegant but unpretentious atmosphere. In the early days, when the lines stretched around the block, the service at Primi Piatti could be brusque, but over time the venerable eatery mellowed, and a loyal following developed that keeps up a steady business.

Celebrities who have dined at Primi Piatti include entertainers such as Madonna, Mick Jagger, John Travolta and Chuck Norris, as well as elite Washington politicians, including Bill and Hillary Clinton, numerous cabinet officers, senators, congressmen and Supreme Court justices. Perennial menu favorites at Primi Piatti include the agnolotti stuffed with ricotta cheese and spinach, topped with pistachio cream sauce; a classic veal saltimbocca in a Frascatti wine sauce; and the signature risotto with truffle butter and mushrooms in a wheel of Parmesan cheese, which Recine has nicknamed OMG for the reaction he gets from patrons who try it for the first time.

Sophisticated Italian restaurants continue to appear in D.C.—Tosca at 1112 F Street Northwest and Fiola at 601 Pennsylvania Avenue Northwest are relatively recent examples—but they are no longer as revolutionary as they were in the 1980s and 1990s. Though neighborhood red sauce joints also still exist, they increasingly seem even more distant. The days when Italian food was an expression of an ethnic identity are long gone, and Italian cuisine is just one of many vocabularies that eclectic contemporary chefs can choose from when dreaming up their next exotic restaurant concepts.

Chapter 14
A COSMOPOLITAN DINING DESTINATION

In recent decades, Washington's restaurants have become far more cosmopolitan and sophisticated than ever before, a reflection of the growing diversity of D.C.-area residents, as well as a general broadening of culinary tastes. But ethnic eateries have been around a long time, far longer than many Washingtonians realize. As we have seen, Chinese restaurants were in D.C. in the late nineteenth century, as were German, Italian and, of course, French. Greek and Mexican restaurants were here in the early twentieth century. Other nationalities showed up over time, often driven by political events overseas. For much of the later part of the twentieth century, the city benefited gastronomically when refugees from politically unstable regions made their way to Washington and opened some of the city's most intriguing and unusual restaurants.

In the early 1900s, more than a dozen Greek restaurants operated on Seventh and Ninth Streets Northwest near Pennsylvania Avenue, an area where Greek immigrants were settling. In 1936, John G. Kritsidimas (1899–1954), a native of Mykonos, Greece, opened the ATHENS RESTAURANT at 804 Ninth Street Northwest. The popular restaurant numbered congressmen and Supreme Court justices among its many patrons and was a favorite of New York mayor Fiorello La Guardia. A menu from the 1940s lists its entrées in both Greek and English and features classic dishes such as lamb kapama, a dish inherited from the Turks; spanakorizo (spinach and rice); beef tas kebab; and yiaourti (Greek yogurt).

Another notable Greek eatery was the ASTOR, at 1813 M Street Northwest, in business from 1945 until 1989. It was owned and operated by Bessie Zaras (1917–2008), a kindhearted hostess who made a point of offering support to Greek immigrants newly arrived in the Washington area. Her easy-going waitresses, mostly from Greece, would call guests "honey" and "dear" in diner fashion, serving them authentic Greek food that was tasty and inexpensive. Zaras's restaurant began as a simple dining room on the ground floor but later expanded with an upstairs room, where Greek entertainers, including belly dancers, performed.

Mexican and Latin American restaurants have a more complex history. Tex-Mex restaurants have been in the city for over one hundred years. A 1901 article in the *Washington Post* profiled the Texas Restaurant, located somewhere downtown, which had been started by a congressman from southern Texas and his brother. The eatery featured chili con carne, described as "a carmine-red chowder, composed of Chile kidney beans and sundry bits of tender meat, the whole swimming in the bright red 'Chile' sauce." The restaurant had its sauce shipped from Texas and served it to the customers "in an odd-shaped vessel of Mexican pottery, set in a bowl equally odd as to color and shape." The *Post* writer further observed that the chili was bitingly hot, and "those who eat, partake freely of iced water on the side, served in a bowl of dull red color."

Chili con carne and hot tamales were the primary offerings at this and other early Tex-Mex houses, including the Ranch, founded by William H. Nichols at 507 F Street Northwest in 1900. Born in Galveston in 1866, Nichols had been a Texas Ranger and state surveyor before coming to Washington in the 1890s. According to the *Washington Star*'s Maureen Dowd, he became fond of chili during his visits to jails in the Houston-Galveston area and brought the recipe for the bracingly hot concoction with him when he moved to Washington. His first restaurant looked and felt like something out of the Old West, with sawdust on the floorboards and long, rough-hewn tables, and apparently it was a great success. Its trademark chili was popular enough to allow Nichols to open four more downtown locations. After Nichols died in the 1930s, his wife consolidated to one spot, 729 Twelfth Street Northwest, which remained in business until 1977, complete with steer horns on the wall, chuck wagon murals and mirrors advertising Mexican beer.

Though the Ranch served other Tex-Mex fare, its famous chili, prepared in a giant steel pot, remained its biggest draw throughout the eatery's seventy-seven-year history and was widely considered the best in town. The recipe reportedly had never changed. Bill Nichols Jr., son of the founder, refused to share it, although he offered several chili-cooking tips, including: 1) don't use any tomatoes; 2) use large chunks of chuck steak, not hamburger; and 3) cook the beans and the chili separately, combining them in a bowl only when they are served. When the restaurant's imminent closing was finally

Cook Cathryn Briscoe stirs the last pot of chili at the Ranch in 1977. *D.C. Public Library, Star Collection,* © *Washington Post.*

announced, crestfallen regulars came by to purchase gallon jugs of the last batch of chili. Bill Nichols and his wife, Eleanor, shuttered their place reluctantly, having been forced out by subway construction.

Despite the niche popularity of chili, Mexican cuisine had only a token presence in the nation's capital for much of the twentieth century. When the LITTLE MEXICO restaurant opened in 1948 at 2301 Connecticut Avenue Northwest, tacos and tortillas were still exotic novelties to most Washingtonians. The restaurant's menu included helpful explanations: "Tortillas are the typical Mexican bread. They are flat corn cakes similar to the American pancakes…Tacos are tortillas filled with either meat or chicken or cheese which are fried in deep fat to a crisp, and covered with spicy tomato sauce and garnished with lettuce and tomato. They are properly eaten with

Little Mexico

2603 Conn. Ave.   AD. 9582, DU. 9270
Washington, D. C. MICHIGAN   0773

A circa 1950 menu from Little Mexico. *Author's collection.*

your fingers as a sandwich." The Little Mexico was a hit, so Washingtonians must have responded well to these strange delicacies.

The city got its first taste of Caribbean cuisine at supper clubs such as the Wardman Park Hotel's CARIBAR ROOM, opened in 1950. Here diners could dance the rumba when they weren't sampling such treats as *pargo asado à la criolla* (Haitian-style red snapper simmered in coconut oil with onions, tomatoes and green peppers over rice), *aguacate relleno à la marinera* (Jamaican half avocado pear stuffed with crab flakes, shrimp and herbs) or *dulce de piña y coco de San Tomas* (pineapple macerated with cordial and topped with a mound of ground coconut). While starting out with an exclusively Latin-themed menu, the Caribar quickly learned that it needed to also offer traditional American entrées or risk losing patronage from the many guests who had a limited tolerance for unfamiliar cuisine.

Peruvian cuisine has been represented in Washington by EL CHALAN, at 1924 I Street Northwest, since 1981. Founded by Pedro and Elsa Espinoza, El Chalan was the first D.C. restaurant to serve exclusively Peruvian food, including favorites such as lomo saltado, ceviche and causa. The menu also includes the refreshing national drink of Peru, the pisco sour.

Beginning in the 1960s, unrest in Latin America brought many new Latin foods to the D.C. restaurant scene. An important pioneer was the OMEGA, at 1858 Columbia Road Northwest in Adams Morgan. Originally a Hungarian restaurant, the Omega was sold in 1962 to Enrique Baez, a Cuban refugee, who converted it into one of the city's first authentic Latin American restaurants. Though bare bones in décor, the eatery produced consistently good Spanish and Latin American food at very low prices. "Señor Castro inadvertently did Washington a favor," food critic Donald Dresden observed in 1969. "Had it not been for his repression, the Omega would not be serving us, and that would be unfortunate." Phyllis Richman particularly liked its pork specialty, *masitas de puerco*, topped with sweet vinegared onions. Also popular were the traditional Latin American meat dishes, such as the Cuban *ropa vieja* (shredded beef) or the Peruvian *lomo saltado* (stir-fried beef with onions and tomatoes). The restaurant became well known even beyond Washington. In 1976, fashion designer Pierre Cardin told the *New Yorker* magazine that the Omega was his favorite. The much-loved culinary institution paved the way for many similar Latin eateries throughout the D.C. region; however, a disastrous fire in 1990 brought it to an end.

In 1968, EL CARIBE opened just down the street from the Omega at 1828 Columbia Road, helping to cement Adams Morgan's Latin accent. Raul Sanchez, another Cuban émigré, and José del Olmo, a chef originally from Spain, founded the new eatery. Both had worked previously at the Omega. This was also a very inexpensive, informal restaurant, furnished with picnic tables and wooden benches, the food served on paper plates. Latin specialties previously rarely seen in Washington, such as ceviche (fish marinated in lime juice), *papas rellenas* (fried potatoes stuffed with meat) and fried yuca (an alternative to French fries), were now available. El Caribe, like Washington's earliest restaurants in the nineteenth century, offered catering services as well, supplying dinners to working couples and families who didn't have time to cook their own meals. The Adams Morgan El Caribe lasted until 1992, after which it moved to the suburbs.

Another pioneer restaurant in Adams Morgan was the CALVERT CAFÉ, now known as MAMA AYESHA'S, at 1967 Calvert Street Northwest in Adams Morgan, which in 1960 was

The Calvert Café (Mama Ayesha's), circa 1980. *Mohammed Abu-El-Hawa.*

one of the earliest Middle Eastern restaurants to open in Washington. Ayesha Abraham (1900–1993), a native of Palestine from a well-connected family, was married at an early age and had been in charge of several large farms in her native land when she decided to give it all up—perhaps under political pressure—and move to the United States, where relatives lived. She first worked as a cook at the Syrian Embassy, where her excellent cooking and outspoken ways brought her to the attention of Washington diplomats and VIPs. She worked for several years at the Desert Inn, a Middle Eastern eatery owned by Charles M. Saah, who would later convert the Iron Gate Inn to Middle Eastern cuisine. In 1960, Abraham had saved up enough money to purchase the old Calvert Café in Adams Morgan, a small neighborhood eatery lined with naugahyde booths and diner-like jukebox players at each table. The café had been a favorite after-game spot for the Washington Senators in the 1940s and 1950s, but it took on a completely different character under Abraham, who turned it into an emporium of Middle Eastern cooking.

While initially the café served primarily the local Arab community, Mama Ayesha's place soon gained the attention of a much wider clientele, helped in part by the patronage of journalist Helen Thomas, who had become a close friend of Abraham's. When the *Washington Post*'s Sally Quinn profiled the restaurant in 1970, it had become a lively bohemian outpost where Henry Kissinger might be sitting at one table and a group of African American college kids at the next, where Middle Eastern businessmen negotiated financial deals and young army recruits found themselves unable to pay their bills (Mama Ayesha would tear up the check).

Abraham's powerful personality dominated the restaurant and ensured its enduring fame. Though overseeing all of the café's operations, from cooking to cleaning, she also presided over the dining room at her reserved booth in the far corner where she could be found from ten o'clock in the morning to late at night every day of the year. She encouraged everybody to have a good time, which Quinn pointed out was "a little different than anywhere else." Abraham had

a dark-haired belly dancer from Boston who starts things off and from then on, you're on your own. When she starts beating her drums and the juke box is whining away anybody can be a belly dancer and often is. There is no protocol and seemingly there are no inhibitions as one is overcome by the haunting Arabic sounds. Often a conservatively dressed, prim-looking lady will be moved to wriggle about between the courses with little interest and no concern from the rest of the guests or the management.

"I don't smoke or drink and I'm not in love with nobody. I don't like men, just food and music and money and I love my business," Abraham told the *Washington Star*'s Vicki Ostrolenk in 1977. "I'll never retire. When I die, the restaurant dies too." That turned out to be one thing that Mama Ayesha, who fancied herself a soothsayer, failed to accurately predict. She left the restaurant to her nephew, and it continues to this day, now officially called Mama Ayesha's. A major renovation in 1994 after Abraham's death created a tastefully decorated eatery that continues to serve classic Middle Eastern dishes in a decidedly less rambunctious atmosphere than had once prevailed.

MAMA AYESHA'S BABA GHANOUSH

Bake 2 medium eggplants in a 400-degree oven until soft. Remove and peel off skin. Sprinkle with lemon juice to keep from turning black. Cool. Then beat with 1 clove garlic, 2 tablespoons tahini, the juice of 1½ lemons and ½ teaspoon of salt. When ready to serve, add a small spoon of olive oil. Serves 4 to 6. Best eaten with warm Syrian bread.

A postcard view of entertainers at the Port Saíd restaurant. *Author's collection.*

Other early Middle Eastern restaurants included the PORT SAÍD, at 1418 I Street Northwest, opened in 1960, and the SYRIANA, at 1214 Connecticut Avenue Northwest, opened in 1964. Both were primarily nightclubs featuring belly dancing and other Middle Eastern entertainment, the Syriana's Harem Room staying open until the wee hours of the morning. Beyond the nightclub circuit, the conversion of the Iron Gate Inn to Middle Eastern fare in the late 1960s also boosted the availability of that cuisine. By the 1970s, Washingtonians could get their hummus, stuffed grape leaves, baba ghanoush and baklava at a wide assortment of both informal and fine dining establishments.

Authentic Indian restaurants were relative latecomers to the nation's capital. A 1979 newspaper article claimed that there had been just two Indian restaurants in 1969 and "only four in the early 1970s." Americans, like the British, associated Indian cuisine with "curry"—a vague, westernized term used to describe a wide variety of spicy dishes. The challenge for Indian restaurants was to get beyond the curry stereotype and introduce Washingtonians to the richness and diversity of authentic Indian cooking.

In 1968, two brothers from the Punjab opened the GAYLORD INDO-PAKISTANI RESTAURANT, at 1731 Connecticut Avenue Northwest in Dupont Circle, one of the city's first authentic Indian restaurants. In a carefully worded 1970 advertisement, the Gaylord offered a classic compromise for wary and inexperienced diners: "Lamb, chicken, beef, and egg curries, spiced and flavored to perfection by true Punjabi chefs await you here, together with other exotic gourmet preparations or, if you prefer, there are all kinds of American dishes." Host Mike Sodhi would charm guests with exquisitely made samosas and then introduce them to Punjabi dishes such as the vegetarian *aaloo mutter*, *palak gosht* (beef and spinach) or *keema mutter* (lamb with peas). Food critic Donald Dresden ventured to visit the Gaylord in 1970 only after a friend who was a Foreign Service officer with experience in India recommended it and volunteered to come along with him to navigate the strange offerings. An unusually hesitant Dresden came away impressed. About the samosas, he wrote, "If the Indians will forgive me, I shall translate this (on advice of several Indians) as a meat and vegetable pie (in small portions) that has been fried in deep fat. It was delicious." Dresden returned in 1972 to find that the food was still excellent.

The TAJ MAHAL, at 1327 Connecticut Avenue Northwest, was another early Dupont Circle eatery, lasting from 1965 into the 1980s. Asha Mallick, a German woman married to an Indian, owned the restaurant. Decorated with imported Indian brassware, the Taj Mahal featured waitresses dressed in authentic Punjabi saris and salwar kameez suits, and it offered equally authentic cuisine.ttt

The 1970s saw the arrival of more Indian eateries. Jagdish "Jack" Katyal, a native of New Delhi, opened first the MAHARAJA, at 1639 Wisconsin Avenue Northwest in Georgetown, in 1973 and subsequently the Nepalese/Kashmiri-themed KATMANDU, at 1800 Connecticut Avenue Northwest, in 1980. The Katmandu, nestled in three small basement rooms of an old town house just north of Dupont Circle, capitalized on the exoticism of its namesake and, according to Katyal, was the only Nepalese restaurant in the United States.

Perhaps most sophisticated of all the early Indian restaurants was APANA, opened at 3066 M Street Northwest in Georgetown in 1972 by twenty-three-year-old Amarjeet "Umbi" Singh and a friend. The *Washington Post* called it "an Indian restaurant of beauty, using color and lighting to effect elegance." Singh, a Punjabi native, had first come to Washington as a child with his diplomat father and knew the ways of Washington's VIP crowd. Guests at his restaurant were seated at cozy banquettes with tall backs that created a romantic, intimate atmosphere. "The pick of the menu includes lemony spiced mushrooms and crusty fried shrimp as appetizers, and fish for a main course, a sublime amalgam of butter, almonds, velvety fish and barely-cooked broccoli," according to the

Post. Apana attracted the likes of Secretary of State Warren Christopher, newsman Sam Donaldson and Arkansas governor Bill Clinton and his wife, Hillary.

After twelve years at Apana, Singh decided to move on, and in 1986 he opened NEW HEIGHTS at 2317 Calvert Street Northwest in Woodley Park, a formal American nouvelle cuisine restaurant that was an immediate hit. Phyllis Richman termed it "the most brazen of the New American kitchens. There is nothing on the menu that leaves you unstartled except the green salad with mustard vinaigrette." Like Apana, New Heights attracted an elite crowd, including David Brinkley, Jim Lehrer, Nancy Reagan and many others. The Clintons reportedly arranged for daughter Chelsea to eat dinner at New Heights while on her first date in public. The restaurant is still in business today, somewhat less formal in style but continuing to offer new and sophisticated dishes.

Like the Kennedys before them, the Clintons liked eating out at fine restaurants, and Bill Clinton was likely the first sitting president to eat at an Indian restaurant. His choice was the fashionable BOMBAY CLUB, at 815 Connecticut Avenue Northwest, which had debuted in 1988. The Bombay Club was conceived by owner Ashok Bajaj as a romantic evocation of the British-ruled India of the 1930s, complete with ceiling fans, lots of palms and other greenery, shutters on the windows and club-like walnut paneling. Musicians played songs from the 1930s and 1940s on a spotless white piano. The "club" served modern Indian food, with tasteful variations on traditional Indian dishes. It also served tandoori dishes cooked in an imported clay oven, as had become standard by the late 1980s in upscale Indian restaurants. Phyllis Richman, writing in 1992, found the cuisine at the Bombay Club "subtle and sublime."

The Clintons' visit in October 1993 cemented the Bombay Club's reputation, particularly after an extensive feature article about the dinner appeared in the *Washington Post*. Bajaj proudly viewed the president's visit as an acknowledgement of the "wealth and complexity" of his country and the broad range of its cuisine. He served Clinton an assortment of his best offerings, culminating with his special "cobra" coffee: "a flamboyant concoction that involves pouring flaming orange liqueur down a snake-like strip of orange peel into a pan of coffee spiked with Scotch." Clinton applauded. He must have enjoyed the experience, as the Bombay Club became a frequent choice for the first family's dinners out. The restaurant, thoroughly renovated in 2009, continues to do a brisk business.

Japanese restaurants in Washington, though relatively few, have generally been very sophisticated. One of the most successful was the JAPAN INN, which opened at 1520 Connecticut Avenue Northwest near Dupont Circle in 1966 and moved to 1715 Wisconsin Avenue Northwest in upper Georgetown in 1971. Opened by Kokei Yoshimoto, the Japan Inn was an innovator for Washington, featuring *teppanyaki*—steak, chicken and other items grilled on an iron plate in front of guests—a novelty at the time. Patrons could also choose the more traditional *sukiyaki*, offered in a back room of the elegantly designed eatery. In 1971, Yoshimoto opened a new, larger Japan Inn in upper Georgetown, a sophisticated, modernist restaurant that remained a Washington fixture for more than thirty years. Nearby, SUSHI-KO at 2309 Wisconsin Avenue Northwest in Glover Park was Washington's first sushi restaurant, part of a flowering of Asian restaurants in the D.C. area in the 1970s.

The war in Vietnam indirectly influenced the ethnic restaurant scene in D.C. through the introduction of Thai and Vietnamese cuisine. The city's first authentic Thai restaurant was the THAI ROOM, which opened in 1972 at 5037 Connecticut Avenue Northwest in upper Northwest. It began as a specialty Asian grocery store with a modest adjoining café, but the successful dining room eventually overtook the store. The restaurant's chefs had been brought to the United States from one of the best Bangkok restaurants, the Sorn Dang, and they introduced Washingtonians to such now-familiar Thai dishes as satay (skewered meat appetizers) and *tod mun* (fish cakes). The restaurant stayed in business for over thirty years, closing in 2005.

Beginning in the late 1970s, many more Thai restaurants began opening in the D.C. area, the majority of them in the suburbs. Vietnamese restaurants followed a similar progression, flowering in the years following the fall of Saigon in 1975. One of the earliest was the short-lived SAIGON WEST at 1509 Sixteenth Street Northwest, midway between Dupont and Logan Circles, which was operating in 1974. Here, Washingtonians who had not served in Vietnam could first sample *pho* (meat and noodle soup) and *chả giò* (Vietnamese spring rolls) and dip their food in *nước mắm* (fermented fish sauce) while being served with impeccable deference by waitresses dressed in traditional silk attire. Other early Vietnamese eateries included LA FREGATE at 2020 Florida Avenue Northwest in Dupont Circle and two cafés located next door to each other in Georgetown, the VIET HUONG CAFÉ and VIETNAM-GEORGETOWN in the 2900 block of M Street Northwest, both operating in 1976. GERMAINE'S, at 2400 Wisconsin Avenue Northwest in Glover Park, was a particularly sophisticated and successful example, combining Vietnamese and other Asian dishes in an elegant setting. Within a few years, Vietnamese restaurants were plentiful, especially in Virginia suburbs such as the Clarendon section of Arlington.

Ethiopian restaurants followed a similar pattern, first putting their imprint on the city's dining scene within a few years of the 1974 revolution that ousted longtime ruler Haile Selassie. The first Ethiopian restaurant in the city—and the country—was MAMMA DESTA, which opened in 1978 at 4840 Georgia Avenue Northwest in Brightwood. It was a humble establishment that took over an old Chinese café in an out-of-the-way part of town near where Ethiopian immigrants lived. It also managed to attract the attention of influential food critics. The unique Ethiopian style of eating, whereby you scoop up *wat* (thick stews of meats and vegetables) from a large communal platter with torn pieces of pancake-like *injera*, was not to every Washingtonian's liking, but it quickly found a following. Mamma Desta herself, an experienced cook who had worked privately for many years in Italy, Saudi Arabia and New York before coming to Washington, was a respected figure in the local community. In a newspaper article in 1979, she said she hoped her little eatery would become famous and that President Jimmy Carter would come there to dine. That didn't happen, but the city's Ethiopian restaurants nevertheless proliferated. Other early examples were the BLUE NILE at 1701 Sixteenth Street Northwest and the RED SEA at 2463 Eighteenth Street Northwest in Adams Morgan.

Restaurants of many nationalities continue to come and go in Washington, just as its inhabitants do, building on the city's changing multicultural communities. While it can now be enormously expensive to launch a sophisticated new eatery downtown, immigrants with more limited resources are still able to open small establishments in outlying neighborhoods and suburbs where they live, keeping the city's dining options fresh and diverse.

CULINARY DISTINCTION

In the twenty-first century, outsiders no longer view Washington as a culinary backwater. Trendy restaurant strips such as Fourteenth Street in the Logan Circle neighborhood or the H Street corridor in Northeast are filled with well-to-do hipsters and "foodies." The sophisticated new restaurants that seem to open on a weekly basis are often jam-packed every night. Many explanations have been offered for this trend—that the city has grown more cosmopolitan in recent years, that more corporations and other large organizations are moving their headquarters here, that businesses fueled by government activity have created a recession-proof economy that is attracting more sophisticated and demanding consumers. These factors are certainly important, but in the context of their historical predecessors, today's restaurants are not really so extraordinary. In many ways, they continue to do the same thing restaurants here have always done: anticipate the latest fashion trends, cater to their customers' wants and needs and offer memorable experiences that will make people want to come back again and again.

SELECTED BIBLIOGRAPHY

Bennett, Tracey Gold, with Nizam B. Ali. *Ben's Chili Bowl: 50 Years of a Washington, D.C. Landmark*. Charleston, SC: Arcadia Publishing, 2008.

Brennessel, Barbara. *Diamonds in the Marsh: A Natural History of the Diamondback Terrapin*. Lebanon, NH: University Press of New England, 2006.

Brown, George Rothwell. *Washington: A Not Too Serious History*. Baltimore, MD: Norman Publishing Co., 1930.

Carson, Barbara G. *Ambitious Appetites: Dining, Behavior, and Patterns of Consumption in Federal Washington*. Washington, D.C.: American Institute of Architects Press, 1990.

Cary, Francine Curro. *Urban Odyssey: A Multicultural History of Washington, D.C.* Washington, D.C.: Smithsonian Institution Press, 1996.

Coe, Andrew. *Chop Suey: A Cultural History of Chinese Food in the United States*. New York: Oxford University Press, 2009.

Denker, Joel S. *Capital Flavors: Exploring Washington's Ethnic Restaurants*. Cabin John, MD: Seven Locks Press, 1989.

———. *The World on a Plate: A Tour through the History of America's Ethnic Cuisine*. Boulder, CO: Westview Press, 2003.

Fitzpatrick, Sandra, and Maria R. Goodwin. *The Guide to Black Washington*. Rev. ed. New York: Hippocrene Books, 2001.

Gelderman, Carol. *A Free Man of Color and His Hotel*. Washington, D.C.: Potomac Books, 2012.

Goode, James M. *Capital Losses: A Cultural History of Washington's Destroyed Buildings*. 2nd ed. Washington, D.C.: Smithsonian Books, 2003.

Green, Constance McLaughlin. *Washington: A History of the Capital, 1800–1950*. Princeton, NJ: Princeton University Press, 1962.

Grimes, William. *Appetite City: A Culinary History of New York*. New York: North Point Press, 2009.

Grover, Kathryn, ed. *Dining in America, 1850–1900*. Amherst: University of Massachusetts Press, 1987.

Haley, Andrew P. *Turning the Tables: Restaurants and the Rise of the American Middle Class, 1880–1920*. Chapel Hill: University of North Carolina Press, 2011.

Hogan, David Gerald. *Selling 'Em by the Sack: White Castle and the Creation of American Food*. New York: New York University Press, 1997.

Hutchinson, Louise Daniel. *The Anacostia Story, 1608–1930*. Washington, D.C.: Smithsonian Institution Press, 1977.

Jacob, Kathryn Allamong. *Capital Elites*. Washington, D.C.: Smithsonian Institution Press, 1995.

Kessler, Pamela. *Undercover Washington*. Sterling, VA: Capital Books, 2005.

Kuh, Patric. *The Last Days of Haute Cuisine: The Coming of Age of American Restaurants*. New York: Viking Penguin, 2001.

Kurlansky, Mark. *The Big Oyster: History on the Half Shell*. New York: Ballantine Books, 2006.

Leech, Margaret. *Reveille in Washington, 1860–1865*. New York: Harper & Brothers, 1941.

Levenstein, Harvey. *Paradox of Plenty: A Social History of Eating in Modern America*. New York: Oxford University Press, 1993.

———. *Revolution at the Table: The Transformation of the American Diet*. New York: Oxford University Press, 1988.

Mariani, John F. *America Eats Out*. New York: William Morrow & Co., 1991.

———. *How Italian Food Conquered the World*. New York: Palgrave Macmillan, 2011.

Marriott Hot Shoppes Cookbook. Boston: Parsons, Friedmann, Stephan & Rose, 1987.

Morley, Jefferson. *Snow-Storm in August: Washington City, Francis Scott Key, and the Forgotten Race Riot of 1835*. New York: Doubleday, 2012.

O'Brien, Robert. *Marriott: The J. Willard Marriott Story*. Salt Lake City, UT: Deseret Book Co., 1995.

Opie, Frederick Douglass. *Hog & Hominy: Soul Food from Africa to America*. New York: Columbia University Press, 2008.

Pearlman, Alison. *Smart Casual: The Transformation of Gourmet Restaurant Style in America*. Chicago: University of Chicago Press, 2013.

Peck, Garrett. *Prohibition in Washington, D.C.: How Dry We Weren't*. Charleston, SC: The History Press, 2011.

Pillsbury, Richard. *From Boarding House to Bistro: The American Restaurant Then and Now.* Boston: Unwin Hyman, 1990.

Rice, Kym S. *Early American Taverns: For the Entertainment of Friends and Strangers.* Chicago: Regnery Gateway, 1983.

Richman, Phyllis C. *Best Restaurants & Others: Washington D.C. & Environs.* San Ramon, CA: 101 Productions, 1989.

Ruble, Blair A. *Washington's U Street: A Biography.* Baltimore, MD: Johns Hopkins University Press, 2010.

Smith, Kathryn Schneider. *Washington at Home: An Illustrated History of Neighborhoods in the Nation's Capital.* 2nd ed. Baltimore, MD: Johns Hopkins University Press, 2010.

Spang, Rebecca. *The Invention of the Restaurant: Paris and Modern Gastronomic Culture.* Cambridge, MA: Harvard University Press, 2000.

Viorst, Judith, and Milton Viorst. *The Washington D.C. Underground Gourmet.* New York: Simon and Schuster, 1970.

Wennersten, John R. *The Oyster Wars of Chesapeake Bay.* 2nd ed. Washington, D.C.: Eastern Branch Press, 2007.

Whitaker, Jan. *Tea at the Blue Lantern Inn.* New York: St. Martin's Press, 2002.

INDEX

INDEX

INDEX

Z

About the Author

John DeFerrari, a native Washingtonian with a lifelong passion for local history, pens the Streets of Washington blog and is the author of *Lost Washington, D.C.* (The History Press, 2011). He has a master's degree in English literature from Harvard University and works for the federal government.

Photo by Austin J. Cuttino.

Visit us at
www.historypress.net

....

This title is also available as an e-book